Macmillan Building and Surveying Series
Series Editor: Ivor H. Seeley
  Emeritus Professor, Nottingham Trent University

Accounting and Finance for Building and Surveying A.R. Jennings
Advanced Building Measurement, second edition Ivor H. Seeley
Advanced Valuation Diane Butler and David Richmond
Applied Valuation, second edition Diane Butler
Asset Valuation Michael Rayner
Building Economics, fourth edition Ivor H. Seeley
Building Maintenance, second edition Ivor H. Seeley
Building Maintenance Technology Lee How Son and George C.S. Yuen
Building Procurement, second edition Alan E. Turner
Building Project Appraisal Keith Hutchinson
Building Quantities Explained, fourth edition Ivor H. Seeley
Building Surveys, Reports and Dilapidations Ivor H. Seeley
Building Technology, fifth edition Ivor H. Seeley
Civil Engineering Contract Administration and Control, second edition Ivor H. Seeley
Civil Engineering Quantities, fifth edition Ivor H. Seeley
Civil Engineering Specification, second edition Ivor H. Seeley
Commercial Lease Renewals – A Practical Guide Philip Freedman and Eric F.
  Shapiro
Computers and Quantity Surveyors A.J. Smith
Conflicts in Construction – Avoiding, managing, resolving Jeff Whitfield
Constructability in Building and Engineering Projects A. Griffith and A.C. Sidwell
Construction Contract Claims Reg Thomas
Construction Economics – An Introduction Stephen Gruneberg
Construction Law Michael F. James
Contract Planning and Contract Procedures, third edition B. Cooke
Contract Planning Case Studies B. Cooke
Cost Estimation of Structures in Commercial Buildings Surinder Singh
Design-Build Explained D.E.L. Janssens
Development Site Evaluation N.P. Taylor
Environment Management in Construction Alan Griffith
Environmental Science in Building, third edition R. McMullan
Estimating, Tendering and Bidding for Construction A.J. Smith
European Construction – Procedures and techniques B. Cooke and G. Walker
Facilities Management Alan Park
Greener Buildings – Environmental impact of property Stuart Johnson
Housing Associations Helen Cope
Housing Management – Changing Practice Christine Davies (Editor)
Information and Technology Applications in Commercial Property Rosemary Feenan
  and Tim Dixon (Editors)
Introduction to Building Services, second edition E.F. Curd and C.A. Howard
Introduction to Valuation, third edition D. Richmond
Marketing and Property People Owen Bevan
Principles of Property Investment and Pricing, second edition W.D. Fraser
Project Management and Control David Day
Property Development Appraisal and Finance David Isaac
Property Valuation Techniques David Isaac and Terry Steley
Public Works Engineering Ivor H. Seeley
Quality Assurance in Building Alan Griffith

(continued)

Quantity Surveying Practice, second edition Ivor H. Seeley
Real Estate in Corporate Strategy Marion Weatherhead
Recreation Planning and Development Neil Ravenscroft
Resource Management for Construction M.R. Canter
Small Building Works Management Alan Griffith
Social Housing Management Martyn Pearl
Structural Detailing, second edition P. Newton
Sub-Contracting under the JCT Standard Forms of Building Contract Jennie Price
Urban Land Economics and Public Policy, fifth edition P.N. Balchin, J.L. Kieve and
    G.H. Bull
Urban Renewal – Theory and Practice Chris Couch
1980 JCT Standard Form of Building Contract, second edition R.F. Fellows
Value Management in Construction B. Norton and W. McElligott

Macmillan Building and Surveying Series
Series Standing Order ISBN 0–333–69333–7

You can receive future titles in this series as they are published by placing a standing order.
Please contact your bookseller or, in case of difficulty, write to us at the address below with
your name and address, the title of the series and the ISBN quoted above.

Customer Services Department, Macmillan Distribution Ltd
Houndmills, Basingstoke, Hampshire RG21 6XS, England.

Real Estate in Corporate Strategy

Marion Weatherhead

MACMILLAN

First published 1997 by
MACMILLAN PRESS LTD
Houndmills, Basingstoke, Hampshire RG21 6XS
and London
Companies and representatives
throughout the world

ISBN 0–333–65765–9

A catalogue record for this book is available
from the British Library

This book is printed on paper suitable for recycling and
made from fully managed and sustained forest sources.

10   9   8   7   6   5   4   3   2   1
06   05   04   03   02   01   00   99   98   97

Typeset by Ian Kingston Editorial Services, Nottingham

Printed in Hong Kong

Contents

Acknowledgements

This book has spanned a wide range of topics and it would not have been possible without the help and advice of a large number of people.

A major inspiration for this book has been the work by Martin Avis and Virginia Gibson. Their reports on corporate property assets have brought the importance of corporate real estate to the attention of many, including me. Ginny has also kindly guided me to a number of US references. I am indebted to them and thank them for their initiative in opening up this important field.

A year as a Sloan Fellow at London Business School helped me to expand the knowledge and experiences I had gained as a chartered surveyor and academic. Many of my fellow Sloans deserve my most grateful thanks, as they provided intellectual stimulation, the benefits of their own professional knowledge, daily encouragement, introductions, blunt realism and fun days escaping all responsibilities! Annabel Sachs deserves a special mention. She said I could do it – so I did, and then she arrived from Australia in time to help me tweak the title to suit everyone! Of other Sloans, Peta Lyn Farwagi, Chris Brunck, Nick Pelly, Kevin Parker and Kent Robertson all warrant an individual mention. Thank you all.

Keeping up to date in the fast-moving world of IT is almost impossible for those not involved from day to day. Without the written contributions and illustrations provided by Bernard Bowles, a communications marketing manager and husband of a lifelong friend, Rosalind, Chapter 5 would never have been completed. I am very grateful.

Making the complexities of finance and accountancy understandable was the challenging aim I set myself. I had help from two accountants to paraphrase the mass of detail – another Sloan Fellow, Simon Paddock, and my cousin, Rosalind Upton. Peter Kelland, a chartered surveyor with Crosher and James helped with the appendix on capital allowances and also gave permission for the inclusion of a table from the practice's Property Taxation Index. Another chartered surveyor, Tim Simon, kindly reviewed the section on securitisation. All have been endlessly helpful by discussing procedures and providing references.

A third of the book would not have happened without the support of the companies who provided the case study material from interviews, documents, site visits and comments on my scripts. I am very grateful for the help they gave. I started at IBM UK Ltd, where the very positive response of their

Property Director, Michael Brooks, was a great encouragement. Later I was delighted to meet Peter Wingrave, who helped show me around their Bedfont Lakes site. Alan White, Director Group Property at BT plc, explained much, organised papers and arranged for Frank Shepherd to show me round Westside, where I met Neil McLocklin. Alan's son Dominic White, now with Henderson Asset Management, provided the illustration on BT's Portfolio Audit.

At Marks & Spencer plc, Chris Williams, of the Property Department, and Peter Stoakley, of the Physical Distribution Department, covered wide-ranging aspects of the company's business operations. Ian Coull, the director at J Sainsbury plc responsible for property, provided the history of their sale and leaseback initiative. David Stathers, Director of Estates at Boots The Chemist Ltd, has implemented many innovative and beneficial developments that have brought strategic benefits for the company's use of real estate – and diversity to my case studies.

John Ritblat, who has expressed his concern that the property and business worlds are too far apart, provided a wealth of information on the activities of the Conrad Ritblat Group. I did meet Ian Harris of Z/Yen Ltd, which may be a disappointment to those who imagined a virtual interview! Again I am grateful for the wealth of information and the visit to the core of their operation, with its surprisingly small amount of IT equipment.

Within the text are brief mentions of innovative developments at a number of companies. While some have been based on published references, many have been discussed directly with the companies concerned. I would like to thank Louise Footner of Barclays Bank plc, Steve Cox of Nationwide Building Society, Andrew Davis of British Gas plc, David Cassidy, Chairman of The Oliver Group plc, and Gordon Edington, Director of BAA plc.

Many people helped with permission to use illustrations and quotations and I would like to thank especially: Ian Cullen of Investment Property Databank for permission to reproduce the graph 'Annual Returns for Equities, Bonds and Property' and for information on the indices; Peter Evans and DTZ Debenham Thorpe for permission to reproduce the graph 'Real Estate Assets' and for information on indices; Tim Dixon of the College of Estate Management for permission to reproduce material developed by Francis Salway; Angus McIntosh and Richard Ellis for permission to quote from the Richard Ellis/Harris Research Centre Report *Occupier's Preferences*; Gary Hamel, C. K. Prahalad and Harvard Business School Press for permission to use quotations from the book *Competing for the Future: Breakthrough Strategies for Seizing Control of Your Industry and Creating the Markets of Tomorrow, Harvard Business School Press, Boston, 1994*; Hugh O. Nourse, Stephen E. Roulac and *The Journal of Real Estate Research* for permission to reproduce the headings from Exhibit 2 in the article 'Linking real estate decisions to corporate strategy'; Franklin Becker, Fritz Steele and publishers Jossey-Bass Inc. for permission to quote from the book *Workplace by Design*; and James

Whitmore and *Property Week* for permission to quote from his article 'Attacking formation'.

For information on property and other indices I would like to thank Robert Wildman of Richard Ellis, Trish Connolly of Hillier Parker and Nigel Roberts of Jones Lang Wootton.

Hunting out information is not easy. I want to thank those who helped me, especially at the library of the Royal Institution of Chartered Surveyors, the Business Section of the Central Library of the London Borough of Bromley, the library of South Bank University and a special thank you to John in the library of London Business School, who made my most trying requests seem reasonable! Mark Davies of Companies House in Cardiff was helpful well beyond normal expectations when some accounts proved hard to access.

Writing a book is a daunting experience, and I doubt I would have got very far without the support and encouragement of the series editor, Professor Ivor Seeley and Macmillan's publisher, Malcolm Stewart. Their guidance was very valuable.

Last, but not least, a big thank you to my family – my husband Peter, our children Elizabeth and Robert, and also my father, Stanley Edwards – for their encouragement and support. Peter's help as proofreader and commentator was invaluable – all remaining errors are mine alone!

Preface

The air is heavy with change, and the property world is not exempt. The property slump of 1989 was felt by many and heralded as a dramatic occurrence, yet it is probably of minor significance compared with the real estate consequences of the information revolution.

The information revolution is rapidly freeing many activities from location and time – they can be undertaken anywhere (or almost anywhere) and be instantly accessed globally.

In the past many businesses had little choice over location, as too many aspects of their activities focused on a specific location. For many, the only issue was to obtain the necessary space as cheaply as possible. As businesses gain freedom over location they also gain the responsibility to use real estate (if it is necessary!) competitively. It has become a matter of strategic importance.

This has meant that business managers, real estate managers and their advisers need to gain new skills. They need to reach beyond their traditional knowledge and learn much more about what drives decisions in each other's fields.

This book has been written to help bridge the divide by introducing business managers and real estate managers to the changing role of real estate in corporate business. The focus is on the importance of real estate, not in isolation but as an integral part of corporate strategy.

However, the book does much more than discuss and illustrate this importance. It has been written to provide active help. The process of reaching the point where a business can make effective decisions that incorporate real estate considerations is explained.

It is then supported by information about new technologies and the way in which businesses are subsequently changing their use of real estate, together with a discussion of the corporate finance issues. The specific features of real estate, such as the choice of tenures and the problems of obsolescence, are discussed. Practical help is also provided to assist real estate and business managers develop, present and implement corporate strategy incorporating real estate. Finally, as some of the UK's leading companies have already began this process, seven case studies review their experiences.

Throughout the book very practical guidance has been given about sources of further information. These range from sources of basic information to sources of up-to-the-minute ideas to help readers continue to keep up to date as the process of change moves rapidly forward.

Everyone is still very much on a learning curve. This book has been written to help develop understanding, to help managers gain new skills and to assist MBA and real estate postgraduate students extend their studies.

The aim is to inspire UK businesses to seek to become more competitive in their use of real estate, not only in order to be profitable in their home markets but also to increase their global competitiveness – both now and in the future – as younger business and real estate managers climb up corporate hierarchies. We need more world-class companies. The UK ranks 6th in the world for its gross domestic product, but in the 1994 World Competitiveness Report was only 14th for national competitiveness. Appreciating the strategic importance of real estate is an important step in the bid to improve profitability for UK companies operating from a densely populated country with expensive real estate.

Marion Weatherhead
October 1996

Part 1: Introduction

1 The Importance of Real Estate

1.1 Real estate – the emerging corporate resource

In recent years, business managers have focused on improving their use of resources, particularly by making use of technology, human resource management, financial and fiscal measures, and information management to make their operations more efficient and customer-focused.

Yet land, or real estate, always highlighted in economic text books as an important factor of production, seems to be forgotten by most as soon as they pass their economics examination. In the USA, where the importance of its role has already been recognised, it was identified by Joroff and his research team at Harvard and MIT in 1993 as the fifth corporate resource, after capital, people, technology and information. They found it a powerful resource: often the second most expensive cost after labour and representing a significant proportion of the asset base – an asset of strategic importance.

Businesses in the UK, a densely populated country with some of the world's most expensive property, have a greater need than most to appreciate the strategic implications of the contribution of real estate to their profits – or losses.

This book presents ideas and methodologies to assist these business managers. It also draws on examples of good practice and innovative thinking to illustrate opportunities to gain the competitive edge and increase profitability by being innovative in the use of real estate, both as an asset and a cost.

It helps those investigating and implementing proposals for their own or a client's company by introducing models and practical advice to help:

- understand the role of real estate in a business
- create a real estate corporate strategy
- develop a corporate strategy *incorporating* real estate

1.2 Real estate is important in a changing world

Historically, real estate has made little significant difference to most ordinary business operations. This has changed. Real estate decisions are now important to most major businesses because computer connectivity has released busi-

3

nesses from the constraints of geography and time. Now including real estate in corporate strategy can bring financial improvement direct to the bottom line. The remainder of this introductory chapter explains what has been happening for those who do not have day-to-day contact with the real estate market and recent research publications from the USA and the UK.

1.3   A rude awakening

The UK business world realised the importance of real estate at the end of 1989. A slump in the property market coincided with an economic recession. Business managers are generally aware of the cyclical nature of both the economy and the property market. However, few could predict the onslaught of the downturn towards recession or the property slump. Even fewer appreciated that they had not suffered both together in recent memory. The varied movement of the different cycles is shown in Figure 1.1.

For many it was a 'double whammy'. Falling property values were reducing asset values at the same time as the economic recession was increasing the need for credit to maintain cash flows (Figure 1.2). Not only did businesses

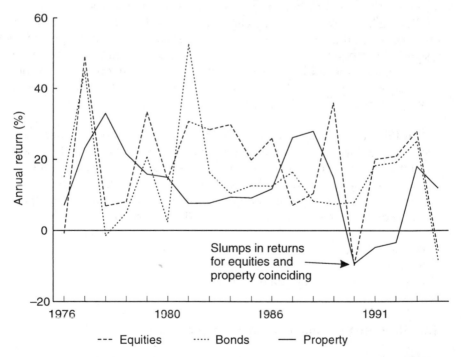

Figure 1.1 Annual returns for equities, bonds and property. Note the different cycles for property and other economic indicators. (Source: Investment Property Databank (IPD) and WM Company, Edinburgh (Gilts and Equity series) (1994)

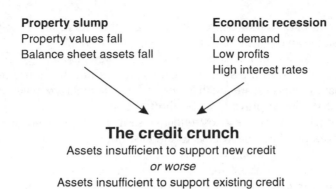

Property slump
Property values fall
Balance sheet assets fall

Economic recession
Low demand
Low profits
High interest rates

The credit crunch
Assets insufficient to support new credit
or worse
Assets insufficient to support existing credit

Figure 1.2 The double whammy.

have insufficient assets to support new credit, but worse, their assets were no longer sufficient to justify existing credit.

There have been credit crunches before, but this time things were much worse. The whole business environment was changing. It was soon clear to the astute that one result was that real estate decisions had become an important aspect of business strategy.

1.4 New technology companies lead

Generally the first to view property interests in a new light were those most affected by the dual slumps and the changing technological environment. Among these, the operators in high-technology industries and communications had the advantage of understanding and believing in the strategic importance of the technological changes. They became the first in the UK to react to the new environment.

1.5 USA experience

The potential importance of the changing corporate real estate environment has been recognised by leading researchers in the USA. Articles began appearing in the US real estate professional journals in significant numbers from the late 1980s. This interest led in 1992 to the Corporate Real Estate 2000 project, undertaken by a team led by Michael Joroff. This sought an understanding about how the shifting business environment was changing the demands on the corporate real estate professionals. In 1993 the first report was produced. It led by explaining that the corporate real estate profession in the USA was being transformed so that it could contribute effectively to corporate goals. It has now been followed by a study focusing on developing the real estate service (Lambert *et al.*, 1995).

The USA was the first country to report on these global changes. Over much of the USA, the pressures on real estate are not as intense as in the UK. Population densities are much lower and mostly rents are lower. It means there is not the same pressure to be thrifty about space allocations. It is in the UK that some of the most cost-effective strategies have been carried out. IBM, for example, have been able to increase their occupation densities in the UK to higher levels than the USA (see Chapter 14).

Another conclusion about real estate from the USA is worthy of note. It comes from Arthur Andersen & Co, who undertook a study of the changing real estate industry across the USA during 1990–1991 called *Managing the Future: Real Estate in the 1990s*. It concluded that the industry was in a profound and fundamental state of change and that the corporate world needed to improve real estate management to sustain property values.

Reporting in 1994 on another survey, *Real Estate in the Corporation: The Bottom Line from Senior Management*, Arthur Andersen, again in the USA, suggested there was a wide horizon of opportunities for many corporations to benefit from managing real estate as a financial asset with a need for a continuing evolution of the corporate real estate manager's function within corporate structure

A summary of US literature about corporate real estate published in 1996 shows that decisions concerning corporate real estate assets have a significant effect on the value of a business (Rodriguez and Sirmans, 1996). Real estate decisions, they concluded, need to be consistent with the overall corporate strategic plan and those making such decisions need to be aware of empirical evidence indicating the financial market's reaction to real estate decisions.

Some influences on the USA real estate market have not been parallelled in the UK, and vice versa. Nevertheless much is similar, including the ability of effective strategic management of real estate to make a valuable difference. European chapters now exist for the main USA groups of corporate real estate executives – International NACORE and International Development Research Council (IRDC).

1.6   Turmoil

Not all businesses were directly affected by the recession or the property slump, but for those managers who needed to address the issues, survival often depended on moving fast. It has created a great deal of turmoil. Those who have time to move more slowly are trying to assess the new structure of the real estate market. They are attempting to plan how the real estate needs of business should be addressed in the future.

The market is dynamic, so this book can only seek to capture the key tenets of change and focus on the fundamentals. There is no doubt that, over time, some recent developments will prove more suitable for business development than others and that some ideas will be superseded.

It is most likely that substantial success will be found by those who seek to understand changing circumstances – managers who think laterally, strive for new strategies and seek actively to make full use of their real estate resources.

1.7   Real estate is an integral part of business

Property is an essential factor of production. It is almost impossible to conceive of a business that does not require some sort of space in which to operate. Even an agent working from a mobile phone will seek free use of doorways for shelter!

This does not mean that every business will own property, but most will incur property costs. For most corporate businesses the cost is substantial. Real estate costs are frequently not well defined. Many costs that are property-related, such as cleaning and insurance, are not seen as such, which masks the role of property as a costly factor of production.

Many businesses are seeking to gain competitive advantage from changing working patterns, such as re-engineering, image processing and 'just-in-time' supply methods. To be effective, each of these has a property implication that must be addressed if full benefits are to be gained.

Additionally, many businesses are now in global markets and must compete with those who operate under very different real estate systems. Some of these systems are more advantageous to business than others, and will attract cross-border investment. The corporate real estate manager making the most active contribution to corporate strategy will be seeking to understand the real estate opportunities and difficulties in a global context.

Real estate may be important to businesses, but real estate management requires skills that are normally different from those needed to run the core business profitably. Focusing on the core business has meant that many corporations have disregarded the role of property – it has been neglected by the key directors and managers. Research has shown that many have very little idea of their property costs, the extent of their property interests or their value (Bannock and Partners, 1994; Avis and Gibson, 1995).

We are now seeing greater concern about shareholder value. Business management is being focused on share price and the importance of creating value in the business that will be reflected in profit growth and share price rises. It can be hard to justify committing shareholders' funds to property ownership when other aspects of the business are creating much higher returns. It means that the most cost-effective real estate arrangements are required, and this is bringing the real estate question before senior management.

For some businesses circumstances are different, and a business may create value just because it occupies a building. This can be because it enhances an area, or because others wish to compete from nearby premises to enable easy comparison of business services and products. This may give a business a strong hand when negotiating for premises (see Chapter 16).

Others have found that property needed for operational reasons can be made to bring in a significant income flow. The prime example is the growth of retail complexes within airport buildings. British Airports Authority's income and profitability from 'other income', which includes the retail provision and property interests, are now greater than from airport charges (e.g. aircraft landing fees) (BAA, 1994).

1.8   The wider economic environment

In 1994, research entitled *Understanding the Property Cycle* was published, which had been commissioned by the Royal Institution of Chartered Surveyors from the University of Aberdeen and Investment Property Databank to investigate links between property and the economy (Investment Property Databank, 1994). Using the somewhat limited historic data available, the study resulted in a time series record of property cycles in the context of the wider economy. This work has now been updated to include the mini-boom and slump of 1993–95. The movement in this latest cycle far exceeds anything from the 1980s (IPD, 1995). The retrospective research assists econometric modellers to highlight correlations and other mathematical features that help develop understanding and eventually strengthen forecasting techniques.

Another move towards understanding the relationship between business and real estate is the research undertaken by Grimley for the Confederation of British Industry. In the fourth of their bi-annual reports, *Survey of Property Confidence and Future Requirements*, they were able to report that trends were starting to emerge (Grimley, 1996). This information is useful, but until a longer series is available it will have to be treated with caution.

The questionnaires supporting the research draw out information on the reasons behind business managers' actions, including the economic scenarios of their businesses. In June 1996, just under half the respondents (47%) reported no change in property holdings in the previous six months and no plans for change in the next six months. Of the remainder, 28% expected to increase holdings and 25% to cut back, which shows an overall positive balance of 3%. The survey gives details of the attitudes of different sizes of firms and the industry sectors where the increases and decreases are predicted. Further information covers site and regional preferences. In this study, the major constraints on capital expenditure on real estate were found to be a lack of suitable property, difficulties in disposing of existing property and inadequate returns. They echo findings in other surveys.

The search for more knowledge by both the property profession and the CBI is a reflection of business managers' awareness of the importance of being responsive to change if they wish to survive. This is hard when many real estate arrangements involve long-term commitments and, additionally, property assets are not very liquid. Property can become like a ball and chain, slowing down a business and making quick response to changing markets almost impossible. Managers, seeking freedom from this shackle against progress, are putting more energy into understanding their property needs and the property market in which they operate.

1.9 Technology changing real estate requirements

Technological change has been very great in the last five years. The internationalisation of the Internet, with the facility for even those working at home to pass files of information cheaply, is perhaps the most dramatic example.

An American health insurance company can fly its paperwork to Ireland, where wages and real estate are cheap. The information is entered into the computer and transmitted by fibre-optic cables back to the USA the following day (Murray-Brown, 1994). Even this development of the early 1990s seems old-fashioned. Information can now be scanned from the written form into computer systems, thereby removing the need to find low-wage operators to type the data.

These are not changes in management style, fashionable one day and soon to be replaced by the deliberations of the next management guru. They are fundamental changes that are changing how businesses use real estate (see Chapter 5).

Substantial change is coming much more quickly than the establishment of the real estate world seems to expect. Of course, not all businesses will be affected to the same extent or at the same speed. Yet those that continue to operate profitably, using their traditional work patterns and operating in the same buildings, will still find that their real estate is affected. The market for real estate and the value of buildings is changing as others implement new technologies.

1.10 Outsourcing brings flexibility

Many businesses are changing their real estate commitments indirectly through the outsourcing of various aspects of the business. Not only does the outsourcing company provide service, it can also provide the necessary buildings.

This means that the users can expand or contract these aspects of their businesses without making real estate commitments. It is the outsourcing company that carries the burden of responsibility for a resource for which disposal can be difficult and expensive. The client businesses can still specify the facilities to be provided.

Outsourcing removes much of the control from the business, so it may not be a panacea for solving real estate problems or for actively making real estate contribute to the business.

1.11   In-house options

When businesses retain full control of their real estate function the changing market conditions supported by new legislation have made greater flexibility possible. Lease conditions can be negotiated to meet the needs of the individual businesses.

Those who commission new buildings, or rent new premises, are now more likely to request greater flexibility in the design. They want buildings that will be more adaptable to the future needs of the business.

Even so, the transfer lead times for real estate are lengthy. This means that successfully matching real estate to the needs of the business will require long-term planning. Businesses have to move fast on occasions, and it is not always possible to develop and implement strategies involving complicated real estate deals. The results are more likely to work successfully if the strategic issues are understood, rather than relying on ill-informed crisis management.

1.12   Real estate in a low-inflation economy

UK business is now adjusting to low inflation, and this particularly affects attitudes to real estate. The level of inflation changes the relationship of real estate to business assets and investment decisions.

For most of the last 50 years property has been a secure hedge against inflation. Many companies have sought to occupy their own freehold buildings so that they would not have to absorb rising rents into their cost structure. As inflation pushed up nominal land values these freeholds increased in value, which pushed up the asset value of the company. As current British accounting methods do not require depreciation to be charged against freehold land, the increase in asset value of the land is achieved without any reduction in profits. Only the depreciation of the buildings is charged against the profit and loss account.

Real estate was important as a hedge against inflation for many businesses. This view of real estate has been so strong that over the years many other aspects of the cost of its use have been overlooked as unimportant.

The onset of low inflation has created a fundamental change for property owners, as real estate values are no longer rising year by year. Low inflation has been maintained since 1992, which is a very short time (Central Statistical Office, 1995). There have been similar short periods of low inflation before during the 20th century, for example the late 1950s (Central Statistical Office, 1991).

There is doubt as to whether low inflation will continue. The result is that property owners are not adjusting their financial management decisions to a low-inflation scenario. This could be wise, but if a longer historical view is taken it will be seen that low inflation or even falling prices are more common (Mitchell and Dean, 1962). Although there has been almost continuous high inflation since the Second World War (and very high inflation in the 1970s), in the historical context this is unusual except in periods of war. Fifty years is not long – although sufficient to colour the views of two or three generations of property owners and advisers.

Economic prediction is fraught with difficulty, yet many real estate decisions will have long-term significance. This means that corporate real estate managers should be objectively weighing up the validity of the various predictions about future inflation before making their investment decisions.

In a low-inflation economy real estate prices will only rise if there is an unsatisfied demand. This will tend to be only for specific types of building and in specific locations rather than generally.

During the 1980s there was a very strong demand for new corporate offices in London, and it seemed that everyone wanted bigger and better accommodation. The culture of the decade was conspicuous consumption. Success was seen to breed success, so it was displayed by fountains, piazzas and palm trees all within the corporate headquarters. There were not enough of such buildings to meet demand and prices rose, encouraging others to develop new corporate headquarters buildings to meet the demand.

Those who 'knew' in 1988 that the burden of the high rents they had just agreed would fall as a percentage of their costs in the coming years were shocked in the early 1990s. They found that real rent levels had fallen as new developments began to balance supply to demand, and demand was also falling as the economic recession began to bite. Tenants with newly agreed leases were burdened with rental levels well above the falling market levels. Not only that, but conspicuous consumption was also out of fashion. Fountains, piazzas and palm trees were more likely to encourage a takeover bid for the business by those who could see the scope for cost-cutting than praise from existing shareholders!

Low inflation changes the role of property in a business. Under conditions of high inflation freehold property is a hedge against inflation, but with low inflation owning real estate is much less attractive. Why should shareholders want their money tied up in real estate, which is making modest returns, when investments in the main core of the business are making much higher returns?

Yet many companies made the opposite decision. At a time of low inflation they have been buying freehold property. This has been a reaction to finding themselves trapped with high rents well above market levels. Yet as capital values rise or fall in the same way as rent levels this does not seem a logical choice. The normal expectation is that the amount at risk will be much greater when real estate is owned rather rented.

However, the structure of rental agreements until the passing of the Landlord and Tenant (Covenants) Act 1995 was so Draconian for the original lessee that the obligations could be more of a burden than those of a freeholder. Prior to the 1995 Act, even if an original lessee was able to assign the lease, the obligations under the lease could remain with the original lessee throughout the term of the lease (privity of contract). Hence the original lessee would have to meet the obligations if the assignee failed to undertake them.

This meant that having signed a lease the only way to become completely free of its obligations before the end of the term was to negotiate with the landlord, who could refuse. Consequently, many felt that it was better to own a property outright, because then it could be sold. Selling at a loss was better than having to meet rent, repair and insurance obligations for 25 years on a building they did not want or which had even been assigned years earlier.

The new Act makes it possible for tenants to negotiate a lease without overburdening conditions, although a landlord in a strong position will resist. Each tenant with less onerous conditions will be balanced by a landlord with a less secure investment than at present.

Now the corporate real estate manager, when choosing between freehold and leasehold property, can focus on the economic factors and market conditions without the choice being skewed by restrictive legislation. Chapter 8 deals with these issues in greater detail. Scottish law has not been changed as these obligations were never part of it.

1.13   Real estate assets of UK non-property companies

Many assume that specialist property companies are the largest owners of real estate, but this is far from the case. Research in 1992 by Debenham Tewson & Chinnock, *The Role of Property: Managing Cost and Releasing Value*, revealed that among the 29 largest real estate-owning companies only eight were property companies. The remaining 21 had a core business that was not property, yet they had responsibility for real estate interests worth billions of pounds (Figure 1.3).

The core businesses of these major real estate owners were very varied, ranging from international conglomerates, through hotels, utilities, leisure, public sector and manufacturing, to banking and retail. Most used real estate for trading locations, but this was not always the case.

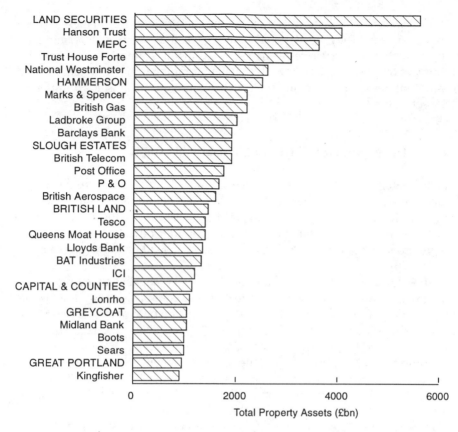

Figure 1.3 Real estate assets. Companies shown in capitals are property companies; the rest are non-property companies. (Source: The Role of Property, Debenham Tewson Research, June 1992)

Many of these large real estate owners have recognised the importance of real estate to their businesses. They have established corporate structures which have enabled them to run this aspect of their businesses efficiently. Most of the case studies in this book are from among this group.

These major companies are already among the leaders in their own business sector. They have gained the economies of scale for their core business. Now they are supporting this with strategies that allow them to have competitive advantage from their efficiency in a non-core area.

Competitors may not have the same magnitude of real estate interests, but they are in competition with companies that have already appreciated the importance of real estate. The smaller companies are now seeking to emulate the industry leaders. For them, the strategic management of their real estate needs has become important.

The smaller organisations are extending the demand for finance and real estate experts. They need people who have the skills to understand the interface between their respective specialisms and the ability to help the formulation of strategic policy. The smaller companies may have smaller real estate interests, but for many real estate is proportionally still an important aspect of the business.

1.14   The importance of UK commercial real estate

In the later part of the 1980s some chartered surveyors were becoming increasingly concerned that neither the business community nor the Government were taking real estate seriously. While well aware of the role of housing in economy, the Government's failure to consider other real estate aspects of its economic policy and legislation was seen as sending the wrong message to industry.

The Royal Institution of Chartered Surveyors, seeking to support their argument about the importance of real estate, commissioned research from the London Business School. The work, undertaken by Professor David Currie and Andrew Scott, was published in the 1991 report *The Place of Commercial Property in the UK Economy* (Currie and Scott, 1991).

These findings supported what the chartered surveyors had realised – real estate was important. Commercial property, essential to the productive activities of manufacturing, services and agriculture, was worth £250 billion in 1989. This was then about half of the value of the total UK equity market. Commercial property accounted for one third of total investment in physical assets, about the same amount as investment in plant and machinery. The broadest measure of the contribution of real estate and construction to the economy as an essential factor of production is estimated to be around 10% of gross domestic product.

The report also allowed the Royal Institution of Chartered Surveyors to do what they had wanted. They took their evidence to the Government, the press and industry and started to promote the importance of real estate.

Over the years, the importance or real estate to business has remained a key component of the RICS programme. In 1992, Douglas McWilliams's report *Commercial Property and Company Borrowing* (McWilliams, 1992), the result of further RICS-commissioned research, was published. This concluded that falls in property prices cause corporate borrowing to be reduced, so that movements in commercial property prices themselves affect the future path of the economy. Not only are corporate borrowing and expenditure patterns affected, as corporate borrowing is an element of money supply the effect follows through to affect money growth and economic activity. Consequently, the report proposed that the government should include a property indicator when interpreting monetary conditions.

In the opening paragraphs of his inaugural address, Jeremy Bayliss, the 1996–97 RICS President, acknowledged that these efforts are having some effect – the importance of property to the economy is receiving greater attention. However, he also stressed the need for many in business to have a greater awareness of the importance of their property assets and how they can be managed as a resource, and not merely treated as a cost (Bayliss, 1996).

1.15   Real estate as a percentage of total corporate assets

Currie and Scott (1991) also looked at commercial real estate in relation to individual businesses. It found that real estate represented on average 30–40% of total assets in the balance sheets of companies. This is a little more generous than the results of research carried out in 1988 and published in *Managing Operational Property Assets* (Avis *et al.*, 1989). This revealed that, on average, 30% of asset value of those UK organisations whose managers were interviewed was held as real estate.

The percentage of assets held as real estate varies from business to business. Those industries that trade with the public from real estate, such as retailing and the hotel industry, will usually have a greater proportion of real estate as a proportion of their assets.

Whether 40% or 30% of the asset base is real estate, it is clear that it represents a substantial proportion for many businesses. This should be sufficient to encourage all business managers to investigate the situation for their own operations.

Many businesses carry real estate in their accounts at historic cost. The valuations of many businesses bear very little relationship to the asset base: their abilities, their brand names, their goodwill and similar matters all contribute much more. So despite the high proportion of real estate assets, it is not surprising that some business managers may relegate real estate until a problem occurs. By then it may be too late (see Chapter 7).

1.16   Real estate as a percentage of total corporate costs

Real estate is an expensive factor of production. Research for Hillier Parker (Bannock and Partners, 1994) revealed that among large UK companies property represented 16–17% of total costs. Again, for those that trade from buildings the percentage is much higher. This runs to millions of pounds for many companies each year – even hundreds of millions for the larger corporations.

Costs are not like assets, which can fade into the background. Costs reduce profitability day-in, day-out. This makes them a very influential aspect of business.

1.17   The real estate market

This book focuses on activating new directions. Any survey of the whole real estate market, or of the commercial users, will reveal that much has not yet changed.

Research by King Sturge & Co. (1995) in 1994 found that proximity to a central business district and a rail station, as well as good motorway accessibility, remain important to occupiers of office buildings. The central business district was important to 73%, motorway accessibility to 78% and a rail station to 81% of their 362 participants, who were based in 11 UK city centres. They also regarded good security, car parking and flexible internal design as the most important factors in selecting office buildings.

At about the same time, Richard Ellis planned a survey undertaken by the Harris Research Centre in which they asked questions about occupiers' intentions, and the answers were rather different from those in the previous research (Richard Ellis/Harris Research Centre, 1995a). The central business district was not mentioned as a destination, maybe because businesses were planning only to move some staff and already had a presence in a central business district. They reported that when relocating offices, air and rail infrastructure linkages were of little importance, and the decision would be based on total occupancy costs, road infrastructure, quality of buildings, security and availability of staff.

Anecdotal evidence collected during the survey from 480 office occupiers found that directors and senior managers suggested the ideal location would depend on

> the right quality of building in a secure environment, well served with car parking and by a good road network in an area of skilled staff, not too distant from the target market.

Interestingly, this is also a description of the new office accommodation used by BT and IBM to provide the flexibility that both need for the 1990s and beyond.

Half the participants in the Harris survey expected change in the way their industries were structured, and these would include:

● expansion into the regions
● squeezing out competition
● growth
● automation
● adaptation to customers' needs

King Sturge & Co. also found changing office working patterns. They reported that around 13% of city centre office occupiers use some form of teleworking, and they reported on office occupiers using shared space or 'hot-desking' (see Chapter 6). King Sturge & Co. predicted that use of both would increase, but more probably by occupiers of business parks rather than offices in city centres. It was noted that some businesses were demanding more headquarters office space to provide for staff from consolidated satellite offices, plus additional meeting rooms and social facilities. Overall desk count has been reduced by hot-desking.

Although the two surveys highlighted differences as to preferred location, both recognised that attitudes and requirements were changing in a variety of ways.

1.18 Summary

This chapter introduces the importance of real estate as a corporate resource which should be included in corporate strategy. It particularly highlights the importance of:

- real estate as a business asset and a cost
- the property slump coinciding with an economic recession, followed by low inflation, for changing attitudes of many to the role of real estate
- business recovery being set against a climate of fast-developing technological change
- businesses gaining competitive advantage from their innovative use of real estate
- outsourcing changing real estate requirements
- appreciating that the low liquidity of real estate makes rapid change difficult, and therefore flexibility needs to be built into real estate arrangements, as long-term planning is often impossible
- research highlighting the importance of real estate in business and the economy

1.19 Further reading

A more general up-to-date overview of change within the real estate industry is found in the weekly journals *Property Week* and *Estates Gazette*. The management, technology and property sections of the *Financial Times* pick up most drivers of change and review many of the latest reports.

The Economic Outlook, a journal published quarterly by Blackwell Publishers (Tel: 01865 791155) and prepared by the Centre for Economic Forecasting at London Business School has a report twice a year derived from a model of the UK property market which was built with financial help from the Royal Institution of Chartered Surveyors as part of the research which resulted in the report *The Place of Commercial Property in the UK Economy*. The model also draws on information from the Investment Property Databank.

Purchasing details of the books by Joroff *et al.* (1993) and Lambert *et al.* (1995) are given at the end of Chapter 12. The Arthur Andersen report *Managing the Future: Real Estate in the 1990s* is a published book, but the second report, *Real Estate in the Corporation: The Bottom Line from Senior Management*, is obtainable direct from Arthur Andersen at Spear Street Tower Suite, 3500 One Market, San Francisco, CA 94105, USA (Tel: 00 1 415 546 8200; Fax: 00 1 415 543 1827).

Property consultants Richard Ellis produce a half-yearly *Corporate Real Estate Bulletin* which contains economic, legal and other information of interest to corporate business (Tel: 0171 629 6290).

The CBI/Grimley *Survey of Property Confidence and Future Requirements* is available from property consultants, Grimley at 10 Stratton Street, London W1X 6JR (Tel: 0171 895 1515) and from the Confederation of British Industry, Centre Point, 103 New Oxford Street, London WC1A 1DU.

Those wishing to focus on business strategy will find the *Harvard Business Review* helpful, and occasionally there are articles about real estate.

Business Strategy Review is a UK journal covering new strategy research findings. It is available from Oxford University Press, Walton Street, Oxford OX2 6DP.

1.20 Sources of information

The library of the Royal Institution of Chartered Surveyors produces the *RICS Weekly Briefing*, the *RICS Abstracts and Reviews* and the *Annual Subject Index*. These are held in the RICS Library and can also be purchased from the RICS Library as *The Information Service* for an annual subscription (Tel: 0171 334 3748).

Property Week is available on *Reuters Textline* (*Property Textline* on *FT Profile*). Reuters' selection of items covers the news and some features. The full *Financial Times* is available online from FT Profile (Tel: 0171 825 7905) and others. *Estates Gazette Interactive* (EGi) is an online subscription Internet service based on their journal *Estates Gazette* (excluding law reports) and with some additional property databases. Details are available from Estates Gazette Interactive, 15 Wardour Street, London W1V 4BN (Tel: 0171 411 2511; Fax: 0171 411 2518). The information page is available on the Internet at the World-Wide Web site http://www.egi.co.uk.

NACORE International (International Association of Corporate Real Estate Executives Inc.) has a European Executive Officer in the UK: Ms Marie A. Heyes, Saxon Court, 502 Avebury Boulevard, Milton Keynes MK9 3HT (Tel: 01908 692812; Fax: 01908 692813).

IDRC (International Development Research Council) does not have a permanent UK address. Their headquarters in the USA are at IDRC, 35 Technology Parkway, Suite 150, Norcross, Atlanta, GA 30092, USA (Tel: 00 1 770 446 8955). There is a European office at IDRC Europe, PO Box 59366, 1040 KJ Amsterdam, The Netherlands (Tel: 00 31 20 607 7155; Fax: 00 31 20 681 8833).

2 Is Real Estate Supporting Profitability?

2.1 Introduction

This chapter shows in greater detail how many businesses have been spending large amounts on real estate without knowing whether the expenditure supports their profitability.

2.2 A central 'free' resource

Typically, the real estate portfolios of corporate businesses have been assembled over time and the actual costs of occupying different buildings can vary tremendously. Traditionally, many businesses deal with this by regarding property costs as a central resource and allocating buildings to the various parts of the business as necessary.

This can mean that managers have no idea of the cost of their unit's accommodation, either as a proportion of the central costs or in real terms. Research for Hillier Parker (Bannock and Partners, 1994) revealed that most finance directors could not even give a general idea of the sum of annual real estate costs.

Similar results were found a year later, when a survey for Richard Ellis showed that only half of those contacted claimed to know the cost of rent, heating, lighting, rates and taxes for their offices (Richard Ellis/Harris Research Centre, 1995a). When it came to the capital value of the offices, 46% claimed to know, but only 17% could quote a figure!

It would seem that it is still common for local managers to be left to make their own decisions as to when new real estate is needed. Although a budget will have to be agreed with someone, most frequently this does not relate to a real estate policy or to the overall business strategy.

Management accounting systems that result in managers treating real estate as a 'free resource' lead to considerable waste. Status is attached to space, and, human nature being what it is, people will tend to overstate their needs. They also covet and acquire facilities and decorations. Many also expend considerable energy ensuring that their new premises are in the most convenient and prestigious location.

When property costs are not charged directly against each unit, there is no incentive to be more prudent than others in the organisation. Lack of understanding will mean that managers will not be aware of how significant real estate costs can be for their operations. Indeed, there is a general attitude that the bigger and better the accommodation, the happier are the unit's staff, which will suit its managers.

This sort of attitude to real estate has been prevalent for many years, and it became even more dominant during the 1980s. Then, the desire for grandiose accommodation went unchecked in many companies because management wanted to display success conspicuously, with the aim of breeding yet more success. The recession and property slump have changed attitudes; conspicuous consumption does not sit comfortably with mass redundancies.

However, trimming the excesses is not the same as implementing structural change, and it is still the case that many businesses are wasteful in their use of real estate.

2.3 Effective cost and profit centres

Only limited amounts of research have been undertaken, so our knowledge is somewhat limited. For this reason it is worthwhile considering US research that provides information on an area not investigated in the UK. In 1987, Peter Veale from MIT undertook a survey of real estate executives (Veale, 1988). The results showed a strong correlation between management attitude and effective management of corporate real estate. Good managers valued real estate and felt strongly about the importance of the function within their organisations.

The results also showed that using profit and cost centres was equally effective in the management of corporate land and buildings. Importantly, companies using either of these methods outperformed companies that did not evaluate their real estate separately from other corporate assets. Not being in the real estate business was the main reason used for employing a cost centre approach. Profit centres were favoured by those who wanted to generate revenue for overall corporate purposes. They were also seen to increase the efficiency of resources and to make for more effectively evaluated property performance. Users of both methods were showing a clear and deliberate choice to account for real estate within a well-defined strategy.

2.4 Lack of management

A report by Martin Avis and Virginia Gibson, *Real Estate Resource Management* (1995) found that in three-quarters of the non-property but major real estate-owning organisations that they surveyed there were no personnel with sole responsibility for real estate. More positively, the number of real estate department heads holding a senior management position had increased substantially since an earlier survey (Avis *et al.*, 1989), from 40% in 1988 to 69% in 1994, with 13% now holding a boardroom post.

Another positive note of the Avis and Gibson (1995) survey was that more organisations, especially in the private sector, now have at least annual reports on real estate resources such as surplus property, repairs, refurbishment and total running costs.

The number disaggregating accounting and budgeting to individual properties had not changed from 1989 and remains at only one-third of respondents. Thirty-seven per cent of the organisations used specific performance measures for real estate, but the measures used varied. About half of the 37% used measures such as return on assets, cost per unit of area, and property costs as a percentage of turnover/profit. This is less than 20% of the 155 organisations participating in their survey, but shows a 20% improvement since 1989, when no organisation could provide this information. It was thought that this could be about to improve, as more organisations now have the basic information systems in place and for the first time are in a position to start to implement the measures required.

Changes during the 1990s have resulted in an increasing gap between those organisations which have addressed the need for corporate real estate strategies and corresponding management requirements and those that have not. The latter are ignoring management of a resource which, on average, is 30% of their fixed asset value. Most typically, the research by Avis and Gibson (1995) found that management of real estate assets is reactive rather than proactive.

An interesting finding from the USA is that the measures used by business units to quantify their real estate performance and the measures used by corporate real estate departments do not always match, even in the same organisation (Lambert *et al.*, 1995). It would seem that information is not being passed around within businesses. Those measures that were most commonly used by both the business units and the corporate real estate teams focused on business and financial objectives rather than on real estate objectives.

Similar research has not been undertaken in the UK, so the situation is not known, but the US results are sufficiently interesting to prompt UK managers to reconsider their own organisations.

2.5   Reducing real estate costs

A key aspect of many real estate strategies is an aim to reduce real estate costs, particularly those related to mature, less profitable, products. As mentioned in Chapter 1, for many of the UK's large businesses real estate expenditure represents 16–17% of total costs (Bannock and Partners, 1994). This is high.

Research for Hillier Parker (Bannock and Partners, 1994) has suggested that a 5% saving in real estate costs will result in up to a 1% saving in total costs. This sounds small until it is realised that some industries, such as advertising, before the recession had net margins of only 7%, so a saving of just 0.65% in costs would increase earnings per share by about 10%.

Not many zany, creative advertising wizards would focus on real estate as important for the success of their business, yet as shown it can be a vital ingredient of success. Real estate is not central to their operation, except perhaps for the image that their office building may create because of its design and location.

It is in retailing, where real estate contributes up to 20% of costs, that a saving of 5% in real estate costs will result in an average 1% saving overall. The figures are less in other industries; for example, 0.45% average total cost savings in manufacturing for a saving of 5% in real estate costs.

Table 2.1 illustrates the situation where real estate costs are 20% of total costs and a saving of 5% of real estate costs is made. Operating profit increases by 9%.

Table 2.1 A 5% saving in real estate costs increases gross profitability by 9%

Existing trading situation

Turnover	100
Total costs:	90
Operating profit	10

Total costs of 90% are made up of:

real estate	20% =	18
other costs	80% =	72
		90

Reduce real estate costs by 5%

Total costs are now:

real estate 18% cut by 5% =	17.1
other costs unchanged =	72
	89.1

New trading situation after reduction in real estate costs

Turnover:	100
Total costs:	89.1
Operating profit:	10.9 (9% increase)

When initial real estate costs are lower and gross margins higher the results of a 5% cut in real estate costs will not, of course, be so dynamic.

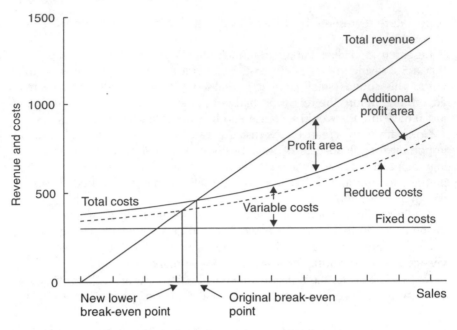

Figure 2.1 Additional profits from lower costs.

Figure 2.1 shows how a reduction in costs will increase profits. It also shows fixed costs separately from variable costs. Real estate costs are normally fixed costs that do not change with marginal changes in turnover. Any reduction in fixed costs applies whatever the level of production. If fixed costs are reduced, then total costs (fixed costs plus variable costs) will fall for all levels of output. It will mean that the break-even point will be achieved at a lower level of total revenue.

If any part of the real estate budget increases or decreases with production, then the costs are variable costs. This could apply to aspects of occupancy costs that relate to the hours that a factory is in use. If production increases owing to longer hours of operation, then these costs will increase, whereas expenditure on, say, rent will not increase.

2.6   Costs related to real estate costs

Real estate as an operational asset will clearly involve a business in expenses for rent (or the initial cost of purchase) plus additional costs such as business rates, heating, lighting, cleaning, landscaping, maintenance and repairs, which may be paid directly or indirectly as a service charge or increased rent.

An effective real estate strategy needs to be based on a consideration of these occupancy costs. However, it needs to go beyond this to include all other aspects of the overall business strategy that have a relationship to real estate. It is unlikely that anyone at boardroom level, other than a real estate director if employed, will have any idea as to what other costs are linked to real estate costs.

Some lateral thinking will be necessary.

Supplies and distribution are functions that can have considerable impact on property requirements. In this field many business decisions will impact on property, so that a saving in one area can increase costs in another. Consequently, the distribution industry is a good example which illustrates the variety of costs that are linked in some way to real estate. Points that may be influential include:

- Location:
  - petrol costs
  - wear and tear on vehicles
  - journey times
  - risk of traffic jams
  - number of drivers required

- Changing legislation:
  - the introduction of a lower speed limit reducing mileage per day
  - fall in demand for premises beyond one day's travel of the Channel ports at the reduced speed

- Changing distribution patterns:
  - improved roads lead to fewer but larger warehouses
  - faster stock rotation and smaller inventory reduces need for storage
  - distribution centres become sorting, not storage, centres
  - just-in-time methods bring satellite businesses around major plant
  - warehouses with permission for 24-hour working are needed

- Changing warehouse design:
  - fast turn-round distribution centres
  - high-bay racking
  - automation
  - pitched roof not required by latest internal designs
  - need for flexibility, especially for easy storing and reaching
  - space for expansion

- Staff requirements:
  - choice of high- and low-wage areas
  - availability of suitable staff and local training facilities
  - local public transport/provision of car parking
  - local cafés, sandwich bars

- Security:
  - 24-hour protection for warehouse and vehicles
  - facilities for drivers while vehicles are parked

- Government intervention:
  - availability of grants
  - infrastructure proposals

- Available properties
  - speculative developments
  - lease conditions
  - planning approval for new schemes

- Outsourcing:
  - facilities available from logistics contractor
  - warehousing can be provided by contractor

Distribution is only a small part of most businesses, unless they are specialist logistics contractors. DTZ Debenham Thorpe reported in *Distribution 2000* that total distribution costs have fallen from 12% of sales in 1983 to under 6% by 1991 (DTZ Debenham Thorpe, 1993). Rent and rates make up only 1.5% of total distribution costs, which is approximately 0.3–0.5% of total sales, well below the overhead for rent and rates in other business sectors.

Clearly, if a business gets it right property costs related to distribution should be small, but there are many who are bearing the costs of empty medium-sized warehouses for which there is little demand. There are those who daily bear high transport costs because their factory is poorly sited and for whom just-in-time methods are just a dream, because they are not located near suppliers, or are too far away to be considered by manufacturers using their products in just-in-time operations.

Using distribution as an example indicates the value of a real estate strategy which ensures that the ideas that are changing business are understood, and hence the need for real estate to be considered at the earliest opportunity and at the highest level. There are considerable first-mover advantages in off-loading properties destined to become unpopular and in locating where success seems most likely.

Equally, planning ahead means that the most cost-effective solution to the changes can be adopted. Attempting to catch up with the competition is not easy when real estate is involved, because of the long lead times. Taking a lease of a speculatively developed building at the height of a property boom will probably result in terms which are a burden during a period of recession. Most directors who are currently ignoring real estate issues will not even consider the property cycle and the likely ensuing property slump, even though they are aware of economic cycles.

It is impossible to predict what will be important in the long term and what should be included in any specific property strategy. What is possible is to include real estate within the business strategy process. Then its interrelationship with other costs can be signalled, the information sought and future possibilities invested long before the need for immediate action arises.

2.7 Summary

This chapter has shown how many companies have not included real estate within their management process, although the situation is beginning to change. The negative approaches to real estate include:

- most companies having no real estate financial information, i.e. no idea of real estate costs (not in real terms or as a percentage of total costs) or the current value of real estate assets
- most companies lacking a real estate policy and having no link between real estate and corporate strategy
- many real estate decisions being reactive rather than proactive
- treating real estate as a free resource leads to waste – there is no incentive to be prudent
- 75% of non-property companies with large real estate holdings having no person solely responsible for real estate
- real estate being, on average, responsible for 16–17% of total costs

The positive approaches to real estate now include:

- those managers recognised as effective having been found to be those who also value their real estate and its function in the business
- 13% of major businesses now giving the head of real estate a place in the boardroom
- 20% of companies now measuring the effectiveness of real estate performance

Cost saving possibilities include:

- real estate savings directly improving profitability, e.g. a 5% saving in real estate costs can increase gross margin by 9% (when real estate accounts for 20% of costs)
- reducing fixed costs so that the break-even point will be achieved at a lower level of total revenue
- linking in various ways other costs (e.g. occupancy costs and distribution costs) to real estate costs and making operational changes that will produce real estate savings

Strategic measures can include:

- including real estate costs in competitor analysis
- considering changing business methods in relation to real estate – keeping real estate up to date and cost-effective
- a proactive approach that includes real estate in the business strategy process and avoids costly panic action

2.8   Further reading

The best information on the latest attitudes to the management of real estate is the research results produced by Martin Avis and Virginia Gibson. Their latest report is *Real Estate Resource Management*, published in 1995. Reference to their earlier report *Managing Operational Property Assets* (Avis *et al.*, 1989), will give a clearer overall picture. A third publication (Oxford Brookes University and University of Reading, 1993), called *Property Management Performance Monitoring* may also assist.

Reference has been made to reports by various property consultancy practices. All contain a range of information on these issues, and it can be expected that these practices and their competitors will produce future reports of interest. New reports are usually reviewed in the property press.

2.9   Sources of information

The annual report and accounts for most major companies are available from the *Financial Times* (order details inside back page of the second section, 'Companies and Markets'). Others are available direct from the corporate offices.

Part 2:
Strategic Overview

3 Real Estate in Existing Corporate Strategy

3.1 Introduction

The body of corporate strategy literature only goes back 25 years (Andrews, 1971). Since 1980 the ideas of Porter (1980), which focus on the competition within industries, have dominated. In the last few years, Hamel and Prahalad (1994) have been very influential, with their ideas of breaking new ground so as to get a business to the future first. The approach being promoted by several writers now focuses on reviewing resources and capabilities and using them to gain advantage in the competitive environment (Collis and Montgomery, 1995). Mostly they have given little thought to real estate.

This chapter looks at the work of these and other strategy writers and applies it to real estate issues. This is possible because corporate real estate is not a separate component in a business but an integral part of the operation, which will affect and be affected by the implementation of strategic policy.

These ideas are helpful in highlighting the factors that make real estate important to a business. This helps indicate the need for a business to develop corporate strategy *incorporating* real estate to gain the competitive edge, as shown in Chapter 4.

3.2 The strategic role of real estate

Joroff and his team, in *Strategic Management of the Fifth Resource: Corporate Real Estate* (1993), showed how corporate real estate competencies in the USA had shifted from the merely technical stage through the analytical, problem-solving and business planning stages to reach the need for real estate experts to have strategic competencies. The real estate managers have moved away from being taskmasters first to being controllers, deal-makers and 'intrapreneurs', finally becoming business strategists. The authors found that real estate experts are under pressure to move very rapidly along this path to become corporate strategists.

The focus on the real estate manager as a person who can make a significant impact is new. In the past, most businesses had little choice over location –

it was governed by customers, raw materials or the need to be close to others in an industry, and there was no need for strategic consideration. The estate manager could be asked to cut costs, but the opportunities were limited and tactical rather than strategic. This has now changed – the real estate manager is now probably more likely to be negotiating within the business to develop and implement real estate options that will support the overall business strategy than be negotiating externally with landlords and vendors.

3.3   Strategic intent

The purpose of developing a business strategy is to focus the operations of the business in ways that are predicted to bring success from gaining competitive advantage.

This advantage can come in a variety of ways. Above all, it is about developing and implementing new ideas ahead of the competition. Implementing ideas that others have tried is mostly about attempting to catch up with the competition and not about first-mover advantage, unless the ideas are being transferred from other industries or different markets.

Real estate has come to boardroom attention mainly because it is now possible to make cost savings. Typically, many of the real estate strategies being implemented during the 1990s included downsizing (or rightsizing!) activities. The success of the estate manager has been measured in the disposal of buildings that are surplus to requirements. The difficulties involved must not be underestimated, as this apparently simple strategy can be extremely complex. Inevitably, the buildings which are of least use to a business always seem to be those for which disposal is most difficult! Matching business operations to the right buildings, maintaining or enhancing corporate culture and ensuring that key staff remain committed to the business add to the complexity of the strategy. It is not a simple real estate disposal exercise.

Many businesses have shed staff and become leaner operations. It follows that many other organisations are likely to follow similar 'strategies'. Quotation marks are used because although these companies will face similar difficulties, the outcome will not be as dynamic or strategically significant. Unless they are the first in their industry to use the approach, all they will achieve by the 'strategy' is to move alongside those who have already experienced these gains and who are by now about to implement new ideas so that they continue to stay ahead.

To gain and keep competitive advantage, real estate strategists will need to offer their business strategy colleagues more than 'more of the same'. They are going to have to be proactive parties to the development of new strategies which give their businesses a new strategic intent. People have very narrow perceptions about real estate, and as already mentioned many managers have had just one aim – cut real estate costs. It is not a bad intention, but it is unlikely to bring sustained long-term advantages once everyone has followed suit. In the coming years, real estate strategy will develop to be more than just cutting costs and will become part of the whole business process. Two comments made by Hamel and Prahalad (1994) are pertinent:

> The new solutions emerge not because the challengers are incrementally more efficient than incumbents, but because they are substantially more unorthodox. They discover the new solutions because they are willing to look far beyond the old.

and

> Creating the future is more challenging than playing catch up, in that you have to create your own road map. The goal is not simply to benchmark a competitor's products and processes and imitate its methods, but to develop an independent point of view about tomorrow's opportunities and how to exploit them. Pathbreaking is a lot more rewarding than benchmarking. One doesn't get to the future first by letting someone else blaze the trail.

Business strategists can continue the cost-cutting models that have been so prevalent during the early 1990s, or they can seek to develop new business and seek out new market opportunities – the method promoted by Hamel and Prahalad. Being a trailbreaker is not easy.

Most strategy case studies are about those that 'got it right'. Little is said about those that tried and got it wrong. Often in these cases the second mover gains by learning from the mistakes of the first mover. The second mover will have lower pioneering costs, and ascertaining the available market will be clear; consequently it will be possible to move faster and more cheaply. Further, where applicable, a later market entrant can select the technical format that is becoming acceptable.

Not all strategic decisions lead directly to a new product or service. It is probable that most real estate managers will not be dynamic trailbreakers. Nevertheless, if a system involving real estate changes does not work it could have considerable repercussions on overall productivity.

Planning to gain the advantages of second mover is difficult. How do you know who to watch? Who will be the first mover that meets difficulties that a second mover can overcome? Who will be the first mover that gets it right first time and moves to an unassailable position in the market?

What is clear is that many businesses that feel that they have a successful formula and are not seeking new strategies find that their market position declines as competitors implement ideas that are better suited to the new conditions.

Much of this book is about methods that have been successful for real estate managers in the early 1990s. Having moved into the boardroom, the challenge for real estate managers in the new millennium will be to contribute new ideas to enhance corporate strategy.

3.4   Critical success factors

Isakson and Sircar, writing in the USA in 1990, proposed this basic strategic thinking process as a way to help business managers recognise the role played by real estate in their business. When real estate management is decentralised, many in senior management do not realise its importance.

They suggest that a real estate manager is included in any team seeking to define the company's mission and supporting issues. These should be matters that are of sufficient importance (whether internal or external to the business) to cause the firm problems if they do not proceed as expected. Hence they are critical success factors.

The paper contains a review of the general business literature on critical success factors and reveals several companies who listed real estate or real estate-related issues as important to their business. They were not able to develop their work sufficiently to be able to offer guidance about when real estate would or would not be of critical importance.

They also found that, even when real estate was recognised as an important aspect of a business and, as a consequence, a centralised real estate department had been created, there was no guarantee that real estate would be incorporated into strategic planning.

Given the lack of interest in real estate shown by many business managers, it is probably wise for real estate managers to conclude that they have to convince very cynical people before real estate is accepted as a strategic component of the business.

3.5   Substitution

Substitution is a concept introduced by Porter (1980). He used an example of a business being under competitive pressure from substitute products and illustrated this with the example of synthetic fabrics being a substitute for natural fibres.

In the context of real estate a business will be under pressure if another can provide the product or service using less real estate. An example is First Direct, the profitable UK telephone banking company that has gained a market share from the high street banks and which does not have the cost of retail premises. This is a substantially different approach from that of reducing real estate costs by marginal changes (for example by increasing the intensity of use).

Business strategies which reduce the need for real estate are the most effective, provided that other costs do not rise to compensate. They also rely on offloading the released real estate.

'Cut real estate' is easily said and quickly forgotten, especially as it reduces the size of the real estate manager's empire!

Not long ago the idea of the successful business cutting real estate was unrealistic, because success and expansion meant that more premises would be needed to reach more customers with more goods and services. Now businesses are expanding using telephony and online systems, goods are moving through the distribution chain so quickly that faster turnover (rather than space-consuming stocks) is the result of increased business, and the trading records are bytes on a tiny computer disk rather than rows of filing cabinets.

3.6 The product life-cycle

Although it is important to think beyond strategies that just aim to cut costs, it is clearly an approach which has been very successful. Therefore, it is important to consider when it will be most effective. A business tool which is useful in this context is the product life-cycle S-curve.

Research has established over the years that industries and products within an industry can be seen to follow an S-shaped life-cycle pattern, which can be used to help plan strategy. This was well described by Porter (1980). He also summarised the criticisms that its usefulness as a planning tool is diminished because the shape of the curve varies from case to case, making it hard to decide the actual situation for the industry or product in question – so some care is needed.

The typical S-shaped curve is shown in Figure 3.1. The first stage of the curve is the period of introduction, when the new industry or product is created. The period of a new venture when establishment takes much of the business's resources and growth is normally slow. This is followed by a period of rapid growth and good profits once the product is established and before competitors enter the market. Maturity is signalled by the introduction of viable competitors, when energies are channelled into maintaining market share and profitability. Competitors and the original entrant are offering similar goods, and competition tends to focus on price. Reducing costs so that prices can be reduced is an important aspect of retaining market share and remaining profitable. Decline follows either for the competitors, who cannot remain profitable, or for the whole industry, because of lack of demand due to causes such as new technology and changing fashions.

These stages do not always occur, and technological change can make a product go into decline soon after it is introduced. The speed of progress varies; a fashion product, for example, can move along the curve very quickly. Not infrequently managers of new products believe that the product has been successfully launched and that they have reached the fast growth stage only to find that progress is slowed by cash flow problems, an inability to expand fast enough or the onset of economic recession. At the other end of the curve are industries which seem to be in decline (for example, passenger shipping,

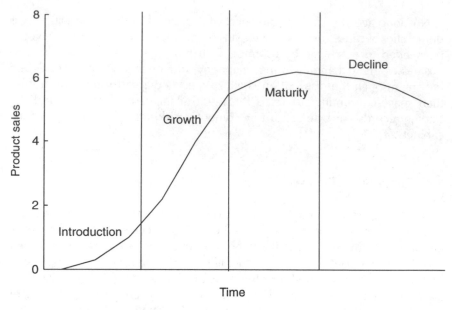

Figure 3.1 The product life-cycle

which was replaced by air travel), but which can later be revitalised, possibly for a different market (which in the case of passenger shipping has been holiday cruising).

Corporate businesses frequently try to buck this curve by introducing new products to replace those in decline.

Clearly, the position of a business in this product life-cycle will influence its needs for real estate and the amount of resources it should expend in ensuring that it has a suitable real estate strategy. Real estate was not one of the costs highlighted by Porter. This is not surprising given the lack of focus on real estate by business managers and their advisers, including economists.

The new venture

Those running successful new businesses are making substantial returns on the money invested. The managers focus on the venture and on growing the business. The managers of many new businesses find that costs are higher than envisaged, and many have cash flow problems. When a new business is successful it is probably because the limited management skill available was aimed at the core business. Spending time dwelling on real estate costs will probably not make the difference between success and failure.

This does not mean that excessive real estate costs should be encouraged; it is merely that they are not a vital element, although all aspects of the business should be fully supporting the core activity. Of course, they become more significant if a high proportion of the business's budget is spent on real estate. Those directors who are supported by experienced venture capitalists, or who have mentors with real estate experience, should be guided towards making prudent real estate decisions.

Change and the growing business

An aspect of real estate that can be vital to the success of a business has less to do with cost and more to do with continuity of production or service. Many businesses need to expand into larger premises. This process should be planned, as it can easily disrupt the trade of a small business (see Chapter 6).

To deal successfully with change the growing business should not be shackled to inflexible real estate commitments. This can arise where a business enters into a long lease or purchases a freehold. As always, there are exceptions, and a business that is tied to a particular location (for example a tourist attraction) may need to ensure that it is secure in that location. For such an operation it could be prudent to own the freehold of the land on which the attraction is sited plus sufficient extra land for expansion.

Those businesses which use expensive fixed plant and machinery could be wise to ensure that the site at which it is fixed will remain within their control for at least the lifetime of the equipment. This security will be perfect provided that production methods do not change; if they do, the burden of the ownership of unsuitable real estate in addition to obsolete equipment may be too great. In a changing environment it is not easy to understand the business needs and ensure that the real estate strategy is supportive.

Mature industries

Mature industries are usually defined by features such as increasing competition, lower prices and lower profits. In these circumstances costs are soon questioned. Surprisingly, until recently this questioning frequently did not include real estate costs, and even now many financial directors are still hazy about the extent of real estate and associated costs. It is those businesses that include products that are mature, especially those which do not also have growth products within their operation, that will be the most interested in the costs of real estate.

Reducing real estate costs may not just help to reduce the cost of producing existing goods. The savings could be sufficient to fund the drive to develop or acquire new products.

A large business has probably added to its real estate in a piecemeal fashion, and during the stages of rapid expansion real estate costs were not a relevant factor for the success of the business.

Many state-run industries had a tradition of heavy use of land and buildings. Somehow, if land or buildings are occupied by a public body it has been seen to be for the public good, provided that facilities for state workers are not too elaborate. Privatisation has resulted in commercial organisations with high levels of real estate either owned freehold or leased. These holdings can play various vital roles in safeguarding the future of the newly privatised company (see Chapter 15).

3.7   Real estate costs and the product life-cycle

Despite all the limitations of the use of product life-cycles for strategic planning, the overall theory is useful when focusing on the role of real estate costs, and can be summarised as shown in Figure 3.2.

Many corporate businesses have a range of products, and their operations consist of overlapping product cycles as new products are developed (or acquired) to replace those in decline. In these circumstances the real estate strategy will need to encompass different approaches to suit the different business strategies.

New business initiatives could be stifled if senior management demands that too much time is spent by the local product manager on real estate issues.

Conversely, it is easy to dwell on the anticipated profits from the new products to the exclusion of looking to cut costs, including real estate costs,

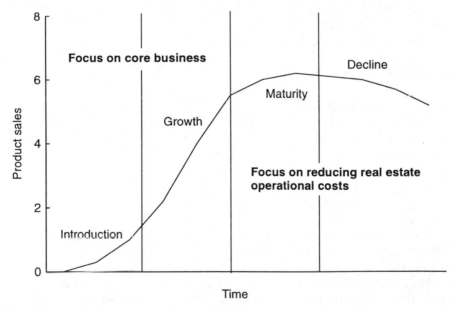

Figure 3.2 Real estate and the product life-cycle.

for established or mature products. It is a considerable drain on the resources available to promote new products if the sales income is first used to meet the excessive real estate costs of mature products with low profit margins.

Real estate strategies must be focused on the specific needs of a company. A central real estate operation may help to overcome these issues, as its specialists can provide advice to the different unit managers according to their needs.

Such a centralised real estate unit could prove unsuccessful if its cost is allocated equally between all parts of the business, whether used or not. This would mean that in-house new business ventures could well have to bear heavier real estate overheads than external competitors. Likewise, mature products may bear unrealistically low real estate costs which masks their true, and declining, contribution to profitability.

3.8   Vertical integration

Vertical integration describes the arrangements when a firm undertakes processes that feed into their main operation, called backward integration, or undertakes processes beyond the main process, known as forward integration (Porter, 1980). For a manufacturing company, an example of backward integration would be to grow or mine raw materials, and an example of forward integration would be to organise its own distribution or retail sales.

Firms that use vertical integration must arrange an internal transaction, or transfer pricing, to replace the market transaction. Porter, who developed this analytical approach, suggested that firms arrange internal transactions because they believe it will be cheaper, less risky or easier to coordinate than contracting out the service.

Again, Porter makes no mention of real estate, but the idea of viewing the ownership of real estate by a company to meets its own needs as backward vertical integration was promoted by Nourse (1990). He proposed that vertical integration applies when a firm purchases accommodation (i.e. freehold) or takes a long lease. If accommodation is rented on a short lease this is not vertical integration but a contract to purchase a service. In the USA, leases where the landlord undertakes the real estate management are more common than in the UK, where this usually only applies to serviced office suites, so the contrast between owning and renting would be greater than in the UK.

Nevertheless, Nourse's work helps to fit real estate into mainstream strategic thinking. Extending Porter's ideas to real estate is a helpful way of bridging the different worlds of real estate and corporate planning.

Porter explains that many vertical integration decisions are framed in terms of 'make or buy?'. When considering real estate, the choice is 'own or rent?', as explained in Chapter 8. Porter emphasises that the essence of the decision is often not the financial benefits of the alternatives but strategic issues that are hard to quantify. Using a real estate context to discuss the strategic considerations that may affect vertical integration decisions draws Porter's work closer to the work of real estate managers. There are two aspects of vertical integration of real estate – the ownership of real estate and the provision of real estate management services.

The strategic benefits and costs of vertical integration of real estate

- *Volume of throughput vs. efficient scale*
  Porter argues that the business must be large enough to support an in-house unit capable of reaping all the economies of scale. If not, then the business must bear the cost of inefficiency. Alternatively, business can sell the excess both by renting out excess real estate capacity and by managing real estate for others. For example, Boots Properties are starting to acquire tenants from outside The Boots Company group (see Chapter 18). These occupy additional capacity in developments undertaken by the company and also use the Boots real estate management services. The strategy is wider than this, because these tenants are selected to widen the retail offer in the development, hence drawing more shoppers to the Boots store.

  Not uncommonly in smaller companies, real estate management is delegated to a manager with spare capacity. Senior management then forgets about it and does not appreciate its importance to the business – a situation unlikely to bring any benefits from the vertical integration!

- *Strategic benefits of integration*
  There are few opportunities for direct cost savings from sharing management of real estate with other business functions. When real estate management is a core skill, as in the case of real estate consultancy, then these skills can be used to manage investments in real estate by the business as well as by clients (see Chapter 19).

  There can be economies from avoiding the market by owning adequate real estate for future needs. The assured supply of accommodation can be of considerable benefit at times of rising rent levels and real estate shortage, when those who have leased accommodation are vulnerable to the demands of landlords (again see Chapter 19).

  The power to have greater influence is another possible strategic advantage of vertical integration. Nourse (1990) gives the example of the McDonald's Corporation, which owns the real estate that its franchisees use. The leases specify that McDonald's may cancel the relationship of any franchisee that does not operate according to McDonald's guidelines.

  Access to the right accommodation is essential for some businesses, such as retailing. Acquiring shops in the best locations takes time, and owning them can give a retailer an advantage. Nourse cites the strategy of owning retail premises as a defensive action which increases the cost of entry for a competitor. Purchase of an ailing retail chain is a way used by large companies wishing to establish a retail business – gaining suitable premises being an essential requirement.

● *Strategic costs of integration*
Nourse points out there is always the risk that capacity and need may not match in volume, location or type. Marks & Spencer experienced this problem when it found it difficult to dispose of surplus warehouse accommodation (see Chapter 16).

Owning real estate increases fixed costs, while some other solutions to providing accommodation can be more closely linked to turnover and be a variable cost. Higher fixed costs make the business more vulnerable to business fluctuations because it is difficult to reduce fixed costs when there is downturn in the market – especially for a non-liquid asset such as real estate.

The business with an in-house real estate operation is dependent on the quality of the management skills of those it employs and on the quality of the buildings purchased. While consultants can be used, the flexibility to switch arrangements for the supply of accommodation is limited. In the past, when most leases in the UK were long ones, the possibilities for switching to different suppliers of accommodation were more theoretical than real. Now that real estate is being provided by property companies in more flexible ways, the ability to switch around is becoming a valid consideration.

Owning real estate, especially when of a specialist nature, can be a substantial exit barrier. Major real estate commitments can mean that a business will have to remain trading in a less than satisfactory industry because it does not have the flexibility to withdraw and invest in more profitable markets.

The main cost of vertical integration into real estate is the high level of capital investment, which is frequently coupled with the lower returns from investment in real estate as opposed to the higher returns of the core business. This can be justified, for example, by a retailer who needs well-placed shops before the higher returns of retailing can be reaped (see Chapter 16).

Writing for the US market, Nourse suggests that increasing returns from real estate could be a benefit of vertical integration. In the UK this is only likely to happen for a declining industry, because generally real estate investments in the UK will probably not be more profitable than investment in the core business.

Porter emphasises the importance of maintaining a balance between the various vertically integrated parts of the business. If the capacity of one exceeds the business's needs, it will affect overall competitiveness. If there is excessive real estate, it must be sold off. This is the situation facing many UK companies as technological changes reduce their need for space, the prime examples being BT, who are disposing of 250 000 to 300 000 square metres of floor space per annum (see Chapter 15).

Another concern of Porter is that the incentive to make profitable choices can be dulled when facilities are provided in-house because of inadequate transfer pricing. In many UK companies the situation has been worse than Porter's fears – real estate has been provided as a free resource with no internal charges. Much of the interest in the strategic importance of real estate is the result of businesses suffering the damaging effects of previously not realising the importance and cost of real estate decisions. Transfer pricing is needed. When market-based transfer pricing is used there will be managerial recognition of the cost of resources used while still gaining the savings from not bearing the transfer costs of market transactions.

There may be other indirect gains from the vertical integration of real estate. IBM and BT have designed and implemented office environments to incorporate new technologies that improve the profitability of their business. They both make use of their real estate successes to market their business's high-tech products (see Chapters 14 and 15).

Porter encompassed the situation of partial integration by the use of the term *tapered integration*. He uses this when a firm has an in-house service but uses the market-place to provide for additional requirements. Nourse used it where the firm owns some accommodation but also rents some on short leases. An obvious benefit of tapered integration is that the firm gains most of the advantages of vertical integration but gains the freedom to acquire additional provision according to need.

Nourse made the assumption that, if a firm owns real estate, it must also have the specialist staff to undertake the work related to ownership. This is not always the case. While in the UK at present the main corporate property owners also have real estate departments to run the operation, some property management services, especially facilities management, are contracted out (outsourced) – a form of tapered integration (see Chapter 12). In the USA (since Nourse wrote) there have been several examples of organisations outsourcing the whole of the property management service (Sinderman, 1995).

Similar situations occur when companies outsource distribution but retain ownership of vehicles or warehouses. This is similar to Porter's *quasi-integration*, but he uses the term for more permanent arrangements, such as joint working or ownership arrangements. In a later work, Porter (1985) extended vertical integration to include activities as well as processes, which gets closer to the real estate situation.

For our purposes, a precise term for every variation is not necessary. What is important is to remember the overriding concept that these arrangements need to be considered in strategic as well as financial terms.

3.9   The value chain

The importance of analysing the value chain (i.e. the value added by each activity) to understand a business is a further development of Porter's theories of competitive advantage (Porter, 1985). Cost analysis of the value chain is useful not only as an analytical tool when considering real estate in the context the ownership of buildings, but also when considering the arrangements for managing real estate. The aim is to consider whether the system in place, or any to be adopted, will bring competitive advantage. The claim of real estate management in many major UK corporations is that incorporating real estate into strategic planning is bringing competitive advantage to their companies. Certainly they are making significant contributions to their businesses by reducing costs. What they will need to be able to do is sustain and improve that advantage when others seek to emulate them.

3.10   Managing real estate to build value

A paper by Apgar IV discusses approaches to real estate management developed by his consultancy (Apgar IV, 1995). This focuses on the role of real estate as a business function. The new ideas are his weighted analytical approach, which centres on five factors – amount, price, grade, area and risk. He uses this to evaluate the client company's immediate real estate priorities. New directions in competitive strategy are linked to long-term real estate decisions that consider how these facilities help or hinder the business's clients and employees.

A second new idea is the formulation of a broad framework that encompasses business functions, time and space. These and their contribution are identified together with the client and later incorporated into a database for detailed analysis. The formulation of the detail of the strategy then follows according to the specific needs of the business.

The paper is also valuable for the debate it contains on the issues involved with incorporating real estate into business strategy and the Dun & Bradstreet case study.

3.11   An alternative approach

Working in the USA, Nourse and Roulac (1993) analysed the various ways in which businesses have tackled the incorporation of real estate into corporate strategy. As a result, they have drawn the attention of corporate business managers to the importance of real estate by focusing on strategic considerations that are relevant to most businesses (see Table 3.1). This highlights the point that there is not just one approach to developing strategic policies. The eventual decisions for each business must relate to its unique circumstances.

3.12   Strategic fit

To be successful, the overall business strategy and its real estate components must fit the organisation, its current position (including intangible considerations such as corporate culture), its resources and the external environment.

Estate managers will find themselves working in many different types of company, especially among the large corporations. The style of strategic planning will need to match the management style. Goold and Campbell (1987) define three different popular types of management control style for the larger organisations: flexible strategic control, tight strategic control and tight financial control. All have their financial and strategic targets, but expect different results, achieved in different ways.

Flexible strategic control companies accept that there are good reasons why targets may not be met, and as long as units are loyally moving broadly in the right direction the centre is satisfied. In tight strategic control companies enforcement is seen to be strict against the annual objectives. The same applies to tight financial control companies, but the terms are set mainly in terms of annual financial performance. In tightly controlled companies, falling below target is considered a failure that will affect career prospects and status.

Those who must meet specific targets are going to be less inclined to propose, or willingly adopt, risky strategies, or to do anything during the year that may adversely affect the target. Where financial targets predominate, strategic planning is pushed down the hierarchy to the individual profit centres;

Table 3.1 Alternative real estate strategies (Source: Nourse, H. O. and Roulac, S. E. (1993) Linking real estate decisions to corporate strategy, in The Journal of Real Estate Research, USA, Fall)

1. Occupancy cost minimisation
2. Flexibility
3. Promote human resource objectives
4. Promote marketing message
5. Promote sales and selling process
6. Facilitate and control productions, operations, service delivery
7. Facilitate managerial process and knowledge work
8. Capture the real estate value creation business

hence real estate may be hived off into a separate company. Strategic control companies will also push strategic development downwards, but will normally seek coordination between units at a higher level, such as the divisional level. The more flexible companies tend to have a higher involvement in strategy by the corporate management, who will coordinate between individual businesses in the group.

3.13 Summary

The main aim of this chapter has been to introduce various approaches to corporate strategy and establish their value when considering real estate. The following points are of general relevance:

- many strategic thinkers have not considered real estate when developing their theories – making these links opens up new possibilities for strategic thinking and hence new opportunities
- academics and practitioners in the USA have spent more time considering these issues than their colleagues in the UK
- to be successful, strategists need to be able to develop and promote their strategic intent
- seeking out the key issues to establish critical success factors is one way forward
- changing the way in which a good or service is provided can bring competitive advantage, and often real estate is a component of the change
- real estate is a more crucial component in a business operation at different stages of product and industry development along the product life-cycle
- an essential consideration is the fit of the proposed strategies to the current business and all its tangible and intangible properties

3.14 Further reading

In addition to books already mentioned, Grant, in *Contemporary Strategic Analysis* (1991), sets out clearly a rational way to develop strategy based on a variety of analytical skills.

The leading writers in the USA provide a valuable source of ideas, many of which are very relevant to the UK. No doubt in the coming years the work being undertaken at MIT will expand and further references will become available (e.g. Joroff and Lambert *et al.*; see Chapter 12).

Until mainstream strategic thinkers include real estate in their arguments, it will remain for real estate experts to look for the possibilities in the arguments they put forward. Thus all new and well-received strategy papers and books could be valuable sources of ideas which real estate experts can develop to meet their needs.

4 Corporate Strategy *Incorporating* Real Estate

4.1 Introduction

Real estate is a major contributor to many business operations. Action to assist one function can hinder another. Corporate strategy must strike a balance – not a mid-point between conflicting interests, but a solution that will drive the business forward.

The corporate strategist needs to be able to identify the contribution of real estate throughout the business and to recognise that even one real estate holding can be influential on the financing and cost structures of many diverse components of a business (see particularly Chapters 3 and 7).

This chapter provides some structures to help real estate and business managers profit from the competitive edge that can be released when corporate strategy incorporates real estate. This becomes possible as the result of a three-stage process:

1. understand the role of real estate in a business
2. create a corporate real estate strategy
3. develop corporate strategy *incorporating* real estate.

4.2 Bridging a divide

First, it may help to go back to basics. Very simply, a business uses funds in an operation with the aim of increasing their value. Once an operation is successfully in progress the added value will be available to be distributed as profits or to be retained and ploughed back into the business (see Figure 4.1). The retained profits and new sources of funds can be used to expand the operation and increase future profits.

The source of funds and the application of funds are for the most part two separate parts of the business – corporate finance and operational management. Clearly, if the operation is not successful there will be no profits to reinvest and individuals or institutions will not wish to invest or make loans to the business. However, for a successful business decisions concerning

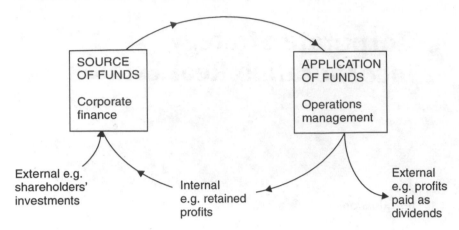

Figure 4.1 Source and application of funds: the divide between corporate finance and operations management.

financial matters, such as the balance between debt and equity capital, relate mostly to considerations other than the actual operation being undertaken – for example, the cost of debt capital and whether the rates are fixed or variable. For the most part, whether it is desirable or not, there is little day-to-day contact between those engaged in corporate finance and those engaged in operational management – both are too busy with their own interests.

Decisions related to real estate frequently, directly or indirectly, bridge the divide between the source of funds and the application of funds. For example, freehold operational premises, such as factories and shops, can be used as security for debt finance (see Chapter 7). Another example is the use of 'sale and leaseback' of freehold operational premises to provide a source of funds, additional to more common sources of equity, debt and retained profits (see Chapter 17).

Additionally, the types of property tenure used will vary the proportion of fixed and variable costs, hence changing the ability of the business to remain profitable if sales fall. Many business are now seeking to reduce fixed costs and increase variable costs to bring greater flexibility (see Chapter 15).

4.3   Real estate in corporate strategy

Those who fully appreciate the role of real estate will consciously make real estate decisions that meet corporate strategy. Those who divorce real estate from corporate strategy are likely to find that corporate plans are hindered by unforeseen real estate considerations. Transaction costs for real estate are high, and the transactions take time to complete. Also, many real estate decisions are long term, and contract (lease) conditions cannot be changed. Business managers who overlook real estate can also find a considerable proportion of their resources focused on a non-core activity.

The business environment is dynamic, and the choices related to real estate and its role in corporate strategy are changing. There is no fixed combination of real estate decisions that can be held out as the ideal approach – businesses are different and vary over time.

It is a two-way process – corporate strategy should include consideration of the real estate implications and real estate management should be undertaken with full regard to corporate strategy.

This is not easy. Figure 4.2 is a model of the process, which involves gaining the information to understand fully the contribution of real estate to the business and will lead to formulating a corporate real estate strategy. These are the first two steps to gaining the competitive edge from corporate strategy *incorporating* real estate. It assumes an existing business. Many businesses will have completed some of the steps and can proceed from these points.

The model isolates the information-gathering processes about real estate from that for the remainder of the business. The corporate strategy component will be in place for most large businesses, but it is positioned within the model because information used to develop corporate strategy will also be needed to develop a corporate real estate strategy. Guidance on acquiring and analysing the necessary information is given in Chapter 11.

The corporate real estate strategy should be based on the internal needs of the business as it implements its corporate strategy. For this reason, information gained from comparison of the business's real estate performance indicators with external sources is shown as only influencing the report on the business's real estate position (i.e. by a broken line) rather than as making a substantial contribution. There is no point in putting resources into matching external real estate achievements unless it will benefit the firm.

Having achieved an understanding of the contribution that real estate makes to the business, it must be realised that a corporate real estate strategy is only the beginning – but an important first step, as without it it is impossible to open up the next stage, which is to develop corporate strategy *incorporating* real estate.

4.4   Corporate strategy *incorporating* real estate

The second stage is to wed the corporate strategy to the corporate real estate strategy (see Figure 4.3). All the companies included as case studies have moved at least this far. It is the point at which a business has sufficient understanding of the role that real estate contributes to the business to be able to include it in sophisticated strategic plans, sometimes as an essential component. Some of the companies, especially those in retail, have been in

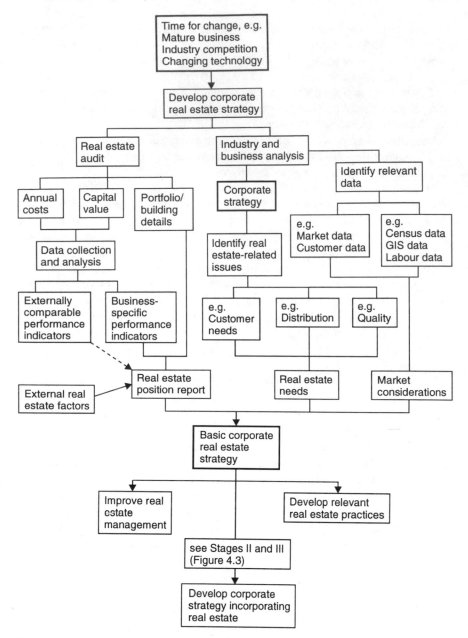

Figure 4.2 Developing corporate strategy incorporating real estate – Stage I.

this position for many years, while others have worked hard to achieve this ability. Z/Yen, the smallest of the companies studied, having been formed at a later point of technical achievement, has taken real estate issues on board

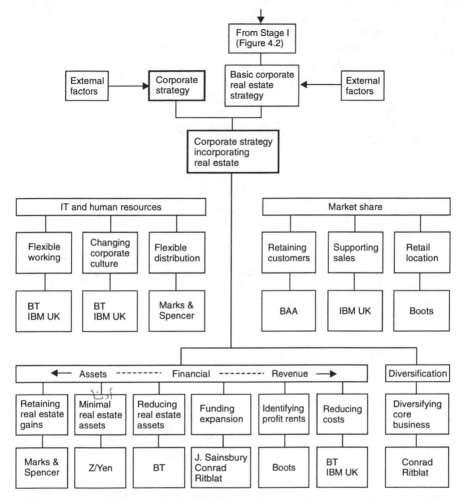

Figure 4.3 Corporate strategy incorporating real estate – Stages II and III (with examples).

from inception – basically by deciding that the business itself would use very little real estate, so that the matter has been 'outsourced' to its individual directors and freelance consultants (see Chapter 20).

These models aim to simplify and focus on the key points so that a structure can be devised that helps show what has been happening and to provide guidance that will be useful to most businesses. The other chapters in this book provide various ideas to help real estate and business managers seek solutions to help their businesses fulfil their full potential from their use of real estate.

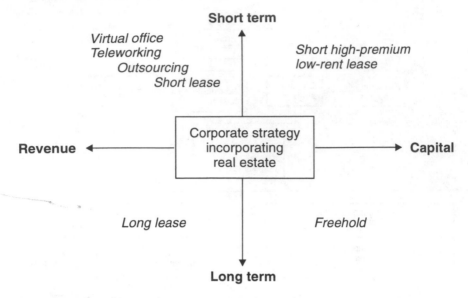

Figure 4.4 Matching real estate to strategic needs.

4.5   Real estate holdings and corporate strategy

Chapter 8 considers the arguments regarding the ownership or renting of real estate. The current ever-changing environment, a constant stream of new IT developments and very competitive markets makes flexibility a valuable attribute for many businesses. As a consequence it is of strategic importance to hold real estate interests – freehold, leasehold, outsourced etc. – that will suit the business. These will vary depending on whether the cost is met from revenue or capital and whether a long-term or short-term use of the real estate is envisaged. Figure 4.4 shows the way in which these influences will pull the operation of the strategy towards different types of real estate holding.

Figure 4.5 goes into greater detail by showing the various ways in which real estate can be provided on a matrix of time and funding. Notes on the model show the ways in which flexibility can be achieved. Long-term commitments are not always the most inflexible. Freehold property which ties up capital in perpetuity offers greater flexibility than a long lease because the freehold can be sold, whereas various contract (lease) conditions usually make it difficult to withdraw form a leasing arrangement.

Such decisions are not made in isolation, and Figure 4.6 shows many of the other aspects that must be taken into consideration. Some were mentioned in Chapter 2 and others are considered in further depth through out the remainder of this book. Many are matters that the business will already be monitoring as part of the strategic planning process.

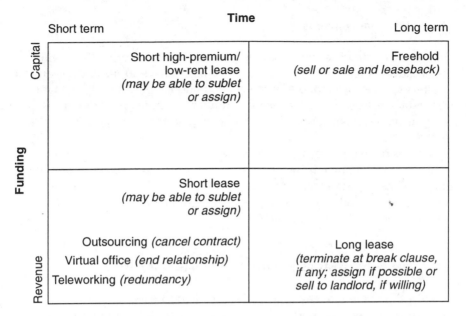

Figure 4.5 *Real estate: funding and time.*

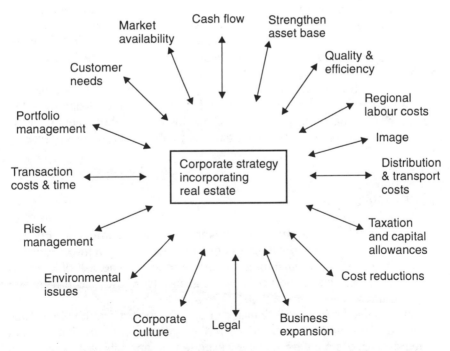

Figure 4.6 *Influences when corporate strategy incorporates real estate.*

4.6   Universal concerns

Many real estate issues are of strategic importance to a corporation, whether or not it owns real estate, because all businesses have to make decisions on matters such as location, use of space and housekeeping. For those that own real estate as freehold or long leasehold interests there are additional issues, such as management of the portfolio (including its future development potential).

Matters related to facilities management are of concern even to those who rent, as most commercial leases require the tenant to take on responsibility for repairs and insurance. Even those who have no day-to-day responsibility for repairs may find that the service charges they are asked to pay cause them to think again about the buildings they occupy.

4.7   Real estate costs as a percentage of business costs

Ideally, the real estate costs should be allocated to each part of the business and be expressed as a percentage of the total costs. A better understanding is possible if the costs are broken down into variable and fixed costs, as discussed in Chapter 2.

It is only when operating and fixed costs are allocated to each of the business's activities that it is possible to see what value the activities are adding to the whole business venture. For example, a business that included manufacture and retail sales might find that the allocation of actual real estate costs to the individual operations shows that retailing is adding little to the business because of high real estate costs for shop premises. This will mean that the value added in the manufacturing process is being used to subsidise the retail operation. Ceasing to be a retailer and distributing to wholesalers or using direct mail might prove to be much more profitable, even at lower levels of sales.

4.8   Finding the new vision

Having a carefully devised structure for planning the development of corporate strategy *incorporating* real estate does not automatically mean the production of the perfect strategy to guarantee the future of the business. It only means that the strategists know their core business and its industry, its drivers and its environment.

They also need bright ideas, which can come as 'bolts from the blue'. They are more likely when the business and its components are known and strategists have open minds, seek new experiences, and mix and match ideas and operations from other industries and ask 'what if?'.

Serendipity will be more likely to work if strategists have a rich background of experience beyond the humdrum. Attempting to strike out to meet the future is hard if you spend all your time within the corporate environment. It is like working in a vacuum.

Given that Peter Cochrane (1995), Head of Advanced Applications and Technologies Research Laboratory for BT plc, has said that:

> The change we are about to witness will overshadow the impact of the printed word, the industrial revolution and physical transport

our day-to-day experiences would not seem to be a sufficient foundation for sparking ideas capable of bringing long-term strategic gains. Strategists need to look beyond their business, beyond national boundaries and their cultural and political limitations; they need to mix ideas from the arts and the sciences; they need to feed their brains with experiences, ideas and debate – and above all they must know and understand the drivers of change.

The spark to be different requires imagination and the ability to consider other options, but importantly also the logic to analyse the possible consequences.

To some extent successful strategy requires that those involved can stand apart from the different interest groups within the company. The goals that are set should be acceptable to all groups. They need to focus on the overarching common interest of ensuring the survival and profitability of the company, even if it realigns the business. The chief executive leads strategy, not only because it is a function of leadership but because the CEO stands apart and can take the overall view, like glancing down from a helicopter.

4.9 The iterative process

Although it needs inspiration, developing new strategy has its more tedious moments. The new ideas have to work. An iterative process is normal. Ideas are moulded by circumstances. This is illustrated in Figure 4.7.

This model follows the situation of a business-generated idea being modified by restrictions coming from the inflexibility of real estate, its expense and the effects of the property cycle. The real estate manager will normally be striving to reduce these impediments to the minimum. Other business components will also contribute to the iterative process (for example, labour supply and distribution). For clarity these have been ignored.

The iterative process can take considerable time, as recognising the possibility of conflict is only one step. Depending on the circumstances, further research and analysis may well be needed to ascertain the magnitude of the problem and to seek ways around the difficulty.

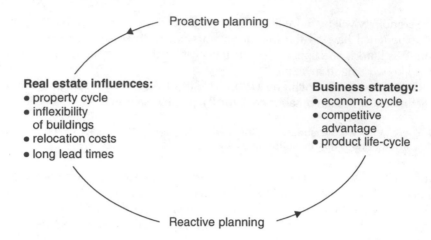

Figure 4.7 The iterative process of developing a corporate strategy incorporating real estate.

4.10   Selecting the strategy

Profitability means earning sufficient to cover the cost of capital (i.e. debt repayments together with the return on equity expected for the risks involved) and an income above this. Ideally, it will mean earning more than competitors or above the industry average.

The real estate strategist will be assisting the business to develop strategies which bring overall competitive advantage. If the company operates in only one industry this is easier to define, but a corporation involved in different industries will be seeking to be above the industry average for each industry in which it operates, hence gaining overall competitive advantage when compared with similar conglomerates.

While the company, as it stands, will have a particular cost of capital, this does not mean that all new projects have to fit in with it. They can be more or less risky, provided that capital can be acquired at a matching cost. After all, the different products (i.e. projects) that make up the business will be more or less risky according to their stage in the product life-cycle. The overall risk will also vary according to the financial risk undertaken. Two similar projects may have the same risk, but the risk to shareholders will be greater for the project with the highest amount of debt finance, i.e. high gearing (or leveraging) is more risky.

In stark and simple terms the choice of strategy should be based on the proposal that produces the highest net present value using discounted cash flow techniques. Strategy, however, is not about the simple. A strategy development may not be about clear individual projects but about repositioning the business to take advantage of opportunities that will arise in the future. This involves a complex financial evaluation combining the various choices and their probable outcomes.

This can be illustrated by consideration of strategies that focus on creating entry barriers for other competitors. This is not about the return on individual projects but about stifling competitors' opportunities. Real estate can play an important role in creating entry barriers. If a business has high real estate needs or if it is needed in particular locations then it is a major barrier to other entrants. Ownership of the necessary real estate will protect the existing players from competition unless a competitor can find an entry route (such as a takeover) that brings it the real estate or, as discussed earlier, if it can find a substitute for the real estate. Entry barrier strategies do not negate the importance of seeking the highest net present value strategy, but they complicate its calculation.

4.11   Risk assessment

The business should be protected from excessive real estate-based risks. Involvement in strategic planning enables the estate manager to take the long-term view in the real estate market.

In locations where premises will be required, the estate manager can seek involvement in development schemes so that developers construct the premises that the business will need. Premises can be purchased or rented ahead of time if market conditions are particularly favourable.

Where possible, the estate manager can seek to have rent reviews on different buildings well spaced so that the business is not hit by several steep rent increases at the same time. Leases can be arranged so that options on renewal arise on a regular basis, giving maximum opportunity for adjusting the size of the estate.

A well-informed real estate manager within the strategy team should be able to ensure that the business moves fast to offload property types that are becoming obsolete before there is a glut on the market: for example, warehouses that will be further than one day's drive from the Channel when speed limits for lorries reduce. Avoidance of property-based risk can be taken further. Although there is little evidence to suggest that this type of risk management is being undertaken by many businesses it is possible for a business with a high rent commitment, subject to frequent rent reviews, to seek to balance the outlay by matching its outgoings with an investment of surplus capital in a property-indexed derivative fund. The income from this fund will rise or fall in line with property overall and should reflect upward changes in the rent commitment. It is not an entirely safe option, because income will fall during a property slump but actual rent commitments will probably remain unchanged. The beginnings of a property derivatives market have been established by Barclays De Zoete Wedd Investment Management Ltd, but fiscal restraints have limited the market, so the prospects for its future development are unsure (see Chapter 7).

Methods of reducing risk have attractions for the nervous, but as shareholders hold equity because they want higher returns than, say, those from gilts, they are prepared to take a correspondingly higher risk. It is not the responsibility of the business managers to abate the normal business risk. This can be done by individual shareholders, who spread their risk by holding a diverse portfolio.

The real estate manager and the other business managers must, however, ensure that they do not open the business to unnecessary risks quite out of proportion to the size of the business.

4.12   Summary

Developing corporate strategy *incorporating* real estate:

- is a multi-stage process
- involves bridging the corporate finance/operations management divide
- will overcome the problems that arise when corporate strategy ignores real estate
- requires that the role of real estate in the business is understood
- will seek to match real estate holdings to financial and time-scale requirements
- helps a business to greater profitability even when real estate is rented or outsourced
- will help to highlight the role of variable and fixed costs
- will need vision and strategists with logical, open minds well served with idea-building experiences
- is an iterative process
- will include strategies mostly aimed at taking the business forward, but can be about making progress difficult for competitors – creating barriers to entry and exit from an industry
- requires risk factors to be assessed before a strategy is implemented

5 New Technologies

5.1 Introduction

New technology developments have underpinned many of the more recent organisational changes in strategic management. Therefore, understanding the key changes in new computer and communications technologies aids appreciation of the possibilities open to the corporate strategist, especially in relation to real estate.

Although Chapter 6 contains most of the practical examples of the application of strategy, explanation is often easier when examples are given. Consequently, some examples have been included in this chapter for greater clarity.

This chapter is mostly about matters which traditionally have been of no interest to real estate managers and of little interest to many other corporate managers. However, nowadays all managers who want to make a valid contribution to business strategy must build up a knowledge of IT, its use by operational management and the opportunities for their sector of the business.

Most of the changes in our need for real estate are linked to management changes that introduce new uses for computers and associated connectivity technologies. These have led to flexibility and efficiency in the way that people work, especially in the office environment but also in manufacturing, distribution, retailing and other industries. This activity is often described as a convergence of the computer, communications and corporate markets and, as shown in Figure 5.1, the time has arrived when none of these can be treated in isolation when considering corporate strategy.

This is a fast-changing environment, in which successful managers will be those who seek out information about new developments, so that they are at the vanguard of change. They will want to gain the competitive advantage of being ahead of the field. This chapter introduces and briefly explains the main factors; those who need to know more about the individual processes can follow up the various references.

5.2 High-tech developments

The first part of this chapter focuses on an overview of the different strands of high-tech developments which have come together to create flexible working practices.

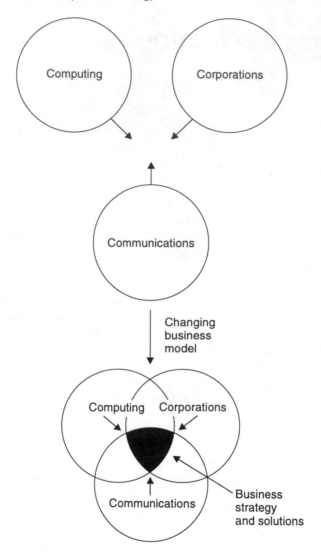

Figure 5.1 The convergence of computing, communications and corporations. (Source: prepared by Bernard Bowles).

Four key fields have generated much of the change, and certainly little would have happened without them. They are:

- the miniaturisation and portability of computer and communications hardware
- the development of networks and the supporting communications systems, known collectively as connectivity

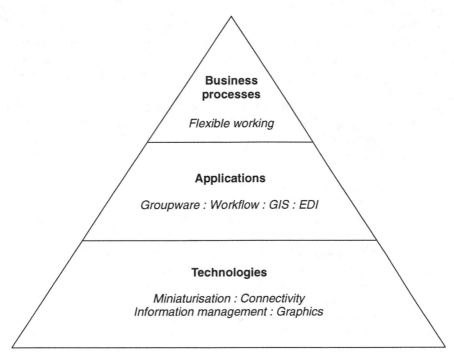

Figure 5.2 Development of flexible working practices. (Source: prepared by author and Bernard Bowles)

- the development of information management systems
- the development of the image and graphics interface

These four have fed into two key software developments – groupware and workflow. In Figure 5.2 these developments are shown in a way that indicates that several technologies are needed to produce an application, and that the various applications are used together to create business processes such as flexible working. The principles illustrated by this model apply in other aspects of business, such as distribution, where different applications, including electronic point of sale systems and geographical positioning systems, have contributed to new operational management methods.

Progress is not uniform, so frequently it is only after advances in several different aspects of technology that a new application is devised using a mix of inventions and developments in technologies which initially had appeared unrelated. For example, greater use of groupware and workflow software is becoming possible because of ongoing connectivity developments.

Spending in the UK on electronic systems is rising fast. For example, the revenue for data communications suppliers in the UK was predicted to rise from nearly US$6 billion in 1995 to nearly US$10 billion by the year 1999

(Frost and Sullivan, 1994). This increased spending is happening as equipment and software costs fall, which means that the changes are more extensive than is at first apparent. These changes are underpinning core business operations instead of being confined to back office functions and the IT department.

Additionally, data and communications systems are working together to enable interworking between remote locations. Thus IT cannot be considered in isolation but must be seen as a component part of a business solution.

5.3   Miniaturisation and portability

The mobile phone was the first step towards portability in the business environment, and it has been closely followed by the miniaturisation of computers. It is not just that the hardware is small enough to carry – it is that the processing power that can be contained within them is constantly increasing and is using less battery power. Laptop computers now have the same capacity as most desktop PCs. At an even smaller scale, 'nanotechnology' is predicted to be the way of the future, when computer chips will be just a few atoms wide (Cookson, 1995).

The travelling worker can use a laptop computer and mobile phone (with the necessary software) to link to the workplace computer and its local area network (LAN) to work on files and download or send data, emails and faxes anywhere in Europe within the GSM (Global System for Mobile communications) network. The results can be printed out on a small portable printer. The dual-mode telephone, which can be used cordlessly but can be connected to a fixed line when in the office or at home means that many people will need only one telephone number.

This mobility means that a business can get closer to its customers. Those that have always travelled, such as representatives and sales staff, can now produce accurately priced tenders, place orders and check on work in progress without returning to the office (and consuming space). The increased productivity has brought competitive advantage to the leaders.

Change is ongoing and rapid. People can now speak to their computers instead of typing in text. Once these sound systems are linked with communications systems, telephones can be answered and queries handled without staff being present. Image-processing scanners can read text, even handwritten text, and turn it into digital information for storage by the computer, to be presented as text on the computer screen or printed as hard copy. Mobile workers will soon need few technical skills, as their computer will react to simple instructions!

The benefits of miniaturisation are not limited to individual travellers – whole sales forces and service engineering teams can be connected by the same methods. British Gas Service is using a private mobile radio network, public cellular networks and portable CD-ROM drive notebook PCs to link their home-based field engineers to customer service, scheduling and parts databases. This has resulted in staff reductions of several thousand and property needs of just seven district offices and the national parts centre, rather than 91 district offices and 300 depots.

Just before we get completely absorbed by high-technology advances, it is worth remembering that 1995 saw the launch of the clockwork radio (Gourlay, 1995). This radio needs no batteries and is to be sold or distributed free via aid agencies in Africa to provide a cheap/free mass communications system. The initial invention was promoted by those who knew of the need to provide information to stop the spread of Aids.

Clockwork radio is not about to change UK real estate requirements, although the transistor radio was the first indication of the future of miniaturisation. However, proposals to extend this simple technology to power mobile phones and calculators suggests that it could have a dynamic future. When one thinks of the changes following in the wake of laptop computers, it may be reasonable to ask, 'What could a clockwork laptop achieve?'.

5.4 Connectivity

A key component of digitised systems is connectivity – the ability to link access to people, data and systems through networks at a speed that does not delay operations. Local area networks (LAN) operate within a building or closely linked buildings. Wide area networks (WAN) link people working in buildings that are geographically dispersed – they can extend around the world and link those working at home or in a hotel bedroom as well as those at the major corporate sites. While LANs generally keep almost constant links open, with information passing rapidly between different users, WANs offer more limited connectivity and performance, although they generally connect many more different machines together.

These networks require three major components: infrastructure, network software and services. Network software, such as operating systems and protocols, controls the flow of data using the underlying physical infrastructure of cables and switches, with the complexity of implementation hidden by managed network services. These three components are now discussed.

Infrastructure

The big problem has always been that the volume of traffic varies. LANs are designed to carry the largest items, but across WANs information has had to be broken down into small 'packets' to be sent and then reassembled at the other end. This is not very satisfactory. Fibre-optic cables now offer greater capacity, but only large organisations can lease their own landlines or have rented space from telecommunications companies. Businesses relying on these connections usually have more than one route between key sites. So London to Los Angeles might be available via New York, which would be the normal route, with, say, Toronto or even via the Far East and the Pacific Ocean as back-up possibilities. In these circumstances, being a large business has strategic advantages.

Others must use systems available for general use. UK cable operators are investing in their infrastructure at the rate of £6 million a day and spent £2.2 billion in 1996 to build a network that passes 9 million homes. The initial strategy has been to focus on the residential sector to provide critical mass before developing processes and systems for business customers. However, it had been expected that UK cable penetration would hit US levels of 60%, but only 21% of homes are connected (Hall, 1996). Cable does not extend beyond urban areas, although a number of operators are forming alliances for greater coverage.

Many large companies, and increasingly small and medium-sized companies, are using public data services either to replace or supplement their private networks. An example is the Integrated Services Digital Network (ISDN), which provides two independent digital channels. This means that one channel can be used for voice and the other for data and/or video. With this service subscribers pay for the initial connection and then for usage.

ISDN has limited capacity compared with some leased line options, and can be too slow for many corporate users, especially at busy times. It is frequently used by these customers to provide a 'pay as you use' service to smaller branch locations and remote workers. Once the phased capital investment is complete, it is likely that prices will fall, leading to a huge growth in market potential, particularly for small and medium sized businesses.

A faster service with a greater capacity uses a new facility called Switched Multi-megabit Data Service (SMDS). This nationally available switched service requires a single access line from the customer's premises to the network to reach another connected point.

This relieves the need for multiple leased lines from one point to every other point. SMDS forms the basis of community networks, as shown in Figure 5.3, and is particularly appropriate for large corporations with many locations of branch sites, service centres, call centres, regional offices, data centres etc. Although already used by major businesses, many more could benefit from its operational possibilities.

SMDS is part of a family of broadband services and is heralded as a major step towards the world-wide Information Superhighway, but its limited quality for voice and video restricts its future use.

The solution to overcome these limitations is imminent, and with it will come new strategic opportunities. For the past 10 years a new network technology known as Asynchronous Transmission Mode (ATM) has been under development. The basis of ATM is that it splits digital packets into small

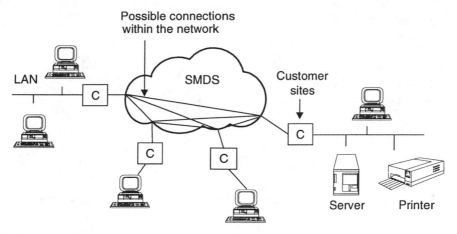

Figure 5.3 Switched Multi-megabit Data Service (SMDS). (Source: prepared by Bernard Bowles)

fixed-length cells which can be treated in a standard manner by network hardware, rather than software. This allows throughput to be increased and network delay to be very small. High-quality voice, video and data can be supported at high speeds without separate physical networks, as shown in Figure 5.4. In addition, multiple simultaneous channels representing a mix of media can be supported with different qualities of service, thereby supporting true multimedia applications.

A new range of services and applications will become possible with ATM technology. The existing narrowband ISDN will become Broadband ISDN (B-ISDN), and applications that were limited to a single or dual narrowband channel will make use of multiple channels with multiple media data representations. It will allow remote users to work and see each other in real time and share common applications and data. It will even allow surgeons to conduct operations remotely. Already many LAN products are now using ATM and the first UK ATM WAN commercial services will soon be operational. These developments create the opportunity for a single network technology from desktop to desktop, as shown in Figure 5.5.

Software

Additional to the physical network infrastructure is the need to control the flow of data from the application across the multiplicity of cables, switches and communications devices. This is the domain of network software, comprising network operating systems (NOS) and network transmission protocols (NTP).

Common network operating systems are Novell, UNIX and Windows NT. These are software components residing on PCs, workstations and servers

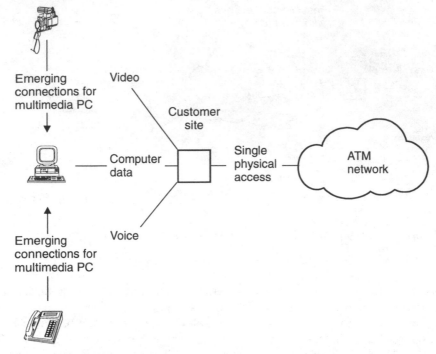

Figure 5.4 Multimedia applications using a single access to the ATM network. (Source: prepared by Bernard Bowles)

which enable end devices to function as if all operations were performed on the same virtual machine. They also enable access to shared peripherals, such as printers, and were initially introduced for local area networks.

Until ATM technology makes real-time WANs a reality, the NOSs have to be able to cope with the limited throughput and data delays of the WANs.

The most widely used NTP is TCP/IP, which lies at the heart of the Internet success story. It is the openness and standardisation of TCP/IP, together with

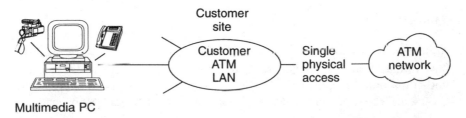

Figure 5.5 A single network technology from desktop to desktop. (Source: prepared by Bernard Bowles)

its performance, that is the basis for its success on the Internet, and it is now common in most corporate networks.

Managed network services

For voice communications equipment costs are the main expense, whereas for data communications as much as 70% of the total costs are in management rather than capital costs. The increasing technical complexity of IT and connectivity is outside the scope of most corporations' business activities, and it is changing at an ever-increasing rate.

While some organisations set up their own in-house teams to manage their systems, many outsource the service. The managed network services (MNS) contractor designs, provides and operates a system to meet each client's requirements, as defined in the service level agreement.

For the smaller customer, bundled network solutions overcome the difficult selection of hardware and software by purchasing an ISDN line and a PC equipped with all the connectivity hardware and software in addition to the application packages. Furthermore, ISDN user groups have collaborated to solve many of the protocol problems, making it easier for independent organisations, both large and small, to link up.

5.5 Information management

'Information management' normally relates to the management of any form of data within a computer environment. The phrase 'Document or record management' is more commonly used when paper is involved, but it is also used in the high-tech environment – processes are moving faster than semantics!

There are two basic types of information, as shown in Table 5.1. The codified information – the facts and figures – has been computerised for years, but is only a tiny percentage of the data held by most businesses.

The bulk of the records to be stored consist of documentary information. Digital methods are now making the computerised storage and retrieval of this an economic proposition and the basis of many flexible working methods.

In addition to creating digital documents by typing them into the computer, text, drawings and photographs can be electronically scanned by image processors and held on a computer disk in digital format. This can then be amended in the same way as computer-generated information. Image processing enables large volumes of data to be stored in very compact formats; some, such as CD-ROM, can be distributed to those without any online connection.

Machines will scan multiple copies quickly, so it is now economical to hold all incoming paper documents on computer disk, from where they can be

Table 5.1 Computerisation of data (Source: based on information in Hendley, T. (1995) An Introduction to Document Management, Document Management Suppliers Group, Worcester)

Documentary information	Codified information
Typically written with conjectures, opinion and assertions that can be interpreted using preferred value judgements.	Factual data, structured data and data analysed by arithmetic and logical deduction which is generally accepted as true.
The computer is restricted to storage, replication, transmission and presentation of the information.	The computer can interpret the data to generate further information.
Normally about 99 per cent of an organisation's information.	Normally only 1–2 per cent of an organisation's information.
Organisations are starting to think about automating documentary information.	Considerable investment has already gone into computerising codified information.

retrieved very fast – almost instantaneously. This means that hard copy records need not be stored unless the original is required for legal purposes. Documents in current use can be kept on live disks and archival material on optical disks or computer-output microfilm. Hierarchical storage management systems automatically sort out infrequently used electronic files and store them in an optical library so that they are not cluttering up the active network. They can be automatically retrieved if needed.

The costs of electronic image processing are falling, but are not yet economical for archive records that are rarely consulted and which are already stored at a cheap location. IBM found that it would not be cost-effective to image process its archival stores held in a Hampshire warehouse.

These changes are the backbone of many new management systems. American Express can deal with customer queries, such as lost travellers' cheques, when the caller and telephonist are in different continents, the travellers' cheques were purchased in a third continent and when the cheques will eventually be replaced in a fourth continent – all the data comes together to deal with the problem and trigger action wherever it is needed.

Additional to all the information that a business has generated for itself is the wealth of data available from many online sources. A variety of specialist services, such as FT Profile in the business world and EGi (Estates Gazette Interactive) in the property world, provide subscription desktop access to commercially valuable data.

5.6 Image and graphic interface

Many users who now use PCs every day to handle a variety of business tasks would have found computers daunting a few years ago. The key to the rapid acceptance of hardware and software developments has been that the screens facing the user are becoming more friendly.

Textual instructions have been replaced by simple pictures on icons. Software writers now focus on the way in which a program will be used and the interrelationships between self-contained software modules.

Another important development is that with increased processor power users can have several programs running simultaneously and can view them side by side on their PC screens. Hence it is possible to see and talk to a colleague at another location while exchanging data files and making changes to a document or drawing.

5.7 Groupwork

Groupwork links collaborating groups of people who work together to create, access and share applications and data using networked PCs. It needs a high-speed network which can support voice, video and data. It embraces a range of applications, such as email, database access, shared applications, desktop video/audio-conferencing and workflow.

Groupwork makes it much easier to keep track of customers' work, to understand the status of various components of a project, to distribute information and to have collaborative free-form discussions of all kinds.

Email is becoming increasingly important for communication in many corporations. In some cases organisations are encouraging the use of email to replace voice calls, and have in many cases eliminated paper correspondence. Documents such as word processor, drawing or spreadsheet files can be attached to the email, with a dramatic increase in transferred data. In many cases communication is informal, with little adherence to a conventional presentation format, thereby enabling the exchange of spontaneous thoughts and ideas which in many cases resembles a casual conversation. Many organisations are having to restructure their LANs to provide greater capacity.

The core of groupware systems is shared databases which can be accessed as necessary and which store the work completed – indefinitely if necessary. These are independent of individual users' email files, which can remain private. The databases are stored on servers and drawn on when needed. The contents of servers are replicated in different locations and are automatically updated regularly at intervals to suit the business. It means that each location is more or less up-to-date and does not have to be constantly connected to all the other sites.

Each database has its own manager who controls access to its indexed documents, which can have up to five different levels of privacy protection

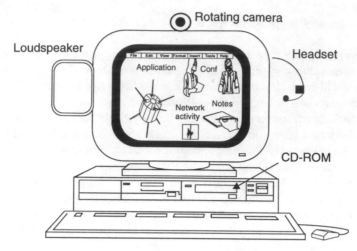

Figure 5.6 Integrated multimedia desktop computer conferencing. (Source: prepared by Bernard Bowles)

(including encryption) although they are designed to be shared. All those who are working together on a project keep their work for that project in the appropriate database or databases. A database can be as small as a departmental phone book or may contain thousands of documents. An individual may be working in several groups and use a variety of databases even in the course of a single day.

There is complete flexibility as to how groups are defined and there are no geographical or organisational barriers to membership of a group. Lotus Notes, probably the most popular groupware product, stores all the documents using Greenwich Mean Time, but will show them at any location around the world at local time.

Increasingly, multimedia PCs are becoming available which can support a variety of media, allowing users to see each other as they talk and exchange application information, as shown in Figure 5.6.

It has been found through a number of tests on human behaviour that the most important medium is voice, so multimedia systems which include good quality voice transmissions are valuable – even at the expense of trading bandwidth from other media. To be effective, systems should have a response time for data of less than half a second. Good systems can cut the time spent travelling to meetings, as these can be held face-to-face online.

5.8 Workflow management

Workflow management encompasses the whole of the documentary and codified information operation of a business in a manner that reflects the work processes. Those arriving as hard copy are imaged into the system, but most will probably be created using a PC.

Workflow is more focused on a particular operation than groupware software. At present, few businesses are completely run by workflow methods. It has been favoured by companies whose business processes include much amendment of records; for example insurance companies that issue policies, send out accounts, settle claims and make payments.

Businesses have used workflow to implement new customer-oriented strategies. A key factor is that users have access to the latest version of the same document at different locations simultaneously, so that a more responsive and accurate service can be provided to customers. An example is the workflow system used by Barclays Bank to reduce the turn-round time of approving a mortgage application by the head office to just 24 hours, so that service to their customers is better than their competitors in a very fierce market-place.

Workflow management has allowed businesses to leverage their investment in IT and people, thereby gaining competitive advantage. As the Barclay's example shows, workflow management will soon be essential to operate effectively in many markets. Sophisticated workflow systems work out what documents will be needed next and prefetch them, hence removing irritating delays while waiting for the screen to change.

Like all operation systems it is essential to avoid bottlenecks and frustrations from delays. The development does need to be well devised to suit the business; to be successful it is necessary to have:

- continuous involvement of the end user in the design process
- backing of top management;
- thorough analysis of documents
- comprehensive indexing
- easy retrieval process
- backup arrangements
- a responsive IT infrastructure

Table 5.2 summarises the gains that a business can expect from workflow management.

5.9 Geographical information systems and geographical positioning systems

Geographical information systems (GIS) store, manipulate and display geographical data on a map, but can also display the data as a table, a graph or in a text report. The data is stored and used in a digitised format, having been input by vectoring or scanning. GIS applications have a high data content and when networked need a high-speed system.

Table 5.2 Gains possible from workflow management

Tactical gains	Strategic gains

● Savings in:
    space
    staff
    storage equipment
    telephone charges
    bill production costs
    data entry costs
● Reduced human error
● Improved cash flow
● Environmental gains from using
    less paper
	● Easy access to information
	● Increased productivity
	● Competitive advantage
	● Improved:
	    customer service
	    quality control
	    management information
	    staff morale
	● Reduced production cycles
	● Faster time to market
	● Increased market share
	● Regulatory compliance
	● Ease of organisational change
	● Supports teleworking
	● Full audit trails

UK users are no longer restricted to Ordnance Survey data; others can now provide competitively priced digital maps, which have led to lower-cost GIS applications. GIS is a high-tech development of direct importance to corporate real estate managers, as it can be used to integrate location with property values, site plans, contract details, journey times etc.

GIS has the capacity to become even more relevant to corporate real estate managers and business strategic planners, because all types of operational and marketing data and information on occupational costs, for example, can be linked with real estate locations. It is an undeveloped area.

Geographical positioning systems (GPS) were developed by the military in the USA during the late 1970s and the 1980s. By taking readings from satellites a position on the ground can be calculated. In 1993, the US government stopped considering GPS as experimental and substantial commercial use began. The US facility became a de facto international utility. By 1995 it was estimated that commercial GPS business was worth several billion dollars per annum and growing, with companies making GPS equipment all round the world, including the UK (Ferguson, 1995).

GPS is a dynamic application of GIS. Operations such as distribution can be tracked and the results recorded digitally and fed into management systems. As businesses are able to keep closer track of stock in transportation and the vehicles in use, so the need for real estate changes.

5.10 Computer-aided design and virtual reality

Computer-aided design (CAD) is peripheral to most aspects of managing and using real estate unless new buildings or refurbishments are planned. The process uses drawing packages linked to design rules and also often linked to rapid photocopying and production. It has helped speed up the design and construction process. Business managers can gain a much better impression of their new building before they make the final commitment.

5.11 The future – virtual cities

One of the most dramatic consequences of the growth in connectivity is the ease with which information can be circulated – the so-called 'information revolution'. Information is no longer the preserve of governments, or even just large corporations. An individual using online databases can monitor an issue world-wide and maintain a personal network via email, fax and telephone.

The resources of multinational companies mean that they already have equal (or better) knowledge than most governments. They are becoming very powerful and operate globally. This means that they can span the world to address their labour and real estate needs for the lowest costs.

Companies based within one or two countries do not enjoy the flexibility in the choice of real estate and other resources available to their global competitors. They are left to seek competitive advantage from a focus on quality and service rather than price. This is not a new concept. Over the years, many western manufacturing industries have declined when faced with low-cost competition from overseas producers. What seems likely in the future is that this will widen to include service industries.

These issues are set to be more important in the future, and many companies' destinies will depend on the IT and real estate components of their corporate strategies. Many IT and connectivity service providers are in business to profit from these developments, and they are going to keep up the pressure for change.

We can see that something will happen, we can even feel that it has started, and we can probably make good guesses as to some of the consequences, but it is still really hard to have the confidence to begin substantial changes to a business based on this somewhat ethereal future. This lack of certainty should not be used as an excuse for doing nothing – competitors will be doing something, and one or more of them will probably gain market share as a consequence.

People are meeting to discuss what the future holds. There is a consensus that change is under way, but natural pessimism and optimism mean that there is a wide range of ideas about the speed and content of the change, as illustrated by the publications mentioned below.

City 2020

Organisations, many with global interests, sponsored and organised a symposium called *City 2020*, hosted by Disneyland Paris in 1995 (Business Publishing, 1996). They were aiming to gain a greater understanding of how the city will develop. The 43 people attending – referred to as the shakers and drivers of change – represented a wide range of interests, extending beyond built environment specialists to technologists, psychologists and social scientists.

An interesting concept, introduced early into the debate, was that life will be simplified in 2020 because many of the technophobes of the 1990s will be dead! (And presumably the younger ones will have retired.)

Delegates were predicting that by 2020 current technology would be affordable and widely used via a comprehensive fibre-optic network. Consequently, location would be much less important than now. Business will become more flexible and decentralised. It was pointed out that the value of information comes from interrelationships at the interface of different bodies of knowledge rather than from the accumulation of knowledge.

Much of the thinking presented emphasised the value of relationships and the importance of getting closer to customers. There seemed to be no doubt that virtual communities – groups of people who know each other and communicate with little concern for geography – were being formed and would grow in importance. Such communities are not fixed to one location and are not under one national government. This is creating new problems of governance – how are conflicts defused and vibrant growth encouraged?

Flexibility is a word used frequently in the symposium report. Delegates could see developments in almost opposite directions; for example, an individual's work might come from the other side of the world, yet it would fit in with the worker's local context. Many comments related to the future need for organisation and management, but by individuals coping with different employers rather than by corporations maintaining their global 24-hour operations.

Most envisaged less work and an underclass who could not find employment while others had work, money and no time. Not only would some people have more time because of less employment, but others would have time to spare because they no longer commuted but instead worked from home and shopped via the Internet.

Many thought that the strength of human attachment and identification with place would create a demand for life in villages, towns and cities – without it, homeworkers would end up with 'cabin fever'. The role of corporate employment as the force underlying cities seems destined to end. The focus of cities will be choice – in entertainment (the festival centre), medicine, education and to some extent business.

It was pointed out that now in the USA more people commute suburb to suburb than into cities, and 60% of office buildings are outside the central business districts. Several discussed the changing requirements for offices and took flexibility further than discussed elsewhere in this book by suggesting that it would mean leasing accommodation, including the electronic 'kit', by the hour, supported by service standards on a par with those of the hotel industry. The concept of pay related to quality of work rather than hours in the office was predicted.

Much of the symposium was spent focusing on the social and lifestyle consequences of new technology, especially the values by which society would be organised in 2020. The mixture of participants and the cross-fertilisation of ideas probably produced some of the best ideas as to how we should plan for the future.

Flexicity

The European Commission has also turned its attention to the cities of the future in a report called *Telelifestyles and the Flexicity* (Hillman, 1993). This does not see a future of home-based teleworkers hunched over computers, but one of people working sometimes at home, sometimes in a neighbourhood office and partly in the company office. The mythical 'flexicity' of the title was cast aside on the first page in favour of an image of more flexible lifestyles and cities.

It was reported that governments are seeing teleworking as having potential benefits for less prosperous areas and of being able to assist in reducing traffic congestion and air pollution. Overall, it is seen as having the capacity to change society if it is desired, an attitude which ignores the power of the market. In the UK, where new developments do not need government approval, change may come more quickly than in other more regulated states in the European Union.

Hillman predicts a limited impact for teleshopping because visiting the shops was seen as enjoyable and providing an opportunity for social encounters, even if there are discomforts. The thinking given in the report is based on the less than convenient online systems currently available; attitudes could well change as the technology improves.

Telebanking is reported as having substantial markets, but Hillman feels that existing investments in land and buildings will slow down change by existing players. The impression given is that this will delay change in the banking sector, but as much has already happened this seems unlikely.

Overall, the report predicts that change will evolve and devolve from the existing structure of development, restrained in part by government and local policies. Hillman predicts that people will use technology as an enabler and not as the purpose of life. Decision-making, she feels, will be slow because of natural inertia caused by the existing patterns of ownership and occupation. Interestingly, Hillman reflects on society's frequent habit of planning to resolve the problems of the past rather than the future.

The report nevertheless predicts a changing demand for inner city space, but Hillman cannot decide whether it will lead to inner city collapse or a return to a more flexible mixed development to create vibrant city centres in which some people will choose to live and work.

Growth in spreading 'cities' at transport junctions, plus a general decentralisation, is predicted to replace city centres other than London, which will survive as an international hub. Hillman sees a demand for short-term meeting space for people to meet in, like motorway service stations.

The image of the future presented by the report is worthy of consideration, but it is not very dynamic. A cynic might well argue that the images are created for governments and their mandarins. They give a sense of security and suggest that there is still time for governments to discuss ideas, develop policies and lead their implementation so that they can direct the way to the future. As governments have yet to tame cyberspace it all seems a little unreal – almost dated, like reading Enid Blyton!

City of Bits

City of Bits: Space, Place and the Infobahn by William Mitchell (1995) is a completely different look at the future. William Mitchell seems to be in the future now. He works where he is – at home, in the air, at MIT, anywhere so long as he has his laptop and a cup of coffee. He writes with the experience of a man who sits in his office in MIT and teaches a class in Singapore.

Mitchell's vision, the City of Bits, is an anachronism for the real estate manager. It is not rooted to any spot on Earth and hence has no land values! It will be shaped by connectivity and be largely asynchronous in operation (messages will be left rather than conversations being held synchronously, face-to-face). It will be virtually constructed from software by logical linkages. Architects and builders will also be redundant!

Already Mitchell lives in a world where his network connections are becoming as important as his bodily location. He sees ahead an era of electronically extended bodies, of occupation and interaction through telepresence as well as through physical presence. It will bring, he predicts, the first opportunities in human history for truly worldwide communities with virtual places to meet, cooperate and be entertained. Mitchell predicts that we will be able to work and compete globally without moving. His book discusses many of the issues involved.

It could all seem too unreal to happen, and it is certainly very different from the gentle change predicted by Hillman. Yet, as Mitchell writes from the experience of one who has started down the path, you end up realising that he cannot be far from seeing the future. Corporate real estate managers will have to hope that we take some time to get there!

5.12 Summary

The major influence on real estate requirements considered in this chapter has been new technology. The key points have been:

- the changes that will occur are not always apparent, as high-tech developments interrelate to produce new opportunities
- miniaturisation and portability of computer hardware have assisted in creating working mobility
- connectivity improvements are making networking more affordable and available within the UK and soon globally
- computerised information management opens up many business opportunities as documents can be accessed simultaneously at different locations
- user-friendly image and graphic interface developments are making computer technologies accessible to those with limited computer knowledge
- groupware and workflow management support flexible working methods and processes that can have major real estate implications
- geographical systems and computer-aided design are closely linked to real estate, but the opportunities are largely unexploited
- global business can now usurp the information-based power of governments and large corporations
- business can operate in low-cost areas and sell direct to high-value markets
- there are many indications as to future high-tech opportunities, but most lack the confidence to be the first to exploit them
- by 2020 (well within the life of a building) the technophobes will be dead (!) or retired
- businesses are moving closer to customers and to addressing their needs
- virtual communities are not a dream – they have started to grow
- some feel that human resistance will slow change, but others are already boasting about their network connections being more real than their bodily location

5.13 Further reading

John M. Griffiths' book *ISDN Explained* (1990) is a useful introduction to connectivity.

For those who want to stretch their minds to think about the future the report on the *City 2020 Symposium* (1995) and the book *City of Bits: Space, Place and the Infobahn* by William Mitchell (1995), both mentioned earlier in this chapter, will help. Both cover much related to our future society as well as work. Bill Gates's book *The Road Ahead* (1995) is a very easy to read entry into the Information Age, and as he is the eternal optimist it encourages positive thoughts – a useful strategic tool.

5.14   Sources of information

Information on communications is available from the business consumer marketing departments of the communication service suppliers. BT plc has produced and published a useful book *Future Business: Engaging Customers Across the Information Superhighway* (BT, undated; available from BT by calling 0800 800 887 or via the Internet at http://www.bt.com).

A specialist service on document management, imaging and workflow is available from Cimtech at the University of Hertfordshire, 45 Grosvenor Road, St Albans, Herts AL1 3AW (Tel: 01707 284691; Fax: 01707 284699). They also produce the *Document Management Yearbook*.

For the individual or small business one way forward is to attend some of the many exhibitions, such as the ISDN Users Show, the GIS Exhibition, the Document Show and the Online exhibition.

The *Financial Times* management pages are a good source of information on the latest management technology and its operations. The individually published *FT Management Reports* usually have a few titles on IT and related topics. They are available from FT Management Reports, 102–108 Clerkenwell Road, London EC1M 5SA (Tel: 0171 814 9770; Fax: 0171 814 9778).

Ovum Ltd is an international market analysis company that specialises in studying the commercial and market implications of developments in computing and communications technology. It produces a wide range of reports. They are available from Ovum Ltd, 1 Mortimer Street, London W1N 7RH (Tel: 0171 255 2670; Fax: 0171 255 1995).

Another leading information provider is Frost & Sullivan, they cover a wide range of market issues in over 300 industries, including IT markets and the effect of various IT applications in different industries, both as published reports and customised services. Reports are available from Frost & Sullivan, Sullivan House, 4 Grosvenor Gardens, London SW1W 0DG (Tel: 0171 730 3438; Fax: 0171 730 3343).

More information on FT Profile and EGi has already been given at the end of Chapter 1.

6 Changing Real Estate Provision

6.1 Introduction

Theoretical ideas for business strategy can seem very distant from the day-to-day issues facing corporate real estate managers. This chapter reviews the practical changes in real estate provision which are the result of corporate real estate and business managers activating their new strategic plans.

This chapter highlights generic changes; while examples are cited, it is the process or policy that is being discussed. These are not guaranteed solutions – what suits one organisation may not be successful when introduced into another. More information is given on those matters that are not illustrated in the case studies in Chapters 14–20.

6.2 Space-saving measures

Most real estate changes being introduced at the present time are to reduce space requirements. When staff were comfortable and located where the business was growing, few gave thought to the costs involved. The focus was on the earning ability of staff – not how much they spent making those attractive earnings. When these firms found that technological changes reduced their profitability, or privatisation had given management more freedom, the costs being incurred in providing accommodation began to be questioned.

Those operating in businesses which have traditionally kept a closer rein on costs will find that there are fewer opportunities now to make startling real estate savings.

Those businesses which introduced change first were pioneers. They had to find the best solutions by trial and error (see Chapters 14 and 15). Those firms that follow can have learned from the leaders. As developers see the way in which businesses are using property they are starting to provide similar buildings – the followers will not have the bother of developing their designs from scratch. There are 'second-mover' advantages.

Many of the cost-saving measures spring from the mobility of staff. Businesses with operations in which the staff are very mobile will have greater opportunities to cut costs than those that need people full-time to operate specific equipment in specific locations – which is a driver to operational changes.

6.3   Internal rents and occupational charges

The aim of internal rents and other occupational charges is to ensure that each user of space understands the full cost of its operations, including accommodation. When this is known there is a realistic understanding of its contribution to the business. Some operations start to look a lot less profitable if the actual cost of the accommodation used is charged against their revenue.

The most market-oriented and efficient way to arrange internal rents is to charge each part of the business the full market rent for the premises it occupies. Various aspects of this issue are discussed in Chapters 14, 15 and 18.

6.4   Intensity of building usage

The need to cut all business costs and the introduction of internal charging do not in themselves reduce floor space per employee; there have to be arrangements in place to help, encourage and cajole people to move closer together. The clear objective of a more efficient business, not chaos, must be embedded in these arrangements and their realisation (see Chapter 14).

Much of what has been written applies only to offices which are normally used for one shift a day, with most people being paid for seven hours of work at their desks (9:00–5:00, with an hour for lunch) for five days per week, even though some may work longer. Annual leave and bank holidays ensure that most occupants do not work more than 48 weeks per year, often less. This means that space in offices is used for less than 20% of the total time available, and when illness, time away at meetings, sales promotions and training sessions etc. are taken into account the figure drops even lower. If shift work is undertaken using the same desks, covering say 8:00 a.m. to 10:00 p.m., seven days per week, then this can increase usage to over 50% of the time or more if desks are not left empty during annual holidays. All this give plenty of scope for even a small increase in the intensity of use to make a dramatic improvement!

6.5   Document management

It is easy to focus on the computerisation of records as a way of saving space and thereby overlook more basic options. The development of computerised paperless systems is still the exception rather than the rule; indeed the use of paper in offices is still increasing by 20% per annum. So improvements in methods of storing paper documents can still produce savings.

The modern document management industry has been driven forward by real estate considerations. The specialist companies add value for their business clients partly by storing records in cheap locations and also by taking over their management, which outsources a non-core function. The gains are sufficient to cover the cost of rapid transit services for records recalled from storage.

As with many changes that affect real estate, there were other influences, such as the legal requirements of the Data Protection Act 1984 (HMSO, 1984), which focused managers' attention on their archival systems. Another was the risk of interruption of business if key records were damaged by accident, natural disaster or terrorist attack. For some, the storage of duplicate current documents was more important than archival records.

In the meantime, the variety of storage options available creates a variety of real estate possibilities for many businesses. Much of this is not very technically advanced and does not extend beyond the traditional method of storage on manually recorded locations on open shelves. The most advanced systems for storing items use bar codes and fully computerised warehouses (ASRS – automated storage and retrieval systems). The automated systems come into their own when original documents are stored and are accessed regularly, for example the deed storage centre of the Nationwide Building Society, which has a fully-automated mini-load system (Alsop, 1991).

When information on paper records has to be stored it is not always legally necessary to keep the original document. In these circumstances the older technique of microfilming (microfiche) and the more recent imaging processing system may be economic.

6.6 Flexible working

New working patterns are emerging together with changing real estate requirements. Simplistically, these changes usually mean that less floor space is required, but at the price of providing sophisticated computer and communications links.

The key reference is a book by Franklin Becker and Fritz Steele (1995) called *Workplace by Design: Mapping the High Performance Workscape*. These two authors are innovative experts in business ecological systems, and their book gives design possibilities for flexible offices, together with examples.

Becker and Steele emphasise that organisational ecology is concerned with the total workplace – not just the desk and its immediate environment, but other facilities, such as the office canteen, the conference rooms, the smoking room, the lecture room and even the fitness centre. For many it will extend beyond the office to hotels, restaurants, airport, car, satellite offices and home – all the places in which one works. They suggest that many

> organisations need to conceive the workplace as a system of loosely coupled settings that are linked by the physical movement of people and the electronic movement of information in a way that enhances the organization's ability to meet its fundamental business objectives.

This is the essence of the changes that are taking place – the workplace can be anywhere and everywhere. Real estate and operational managers are starting to come to grips with the opportunities through a number of new arrangements, such as teleworking and hot-desking. For convenience they are described separately, but most frequently working arrangements include both to a greater or lesser extent.

Teleworking and homeworking

More common these days is for people to work at home and still be accessible by telephone, fax and online links – called teleworking. This is not a cheap alternative, as staff must be provided with computers, modems and (frequently) additional telephone lines or, for digital communications, ISDN connections plus a supportive corporate culture.

The authors (Gillespie, Richardson and Cornford) of the University of Newcastle's *Review of Telework in Britain: Implications for Public Policy*, published in 1995, reviewed various attempts to calculate the numbers teleworking from home in the UK. The probable figure for teleworkers was around ½ million, with only 100 000 home-based teleworkers. It was suggested in 1993 that there could be over 2 million mobile or nomadic workers in the UK (Gray, Hodson and Gordon).

Some operations are basing their staff at home because it is not necessary for them to be in any specific geographical location. A key aspect of full teleworking arrangements is that telecommunications links are not used just to keep in touch with the corporate headquarters but as an ongoing and, more or less, constant link along which work passes. For example, home-workers update the company's database as they work, just as if they were in the office and fully integrated into a document workflow management system.

Teleworking also works globally. Once linked, the two people can be operating from different continents. Firms no longer need to obtain work permits to engage overseas staff – they can work from their home countries receiving local wages, yet directly service a high-wage economy.

Some see it as futuristic, but it is not a distant dream. The virtual office exists. Already whole businesses operate with little more than a single office, and even the boss is rarely there (see Chapter 20).

Hot-desking

It is becoming more common to employ part-time staff and consultants who need desks when they are in the office but not at other times. This also applies to sales staff and customer service personnel. If they all work together at some time in the week then accommodation will be needed for all of them. However, it is frequently the case that never more than 30% are in together.

In this situation, shared desks, more frequently called hot-desking, can become beneficial (see Chapter 14). There are various versions, but the key feature is that the staff concerned do not have their own desks. Instead, individuals will have a small store for personal and work items, and nearby will be workstations, tables with computers (or docking points for laptops) and telephones which they can use. When staff arrive they will key into the telephone system so that their calls are routed to the table that they are using. Some more advanced systems provide staff with their own cordless phones.

To work well, the provision of workstations must be adequate for the number of staff using the space. Often staff will use the same desk every time *ensure* they are in the office – they will barely be aware that it is also used by someone else.

People will normally sit in groups comprising those doing related work; around them on the walls will be relevant information. There may well be some staff who are permanently in the office.

Researchers undertaking a review of the workplace for Richard Ellis concluded that hot-desking will become very widespread in the future (Richard Ellis/Harris Research Centre, 1995b). Of the companies they interviewed, 37% confirmed that 10% or more of their staff already shared desks, and in 11% of companies over 70% of the staff currently shared desks. How many people this represented was not given.

The furniture being designed for these arrangements is becoming less formal, *reamed in* with some companies investing quite heavily in attractive purpose-made designs which include comfortable seating for small meetings and relaxation away from VDUs. The aim is to create an attractive place to meet and work whether in an open plan office or in individual rooms – a scheme known as 'hotelling'.

At this relatively early stage of hot-desking in the UK the need by existing users is for information about its acceptance by staff and its effect on productivity. This is not easy to judge (see Chapter 15).

The decision to implement some or all of the components of flexible working should be a strategic corporate decision. Attempts by real estate managers to promote space-saving initiatives that are not fully planned and accepted by business managers will be counter-productive. The tactics of hot-desking and teleworking, which are valuable components of flexible working, will achieve little unless part of a business re-engineering package that has the support of senior management.   *flexible working [hot desk / teleworking*

6.7   Offsetting computerisation against air-conditioning costs

The provision of air-conditioning is a major issue for future consideration. Air-conditioning was deemed necessary by letting agents in the 1980s and early 1990s. They claimed that it was essential if a building was to be let. Now the necessity has been questioned by many occupiers, who have not enjoyed working in sealed air-conditioned buildings. The major argument in favour of its provision has been the need to disperse the heat emissions from electronic office equipment.

For most of the year in the UK opening windows is an effective way of dealing with excess heat, although this does not apply in noisy city centres, where opening windows can be deafening. During the winter of 1994/95 many were promoting a move away from the automatic provision of air-conditioning in major new office developments. It was one of the most talked about suggestions in a *Specification for Urban Offices* produced by the British Council for Offices in July 1994 because it would be a major cost saving for developers, which could be reflected in lower rents. The recommendation has been questioned by many developers, who still believe that quality offices would not let without it. No doubt their view has been strengthened by subsequent hot summer days. However, as few are building new offices, the debate is somewhat academic.

The argument is more complex than whether or not air-conditioning should be provided, because much of what is provided does not work well. Hill, from the Building Research Laboratory, has shown that many designers base air-conditioning systems on the nominal power ratings of office equipment and often use even higher figures to allow for the future use of even more equipment (Hill, 1995). In reality, the consumption of power by office equipment and the subsequent heat emissions are much lower. As a consequence, many air-conditioning systems are over-sized – some are up to five times as powerful as necessary and never work efficiently (Lawson, 1994). This situation is likely to get worse rather than better because computers and other high-tech equipment are becoming more energy-efficient, hence increasing the over-capacity of the air-conditioning plant.

6.8   Just-in-time and distribution logistics

The just-in-time (JIT) operation management system was developed in the Japanese automobile industry as a planning and control system applicable to manufacturing industry. It is a 'demand-pull' system resulting in goods arriving at the shop just in time to be sold, components arriving just in time to be assembled, and materials arriving just in time to be made into components.

It is a uniform rate flow system driven by the end user calling products through in an even way and instigating the development of the system and contracts with suppliers. There are no stores and no stocks waiting to move; the work in progress inventory is kept to a minimum.

Once set up there will be a series of small factories (300 employees or fewer) each delivering to the next in the successive stages of production until the final assembly plant, which will deliver to the shop or consumer. The lead time is one day and nothing is retained. Suppliers must be geographically close to customers to enable regular deliveries to be made.

The Nissan factory in Wearside works on this principle, and suppliers have set up factories nearby. The importance of regular deliveries caused Nissan to object to the siting of the Sunderland Football Club's new ground next to the main factory because the crowds on match days could cause traffic jams and disrupt production (Tighe, 1995).

It follows that JIT is not suitable for irregular and low production situations or markets with uncertain and intermittent demand, such as retailers who experience double the volume of trade before Christmas. These businesses are faced with installing a system that cannot cope with peak demand or one that operates at half capacity for most of the year.

JIT makes use of Electronic Point of Sale (EPOS) information systems which start the reordering process the moment goods are sold. Electronic Data Interchange (EDI) enables the exchange of information and payments between participants in the JIT chain. Import and export agents, ports, airports, haulage companies and couriers are all linked by EDI, making a comprehensive logistics network – goods can be tracked as they travel, often helped by bar code readers, GIS and GPS (see Chapter 5). These can be used in conjunction with data on deliveries, collections, route schedules, timetables and road traffic conditions to ensure the most efficient use of all facilities. These systems work most effectively when the number of sites is limited, and they have already resulted in warehouse rationalisation (see Chapter 16).

Distribution centres are being used for transhipment rather than storage. This requires clear floor areas for rapid cross-docking using fast sortation conveyors. For some, high floor-to-ceiling heights and high-bay storage are less relevant. When floor areas are more important than storage volume, reducing aisle widths and using narrower trucks can save costs.

Sites with planning consent to operate 24 hours per day and seven days per week are highly valued. The distribution industry, just like office users, is demanding flexibility in both design and hours of operation.

The distribution sector has also been influenced by legislation; for example, planned changes in speed limits will reduce the area of the UK that is within one day's drive of Channel and North Sea ports (Thame, 1995b). Some existing warehouse locations will become excessively expensive for importers and exporters after the change. Those businesses with warehouses in these zones have experienced a loss in property values. Other parts of the country, such as the M1/M6/M42 golden triangle, are popular because most of the UK population is within one day's return drive. New roads or increasing congestion can affect marginal sites in these key areas. For example, the opening of the A14 has extended the golden triangle of the M1/M6/M42 east to Kettering and Huntingdon, which are now also within easy reach of the East Anglian ports.

Another development in distribution reported by DTZ Debenham Thorpe (1993) has been the replacement of medium-sized warehouses of about 5–10 000 m^2 (50 000–100 000 ft^2) with national distribution centres of 10 000–45 000 m^2 (100 000–500 000 ft^2), supported in some instances by satellite depots of approximately 2–4000 m^2 (20 000–40 000 ft^2), which are buffers to assist in overcoming any disruptions.

The development of the Single European Market has encouraged the development of large manufacturing sites serving several countries, and these are often coupled with large distribution centres. Many businesses plan to serve the developing central European economies without new distribution centres in the region.

Other EU initiatives will enforce recycling of packaging, which will mean more plant and equipment at warehouses – hence favouring larger operations which will bring economies of scale.

6.9   Retailing, banking and other consumer services

The effects of new IT-based operational methods are already being noticed in financial services, where businesses, such as First Direct in banking and Direct Line in insurance, have grown to be very profitable. They have been at the vanguard of what can now be seen as a massive restructuring of the operation of consumer financial services. Most other leading banks and insurance companies now offer telesales services. The number of bank branches has been declining on average at the rate of almost two per working day for the last five years (British Bankers Association, 1996). The large building societies now seem to be following the same route as branch closures follow amalgamations.

The future of the retail sector is uncertain, with various predictions as to the likely uptake by the public of online electronic shopping services. It seems that this will depend on which providers get their infrastructure in place and in use by a critical mass of users first.

Many holidays are now booked after the details have been seen on teletext. This is just one small aspect of electronic shopping, or teleshopping. The development expected to cause major disturbance to shopping habits is the widespread introduction of online services. These are accessed via a PC (or possibly an adapted television screen) and a network connection. The consumer can then select a shopping service and choose from the products on offer.

Videos of holiday destinations and hotels would seem to be the logical development for these services. This will be an improvement over other holiday selection methods and an example where online services could be significantly better than existing methods. It has already been noted that users of the World-Wide Web on the Internet have a profile that matches the most desirable travel market (Pollock, 1995).

Teleshopping of all types in the UK in 1994 accounted for just 0.02% of retail sales (Buckley, 1995a). Currently, this small market mostly uses cable television and telephone ordering, although Internet-based services are increasing. While connectivity is speeding up between commercial users, domestic computer users are mostly using modems that are quite slow. Using these to browse through electronic shopping pages is 'like a double decker bus in a country lane' (Taylor, 1995).

Two main ways in which online shopping may reach and be used by a critical mass of shoppers are:

- The speedy installation of ISDN or fibre-optic cable followed by households connecting to the services. This could be more wishful thinking than reality, as cable only serves 21% of homes at present and subscribers are more interested in telephony than television services (Hall, 1996).

  Those promoting this view see a half-way solution of using CD-ROM catalogues for browsing (which speeds up the selection process), with online links, or even the telephone, being used for ordering. Software writers are hard at work developing methods to provide security for the ordering and payment of services online.

- The final stages are in hand to develop systems that will make use of the existing copper telephone wiring. As most homes are connected to a copper telephone line, the basic infrastructure is already in place. All that is needed is the final development of a system which will make use of 'asymmetric broadband' communications and the availability of low-cost conversion boxes for televisions or home PCs.

  Asymmetric broadband will make almost full use of the wiring to send high levels of information about the available goods out to the home and will dedicate only a small amount of the data-carrying capacity of the wiring for the limited return traffic to select the items to be shown or the orders to be placed.

In 1994, Home Shopping Network, the US cable television shopping channel, acquired Internet Shopping Services. The aim was to produce the first large-scale online electronic shopping mall, accessible to millions of personal computer users. They were attracted by the 25 million people already using the Internet. The predictions are that eventually the planned Internet service will be surpassed by an interactive television shopping service (Kehoe, 1994). Further predictions are that Home Shopping Network will find the market-place crowded, as many other computer groups are eyeing the opportunities (Lex, 1994).

In the meantime, a BT trial in Ipswich and Colchester is testing a mixture of services, including shopping, video, games and information, in 3000 homes. As this is the largest test in the world, it may be wrong to think that developments in the UK will follow those in the USA and elsewhere; it could be that new ground will be broken here first!

J Sainsbury plc has developed a computer model of a virtual shop (Buckley, 1995b). It is being used to assist in the design of new stores. It has also illustrated what could be the possible experience of the Internet home shopper 'walking' through a virtual shop that mimics the real shopping experience of strolling and browsing. Sainsbury's has no plans to develop its initial model. Yet the cost of headsets for virtual reality has already fallen from £9000 to £500, which is still considered too expensive for buying groceries but, nevertheless, no more than some white goods. It is perhaps more likely that the virtual reality headsets will be purchased for entertainment use and then be available for more mundane uses. If current practice continues it will probably be the case that a bundle of services, including both games and shopping, will be promoted in the future.

Goldman Sachs (Blackley et al., 1995) foresee profound long-term implications from electronic shopping for traditional retailers (including supermarkets), because a 10–20 percentage point shift in the retail market from the high street to the home could eliminate most retailers' profit margins.

Many may dismiss virtual reality because it seems too unreal, but there is a strong feeling that food shopping will change. A conclusion of importance to real estate can be drawn from the recent research, *The Future for the Food Store: Challenges and Alternatives*, undertaken for the Coca-Cola Retailing Research Group – Europe by Coopers & Lybrand (1996). It predicts that in the next 10 years food retailing stores and locations will be replaced as the greatest assets of a supermarket chain by customers. The customers will be attracted by convenient local services that overcome the current problems of shopping being time-consuming, complex and tedious.

Coopers & Lybrand predict the erosion of mass marketing and its replacement by mass customisation – dealing with large numbers of customers as individuals. The real estate implications of dramatic changes in the current supermarket chain marketing channels must surely ripple out throughout retailing and probably into production and distribution. New entrants may operate completely differently from anything we have yet experienced and with completely different real estate needs.

The British Council of Shopping Centres conference in 1995 was told that the company which sells more compact discs than any other firm in the world grew from a standing start in just five weeks by using the Internet (Neate, 1995). It was also pointed out to the conference that 81% of Internet users in the UK are from the ABC1 groups which shopping centres want to attract (Brown, 1995). It would seem that change could come quickly.

Even within the home shopping sector there is considerable cost variation. Goldman Sachs (Blackley *et al.*, 1995) report that in the USA the cost to process a consumer order on a toll-free number is about $5, compared with 50 cents on a consumer online service and less than 20 cents on an Internet-based service.

A report from Andersen Consulting (Hollis, 1995) points out the difficulty of defining particular sectors when there is industry convergence across retailing, financial services, entertainment, telecoms and information services. They foresee huge competitive issues and uncertainties as they seek to meet consumers' demands for the best value deal on every occasion. Tweaking the system will not be sufficient – managers will need to rethink their business strategies fundamentally. It looks as though the changes will be dynamic and will have to involve real estate.

Market research and forecasting

Retailers have always attempted to forecast market demand, but now the market leaders are becoming much more sophisticated. They are matching their forecasts for their own and other retailers' products directly to each high street and shopping centre. They are measuring supply against demand and matching this to the retail real estate and its rent levels in each town centre (see Chapter 18). The results, together with other marketing data, are used to assess the future strength of each retailing location, a process that is also being undertaken by some shopping centre developers and owners seeking to enhance or just maintain the value of their retail investments (Doidge, 1995).

There is considerable nervousness that while many prime retail locations will grow, changes in retailing will result in the decline of many weaker shopping centres.

6.10   Outsourcing of non-core processes

Rapid change makes it very difficult for businesses to invest with confidence in expensive operational systems, because there is a very real fear that new developments, whether technological or market-driven, will make the investment redundant before it has made a profitable contribution to the operation.

Using outsourcing contractors who also provide the necessary accommodation allows businesses to expand before undertaking the commitment of new permanent facilities. If they find that their predictions were erroneous they can quickly step out of the extra space and are not lumbered with the need to offload real estate.

In these circumstances the specialist contractors bear the real estate risks. They will aim to keep their real estate fully occupied by replacing clients who leave with new ones. The corporate real estate strategies of a storage, distribution and warehouse outsourcing contractor will be different from those of their clients.

6.11   Government grants and other intervention

Governments, including local authorities and those in Parliament and Brussels, often aim to influence economic processes through the provision of grants or subsidies. These come in many forms, from milk quotas to mortgage tax relief. Most commonly, industry and commerce are assisted by grants and subsidies that are related to real estate. A variety of different methods are used to make some locations more attractive for economic development. Fiscal policy can be very influential on real estate, especially where development is being promoted (e.g. Enterprise Zones) (see Chapter 7).

Government intervention can be very beneficial to corporations, but the business has to be able to remain profitable when the subsidies end. This has an effect beyond an individual firm, because although a business may be viable, others in the area may not. As these fail, real estate values are likely to decline. Those firms that are profitable may have debt finance secured on real estate fixed assets, which may fall in value in line with the local area to the point where the value may not be sufficient to support the debt.

The possible consequences of government intervention are not always considered, either by government or by the corporations who take decisions based on the benefits that they appear to offer at the time. Corporate strategists should be able to see these possibilities, and this will be more likely if real estate experts are involved in the initial decision-making process.

Those basing their decisions on current government policy should be aware that politicians are more frequently concerned with winning the next election than in long-term prospects. They are only concerned with the effect of giving a grant today and not in what will happen when it ends.

6.12   Churn (staff movements)

The cost of 'churn', or moving staff, is a major one for many businesses which, for operational reasons, find that staff need to move very frequently. In a survey of office occupiers undertaken for Richard Ellis (Richard Ellis/Harris Research Centre, 1995a,b) it was revealed that on average well over 30% of staff had moved within their existing building during the previous year. For many businesses this figure will be higher. They also found that a majority of respondents did not know the annual cost of churn. In addition to this internal churn, a third of all occupiers claimed that they expected to relocate their offices with the next five years.

The costs of moving staff often fall to budgets other than those of the real estate manager, such as portering, post rooms, printing, IT and removal contractors. The total cost is never seen on one budget and no one is particularly interested in attempting to add it up a reveal a figure that they feel powerless to reduce. Many business managers just shrug their shoulders and accept the cost as a burden not worth arguing about. They do not like what appears to be the only answer – not moving staff. At BT's new flexible offices, where churn costs have dropped from around £2000 per worker moved to £150, moving staff is commonplace (see Chapter 15).

A majority of the companies in the Richard Ellis/Harris Research Centre survey (1995a,b) had less than 50 employees. Even at this level moving 30% of staff at a cost of £2000 each totals £30 000 per annum. For the larger companies surveyed, who had over 1000 staff, the cost would be over £½ million per annum.

6.13   Summary

This chapter has reviewed some of the latest changes in the provision of real estate, many of them linked to new working practices and operational methods. A very common feature was that the new systems required less real estate than previously and are often in less expensive locations. The main points were:

- greater flexibility and mobility for office-based workers from the use of IT and connectivity means that less office space is needed
- there is a major role for corporate real estate teams in assisting in the implementation of flexible working and space-saving measures
- various knock-on effects occur with change, including changing air-conditioning requirements;
- changing industrial and retail methods are also bringing changes to real estate requirements
- government invention is influencing some real estate decisions
- the cost of moving staff to meet all these new objectives is being influenced by corporate real estate decisions

6.14   Further reading

Franklin Becker and Fritz Steele's book *Workplace by Design: Mapping the High Performance Workscape* is an excellent source of detailed and well-illustrated examples of how workplaces can be reorganised to make the most of high technology for the benefit of employers and employees. Guidance is given on all aspects of the changes involved, including working and management methods.

The report by the team of Richard Gillespie, Ranald Richardson and James Cornford at University of Newcastle Upon Tyne, *Review of Teleworking in Britain: Implications for Public Policy*, prepared for the Parliamentary Office of Science and Technology, is very comprehensive. It is well referenced and is a good introduction to the development and use of the process up to early 1995.

For those who seek guidance on introducing teleworking, *A Manager's Guide to Teleworking* written by Ursula Huws (undated) on behalf of the Department of Employment should prove helpful, especially as it contains a list of other relevant documents. It is available from Cambertown Ltd, Unit 8, Goldthorpe Industrial Estate, Goldthorpe, Rotherham, South Yorkshire S63 9BL.

Of the many operational management textbooks on just-in-time methods, *Production/Operations Management* by Terry Hill (1991) is a useful introduction to the development of just-in-time and the role of inventory in business competitiveness.

Leading retailers, Internet providers, cable TV companies and communications companies have been undertaking their own research, either in-house or by consultants, but little has been made available publicly. Three useful publications have been mentioned in the chapter. The report produced by Coopers & Lybrand for The Coca-Cola Retailing Research Group – Europe, *The Future for the Food Store: Challenges and Alternatives*, is available from The Coca-Cola Retailing Research Group – Europe, 1 Queen Caroline Street, London W8 9HQ (Tel: 0181 237 3845; Fax: 0181 237 3709). The Goldman Sachs report *The Electronic Retailing Market Place*, by Blackley, Lamming and Parekh, is available from Goldman Sachs, Peterborough Court, 133 Fleet Street, London EC4A 2BB (Tel: 0171 774 1000). The article by John Hollis is in the Autumn 1995 issue of the Andersen Consulting publication *Retail Technology: Smart Store Europe*, which contains information on a number of retail issues. It is available from their office in Windsor (Tel: 01753 605 000).

6.15   Sources of information

Information on air-conditioning systems for buildings is available from BRECSU at the Building Research Establishment, Garston, Watford, WD2 7JR (Tel: 01923 664258; Fax: 01923 664787). For information on air-conditioning for industrial projects contact ETSU, Harwell, Oxfordshire OX11 0RA (Tel: 01235 436747; Fax: 01235 433066).

The National Materials Handling Centre and Cranfield Centre for Logistics and Transportation have specialist logistics and distribution library facilities at Cranfield University.

7 Real Estate and Corporate Finance

7.1 Introduction

A company's annual report may not appear very strategic, yet it is here that the results of strategic policies become public, where the financial consequences of the activities of the business are recorded for all to see.

This chapter views company finances both from the view of the managers who want to improve their business performance and from the view of inquisitive outsiders who wants to know how the business is performing and why. It is not always an easy task, as the annual report contains the cumulative effect of all the financial arrangements of the company. Success in one area may be offset by losses elsewhere and vice versa. Even where financial changes are apparent the cause may not be clear unless specifically described in the Directors' Report or other statements published with the statutory accounts.

Introductory notes on the inclusion of real estate in company accounts is given in Appendix A, information on the key aspects of valuation methodology in Appendix B and brief details about fiscal allowances, especially capital allowances, in Appendix C.

7.2 Accountancy indecision

The accountancy profession is far from united as to the way that company finances should be reported and is engaged in a major debate on future accountancy practice. The main pivot of the debate is whether the balance sheet should be based on the traditional historic cost (cost of acquisition or production) or on a current valuation of the assets. In very simple terms, when historic cost is used the profit and loss account shows realised profits or losses.

A total valuation-based approach, which is not used at present, defines profit as the change in wealth of the business during a period and includes increases in value which have been identified but not realised.

The debate has been explosive, and eventually some decisions will have to be taken (Paterson, 1996). While companies use historic cost at present, many also include assets, most frequently real estate, revalued to take account of general changes in price levels, and they are also obliged to include at 'fair value' assets acquired as part of the acquisition of another business.

These issues are clearly very relevant to corporate real estate managers and their financial directors because there are also a number of tangential debates on the recognition of the value of a company's real estate. Valuers have expressed fears that the accountancy profession will move away from revaluation and back to historic cost, because this would have a significant effect on a major source of valuation instructions (Waters, 1996).

Accountancy requirements are not fixed and companies select different approaches, so practice varies. The methods currently in use are given in *Generally Accepted Accountancy Practice in the United Kingdom*, better known as *UK GAAP* (Davies *et al.*, 1994).

7.3   Fixed assets

Fixed assets are used on a continuing basis in a business's activities, yet normally they have a finite useful economic life and will eventually need to be replaced. The term 'fixed asset' is not restricted to immobile items, and can include items such as aircraft. Freehold land (not buildings), unlike other fixed assets, is normally regarded as remaining forever, but there are exceptions, such as mineral extraction and limited life planning permissions.

Depreciation

To create a true view of the effect of the finite life of fixed assets, a charge is made against the profit and loss account each year by way of depreciation. It is calculated to ensure that a fair proportion of the cost, or value, of the asset is allocated in each accounting period expected to benefit from its use. It is based on the cost or value of the asset and also the estimated residual value that may exist at the end of its useful life. Normally no depreciation is charged for freehold land, and this includes the land element of any freehold property. The requirements are given in *Statement of Standard Accounting Practice 12* (Accounting Standards Committee, 1987).

Depreciation in this context is not about an asset losing its value. It is about conserving the capital. A sum held back from profits stops a company from boosting profits by draining its ability to maintain the assets on which it bases its operations. In theory, buildings are no different from other fixed assets, except that they have a longer useful life and are therefore depreciated over a longer period. Amortisation of leasehold interests over the period of the lease is similar to depreciation.

Some assets do not wear out, generally because a company is spending money maintaining the asset. This is often the case with well-maintained real estate assets. Companies that do this often argue that the value of the estate is not being impaired by the passage of time. They also point out that they are spending large amounts to ensure that this is the case – costs which are charged to the profit and loss account. Therefore they argue that depreciation is immaterial and they do not make any provision for it in the accounts with respect to their real estate.

However, buildings often suffer from obsolescence because they do not meet current needs, even though the fabric may be in good condition(see Chapter 9). Obsolescence has affected the real estate assets of many companies, and as a result of the impairment in real estate values attitudes are changing to the role of depreciation charges and some companies that discontinued them have reinstated their use. There is no uniform approach, so the accounts must be read to find out the practice adopted for each company.

The value of fixed operational assets

The value of the fixed assets recorded in the balance sheet can be the historic cost or a current valuation according to various criteria. When valuations are undertaken they must follow the requirements of the Royal Institution of Chartered Surveyors *Appraisal and Valuation Manual* (1995) (see Appendix B).

As real estate values change over time, using historic cost can be very misleading when attempting to understand the current position of the company. Changes in nominal value will occur if inflation is high and/or changes in real value occur (up or down) when, for example, local market conditions change, say due to a new road.

It is best for most shareholders if the real estate interests are revalued regularly and the latest figures are included in the annual accounts. Clearly, surveyors have a vested interest in promoting regular revaluations of real estate, but real estate is unlike most other fixed assets. In the long term the land element, especially, and often also the buildings, can retain their value (despite the rises and falls of the property cycle). Real estate, unlike most other fixed assets, can have a resale value greater than the initial price, although obsolescence means that it does not always happen.

This is very close to the issues being discussed by the accountancy profession. Suggesting that businesses should be very open about the value of their real estate assets does not mean that current cost or current valuation accounting is essential. What is important is that shareholders and managers should understand the value of the assets tied up in the company. Not appreciating, or attempting to hide, the value of real estate assets can lead to takeover bids (see Section 7.11).

Shifting real estate values

Real estate values do not always rise. If there is supplementary depreciation due to a valuation downwards this will be shown on the balance sheet, not the profit and loss account. The net book amount should be written down immediately to the estimated recoverable amount and then be written off over the remaining economic life of the asset. Where material, the adjustment of accumulated depreciation should be separately disclosed and may also be shown in the accounts as an exceptional item.

Exceptional items have been necessary for buildings that have suffered from a sudden decrease in value due to economic or technical obsolescence. Freehold land can suffer from a permanent diminution in value owing to factors such as changes in the desirability of its location or soil contamination, and will then generally have to be written down and charged to the profit and loss account (any reversals will be credited).

It is easy to appreciate that decisions over temporary and permanent diminutions in value (or the reverse) can be hard to define, so the decisions on accountancy practice can be equally difficult and therefore vary from company to company.

If an asset is revalued upwards, the amount charged to depreciation will also increase. This means that the amount of depreciation charged to profit and loss increases, hence reducing profits and giving lower earnings per share. It will also change balance sheet ratios, such as return on capital – as the assets go up, the return on capital goes down (assuming nothing else changes). Those companies that remain with historic cost figures do not have this difficulty.

Companies often revalue some assets and not others. The periods between valuations can be arbitrary, although most companies seem to be guided by whether there has been a generally recognised change in value for the type of real estate that they own. If directors fear that values are falling they may well feel inhibited from commissioning a revaluation (Waters, 1996). Some companies have a continuing rolling programme of real estate asset revaluation which can help overcome such pressures.

7.4   Investment property

If real estate is owned by a business not for operational purposes but as an investment, or is set aside awaiting disposal, it will be treated in the accounts according to the requirements for investment property which are given in *Statement of Standard Accounting Practice 19* (Accounting Standards Committee, 1981). Investment properties are included in the balance sheet at open market value.

An investment property is one on which construction work and development is complete, which is held for its investment potential with any rental income being negotiated at arm's length, is not used by the business operation and the disposal of which would not materially affect any manufacturing or trading operation. Consequently, it is the current value of the real estate held as an investment that affects the value of the business, not the level of depreciation.

Annual depreciation is not charged to the profit and loss account except for short leasehold interests. This means that higher profits are declared each year.

This is not in line with the general requirements of company legislation, but is possible because this legislation allows for not including depreciation if it can be argued that it would not give a true and fair view. A statement to this effect can be found in annual reports where the company owns investment properties.

This arrangement is also under review by the accounting profession. Again the property world is concerned, firstly because property companies would suffer most, since depreciation provisions would reduce profits, and secondly because such a change could also reduce the need for valuations (Waters, 1996).

Changes in value are shown as a change on the investment revaluation reserve, often just called the revaluation reserve or even the unrealised capital reserve. They will also be taken to the statement of recognised gains and losses.

If a change for an individual building is considered to be permanent the loss (or its reversal) should be charged (or credited) in the profit and loss account. This does not always happen, and many recent annual reports do not make it clear whether the recorded diminutions in value are considered to be temporary or permanent – no doubt many finance directors hope for the former and fear the latter!

The legal requirements for valuations are not onerous, and, unless investment properties represent a substantial proportion of the total assets of a major corporation, a qualified valuer need not be used. In reality, most companies do use qualified valuers and have regular external valuations, although it is not uncommon for the directors to adjust values in the intervening years. When chartered surveyors undertake these valuations the requirements of the *Appraisal and Valuation Manual* (Royal Institution of Chartered Surveyors, 1995) apply.

There are specific requirements for organisations such as property unit trusts, pension funds, insurance companies and charities.

Properties that are let and occupied by another company in the same group cannot be included as investment properties in the group accounts. This is unpopular, and companies such as The Boots Company plc have expressed their discontent (see Chapter 18).

When properties are transferred from operational use to investment or vice versa, there are a variety of accounting practices which can be used to incorporate the change into the annual report. These are well covered in the *UK GAAP* (Davies et al., 1994).

With the USA leading research and development in the field of corporate real estate it is worthwhile noting that in the USA there are no special accounting arrangements for investment properties, so this is never mentioned in US publications.

7.5   Core business and real estate investment

Generally, businesses are seeking to maximise the potential of their core operations. For non-property companies, holding investment properties would tend to suggest a diversification away from core business (for exceptions see Chapters 18 and 19). Property investments should be justified for sound business reasons, such as gaining an income from real estate that will eventually be needed as an operational asset, or because it is part of a deliberate diversification.

7.6   Strategic implications of valuation methods for accounting purposes

While standard ways of proceeding are vital for shareholder confidence, they cannot cover every aspect that affects real estate within dynamic businesses operating in dynamic markets, even though the rules are updated to deal with new situations.

It will probably always be necessary for corporate strategists to think beyond the figures produced by the standard valuations if they want to maximise the potential of the real estate used by the business. A business's own internal valuers can produce valuations for internal use on any basis they wish. They can build different 'what if?' scenarios and make valuations using assumptions not permitted in more formal circumstances. Just as businesses undertake economic and trading forecasts, so they can forecast property values to assist in their decision-making.

We have already seen that many directors do not know the value of their real estate interests (see Chapters 1 and 2). Those that do probably focus on the values given in the annual accounts, but there could be additional value in different circumstances. For example, if additional value depends on acquiring planning permission for new uses or disruptive construction works, the potential will not have been included in the Existing Use Value and would only be mentioned in the accounts if appreciated and if significant in relation to the total real estate valuation. Directors who have not focused on real estate will probably not have noticed the creeping changes and increased potential.

Some development possibilities are far from obvious, especially to a valuer who believes the existing business will continue to operate on the site in question. It can need imagination to envisage an area without the dirt, noise and traffic of the business operation to appreciate the possibilities. Demand for new types of building arise from time to time so that what was an edge-of-town warehouse could be a potential out-of-town multiplex cinema or fitness centre. When development potential is recognised it can be enhanced, or even created, by purchasing properties surrounding a real estate holding to create a large development site of major significance and market attraction.

Retailers who tend to change their trading locations frequently can gain significantly from understanding the full potential of all their real estate. Forecasting should include the potential for surrounding buildings to help judge whether an area has growth potential not only for trading but for real estate values (see Chapter 18).

A recent example of the effect of new planning permission on share price is The Oliver Group plc, a shoe retailer.

A period of retrenchment in 1993 for The Oliver Group plc was followed by growth during 1994. It was reported by the Chairman that the company was still awaiting the decision of the Secretary of State with regard to planning permission for change of use of their headquarters site (Oliver Group, 1995a). Share prices during the summer of 1995 stabilised at 92p, although they slipped a little to stand at 87½p at the end of August (Figure 7.1).

On 4 September 1995 the company announced poor half-year results (Oliver Group, 1995b). Trading had improved, but the rate of growth was

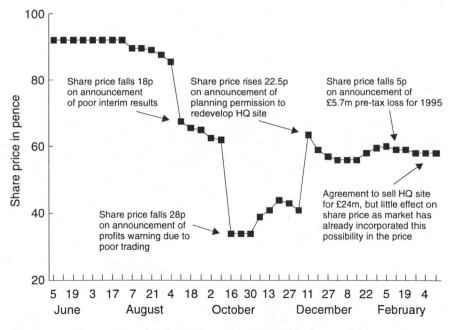

Figure 7.1 Share prices for the Oliver Group (weekly from 5 June 1995 to 11 March 1996).

lower than expected, leaving the business with capital tied up in unsold shoes. The company also announced that it had gained planning permission to redevelop its head office site, but the decision was being challenged on a point of law in the High Court. This meant that redevelopment could not go ahead while the case was outstanding and would not go ahead if the appeal to the High Court succeeded. As the poor trading could not be offset by any property value gains the share price fell to 67½p. Summer trading was also bad and the sales of the autumn ranges were disappointing, and following a profits warning issued on 9 October the share price fell dramatically again to 34p (Oliver Group, 1995c). The share price picked up a little in November.

On 8 December, Oliver announced that the appellant had withdrawn the appeal to the High Court and that the company was free to sell the head office site for considerably more than the current book value of £9 million (Oliver Group, 1995d). It was reported separately that the sale price was expected to be more than £15 million and that the gain would be invested in the company (Harding, 1995). Share prices rose to 63½p.

The share price fell 5p on 22 February 1996 when the annual results revealed a £5.7 million pre-tax loss for 1995 (Oliver Group, 1996). Early in March it was announced that the sale of the land for £24.9 million had been agreed. These last two announcements had less effect on the share price because the market had been expecting them. Share prices change when the unexpected happens, as with the initial announcement of poor trading. They also change when something like the planning permission is confirmed – it was known to be a possibility, which was already reflected in the share price, but the market was very unsure as to the likelihood that it would be granted.

7.7   Fixed assets are investments

Although operational real estate is treated differently in the accounts from investment properties, this should not be allowed to mask the fact that the capital could have been used to acquire different properties or the business could have invested in other factors of production, such as labour or plant and machinery.

7.8   Leveraging real estate

While the money used to acquire real estate could have been invested in other factors of production, the decision to invest in real estate need not tie up the capital.

Although real estate comprises fixed pieces of land and specific buildings, it can be very flexible. The flexibility comes from being able to use its intrinsic value to support a variety of financial arrangements. Good quality, well-located real estate is attractive, and ownership of the freehold of such buildings generally enhances a business, even if it is highly geared. This is because if the business fails good real estate assets can be sold, and their value will not decline with the business's decline.

Real estate, as well as being an operational asset, can be used as security to raise finance. It can be sold and leased back, releasing capital for other investments. Sometimes the activities of a business can increase the development potential of its real estate. This can then be released by a sale or captured and turned into cash through its role of supporting debt finance. To extract the best value-making potential from real estate assets while they are being used as a factor of production needs carefully strategic management.

7.9 On or off balance sheet

Recent changes aim to ensure that the substance of a company's transactions are reported in the annual report and other financial statements (HMSO, 1989; Accounting Standards Board, 1994). Consequently, most legal but somewhat unscrupulous off-balance sheet provisions have ceased.

Now the most common way of moving freehold real estate interests off balance sheet is a sale and leaseback arrangement. The deal removes the premises from the balance sheet when they are sold, but allows the company to continue to use them in exchange for rent. As illustrated in Chapter 17, this will reduce gearing, but the arrangement is clearly shown in the annual report and nothing is hidden.

A company can hold freehold and substantial leasehold interests in separate companies. If they are in a separate subsidiary, they will not be included in the balance sheet of the core business, but will feature in the group accounts and nothing is hidden from investors (see Chapter 18). Except for some tax considerations, it really does not make a great deal of difference for accounting purposes, and the deciding issues could well be organisational, not financial.

It is beyond the scope of this book to consider the holding of assets offshore and in tax havens. As recent events have shown, even large and well-known listed companies have undertaken less than satisfactory arrangements – although this is becoming harder to achieve.

7.10 Valuation for lending purposes

It would be misguided to look at the accounts valuation of real estate fixed assets of a business and think that it represents the only figure that could be used as security for loans.

A lender might agree a that higher valuation based on Open Market Value could be relevant, because if the business fails the site will be repossessed and vacant and could be used for a different purpose, which could not be reflected by an Existing Use Valuation. The difference will probably not be large, because otherwise the business would probably realise the development potential itself. It could be sufficient to encourage a lender to make a loan in circumstances that are otherwise risky. All the circumstances must be clearly stated in the valuation, which again must be carried out according to the RICS *Appraisal and Valuation Manual*.

7.11   Corporate raiders and takeovers

Many businesses which pay little attention to real estate can find that others are keen to purchase the company. It is not the profit streams created by its operations that interest purchasers but the real estate assets that could be sold off for considerably more than the balance sheet has revealed. Real estate interests that seem out-of-date and of little value to the owner may be seen in quite a different light by others.

Research in the USA based on the first half of the 1980s found that corporate real estate played a significant role in determining the likelihood of a business becoming a takeover target (Ambrose, 1990).

A company that wishes to use real estate in a way that does not directly exploit its full economic potential may be able to use this potential to secure a loan which could be put to more profitable use in the core business. Thus the value of the asset is exploited.

Where a company is considering acquiring another business, the real estate issues should be thoroughly investigated – matters such as ownership and planning consents, as well as financial obligations, must be considered. It is not only real estate currently owned or leased by a business that needs to be considered, but also any obligations that could arise if the assignees of assigned leased buildings subject to privity of contract fail to meet their obligations. This is discussed in greater detail in Chapter 8.

When takeovers and mergers are under way, the requirements for valuation of fixed assets including real estate are governed by the Stock Exchange in the *City Code on Takeovers and Mergers* (Panel on Takeovers and Mergers, 1993). This is well beyond the scope of this book other than to point out that the rules are tight and it is far too late to panic about previous under- or over-valuations.

7.12   Real estate and financial instruments

There are a number of ways in which real estate is used, directly or indirectly, to provide security for debt finance. Business managers will be mostly interested in ways in which their real estate can be used to secure reasonable debt finance. However, most of the developments in the market-place are driven by investors, who want more variety in the ways in which they can invest in real estate.

Methods are being evolved to enable investors to gain exposure to the real estate market without the need to buy specific property. For those who cannot diversify by acquiring several buildings the risks are higher than average, and added to this are the disadvantages of high transaction and management costs, together with high illiquidity. Owning real estate through shares in a property company is inefficient for tax-exempt investors, such as UK pension funds and charities.

The following sources of finance related to real estate could be used to implement corporate strategies involving real estate. Various limitations mean that most are not currently used directly by businesses to raise finance, but this seems likely to change.

Securitisation

The main purpose of securitisation is to convert assets into marketable securities that are sold to various investors, who take a smaller stake than the whole security. An essential component in the arrangement is development of a market, a recognised exchange, in which the securities can be traded freely. The interest payments are serviced from cash flows on the assets.

Would-be real estate investors want to purchase interests that are smaller than a single building and based on a selection of real estate. Methods exist in the USA and Australia, but in the UK tax laws generally make similar arrangements unattractive. If the taxation regime improves, investment banks, investment managers and others would develop a wider range of debt instruments.

A recent report on securitisation of property produced by the Investment Property Forum (1995) has attracted considerable interest. This, and reports such as that by Currie and Scott (1991), mentioned in Chapter 2, are resulting in greater government and City awareness of the role of real estate.

It is a complex market, and the securities are often placed with specialised groups of investors, such as those developed for tax-exempt UK pension funds and charities, rather than being offered to the public. Some landlords have been involved in offering securitised loans. The buildings involved are usually let to government or corporate tenants with a high credit rating. Securitisation is also well known in the mortgage market, where the receivable payments from mortgagees provide the interest payments. So far, most of these instruments have only very limited trading potential and do not create a securities market.

The proposal by the London Stock Exchange to list authorised property unit trusts (APUTs) could be a move towards opening up a market (London Stock Exchange, 1996).

Whatever the basis of the security on offer, investors want to be sure that the income is secure. To gain the best terms securities need to carry an AAA rating, although instruments with lower ratings have also been created. Where real estate incomes have been involved credit rating companies such as Standard & Poor or Moody's have had to rate the cash flows. In the UK rating commercial property debt is a new process. The concern has not been the borrower as much as the credit quality of the underlying tenants and the details of the lease under which the rent is paid.

Securitisation offers companies another route for making real estate arrangements work for their businesses. It is expected that in time it will become part of the financial apparatus normally available to corporate business. The real estate assets could be taken off balance sheet to become the assets of investors in the securitised debt. The business would continue to occupy the accommodation, but would pay a rent which will form the investors' income.

Corporate bonds

Major businesses are able to raise loans directly in the finance markets as bonds. These are cheaper than bank finance. They also provide businesses with more certainty than bank finance. No bank can offer finance to match a long-dated bond of, say, 20 years at a fixed rate of interest.

The market for issues available to the general public requires raising at least £50 million, but smaller companies can form joint ventures in order to reach this level (London, 1991). Sums of £10 million are possible from private placings with institutional investors, but these cannot be traded and cost more than public issues, although still less than bank borrowing.

The terms of bonds and the security offered varies. They are normally issued as debentures created to give holders a floating charge over the company's undertakings, with or without a fixed charge on the real estate (normally a mortgage on freehold property). Real estate supporting a debenture cannot be sold without the agreement of the debenture holders. This will increase the inflexibility of the real estate assets. An example of such a bond is illustrated in the 1995 accounts of Marks & Spencer plc, where the various debt instruments are listed including a 7¾% debenture 'secured on certain freehold and leasehold properties'.

Synthetic and derivative property instruments

These are tradeable securities that derive their value from other financial assets. The asset can be owned by those issuing the instrument, but this is not always the case. There has been much discussion about their use to create instruments based on real estate investments, but no progress until Barclays Bank developed the first real estate synthetic in 1994. Their product reflects the real estate market, but for investors the security is based on the financial rating of Barclays Bank rather than actual real estate assets. It is a synthetic because it tracks a property index rather than being linked to a financial asset in the way that a warrant is linked to a share, for example.

Barclays De Zoete Wedd Investment Management Ltd, acting for Barclays Bank plc, set up a real estate-based synthetic to offset the risk Barclays Bank was carrying by having 9% of its loans against real estate. Its exposure to real estate was too high, but it could not rapidly sell off the loans to others without destabilising the market and suffering loss.

The first issue of the synthetic, known as Property Index Certificates (PICs), was sold in tranches of at least £250 000 to institutional investors. The PICs were not listed, and any trading had to be on the basis of matched bids. The issue was fully subscribed, and in 1995 a second tradeable issue (PICs 2) was launched. This raised the total fund from £150 million to £250 million. Original investors were able to change to the new tradeable product. The PICs have proved successful and have traded at a premium.

The PICs are linked to an Investment Property Databank (IPD) index based on the movement of £45 million of commercial property. The investors are paid an income based on the yield of the index. The capital repayment after the fixed term of three or four years is also based on the index. Investors will be paid a premium on redemption if the capital value of the index rises. If it falls, the investment will be only partly repaid.

It is a hedge for Barclays Bank against the risk of the value of their real estate loans falling. The price they pay is the cost of the premiums on redemption if real estate values rise. A contingency is held as a provision in the Barclays Bank accounts in case this happens. While in theory the real estate could rise in value by more than the contingency fund, the risk is limited by the short, three- and four-year life of the PICs.

The PICs cover Barclays Bank's downside risk. Without a hedge, Barclays Bank would have had considerable concern if real estate values fell. Such a fall would probably be linked to business failures and lead to the bank having to repossess some of the properties securing the loans. There would be the possibility of the property values falling below the outstanding debt, and causing Barclays Bank to lose money. With the PICs in place the bank would be able to offset such a loss from the capital retained because the PICs would only be partly repaid, as the IPD index would also fall.

If real estate values rise, the risk of repossessed property being insufficient to cover the outstanding debts falls. At the same time the need for repossession is also likely to fall. The only commitment will be the premiums for the PIC investors, and these have been covered by the contingency.

Investors are attracted because they can have an exposure to commercial real estate without buying and managing a whole building or using expensive unit trusts. The exposure to real estate allows investors to diversify the risks in their investment portfolios.

The synthetics have only been used to cover part of the loan exposure, as some exposure is normal and part of the bank's normal balancing act to diversify risk. The strategy of hedging the excessive part of its existing property loan portfolio means that Barclays Bank has been able to remain in this market and continue to offer real estate-based loans to its customers.

The property derivative market has yet to develop – to date there have been very few products, most of them short lived. It is an area that is attracting activity, and new products could soon become available.

With the lack of products it is not surprising that corporations do not hedge their real estate holdings, but there is considerable speculation that it will happen. As already discussed, many non-property companies, especially retail groups, have high exposure to the real estate market. Many already hedge their exposure to foreign currencies, so doing the same for real estate is evolutionary – not revolutionary.

7.13   Capital allowances and other fiscal measures

Although very much an aspect of detail rather than strategy, the financial benefits that come when various allowances are claimed and agreed by the Inland Revenue can make the consideration of capital allowances a component of establishing strategic plans. As it is an important and often overlooked subject, some of the main points are worthy of further consideration. These allowances, which are subject to change by the Inland Revenue, can be claimed when real estate is purchased, developed or refurbished – each action creates an opportunity for making a claim. Introductory details on the opportunities offered by fiscal allowances are given in Appendix C.

The attractions of capital allowances for particular buildings must always be balanced by an equally careful consideration of the suitability of the building for the operation of the business or investment performance. The benefits of the tax allowances can be negated if the building is inefficient for the business's operation.

7.14   Financial motives

Liow has attempted to seek explanations as to what financial factors predispose retail companies to acquire and dispose of real estate. He found it difficult for a variety of reasons, including the limitations of the available evidence. He concluded that it was likely that the decision is not just financial but relates to the context of the whole firm, suggesting that real estate is a strategic asset for the non-property company (Liow, 1995).

7.15　Summary

This chapter has shown that an understanding of the role of real estate in the balance sheet of a company is a vital component of developing corporate strategy that includes real estate.

It has focused on:

- the importance of understanding the requirements that govern the accounts valuation of fixed real estate assets, as these may not reflect the most profitable uses and conversely can be higher than open market value
- some of a company's real estate possibly being investment property with different accounting requirements
- the value of corporate strategists thinking beyond the limits of asset valuations and considering the 'what if?' scenarios that asset valuers must ignore
- the analysis of competitors' use of real estate
- using real estate to extend the core business
- remembering that real estate fixed assets represent an investment in the business which must be justified
- the fact that real estate need not tie up the use of capital because real estate fixed assets can be used to secure debt finance
- the limited opportunities for taking real estate off balance sheet
- the risks of ignoring real estate and leaving the business exposed to a takeover bid
- the development of financial instruments which could eventually be used as a part of the tactics to increase strategic opportunities
- the financial gains available from capital and other fiscal allowances
- real estate being a strategic asset for the non-property company

7.16　Further reading

Those wishing to know more about the issues related to the securitisation of real estate can consult the report *Property Securitisation* by the Investment Property Forum. It explains a variety of securitisation possibilities, including those that would be successful if the tax regime changed, and is illustrated with case studies. It is available from the Secretary of the Investment Property Forum at the Royal Institution of Chartered Surveyors, 12 Great George Street, London SW1P 3AD (Tel: 0171 334 3799 or 0171 222 7000).

Those wishing to investigate property finance in greater depth should consult the quarterly *Journal of Property Finance*, available from MCB University Press, 60–62 Toller Lane, Bradford, West Yorkshire BD8 9BY (Tel: 01274 777700).

7.17   Sources of information

The *UK GAAP* or *Generally Accepted Accounting Practice in the United Kingdom*, written by Davies, Paterson and Wilson, sponsored by Ernst & Young and published by Macmillan Press provides a basic reference and analysis of the way accounting is undertaken in the UK.

The Royal Institution of Chartered Surveyors *Appraisal and Valuation Manual* (1995) is available from the RICS bookshop (Tel: 0171 222 7000).

Financial Reporting Standard 5: Reporting the Substance of Transactions, *Statement of Standard Accounting Practice 12: Accounting for Depreciation* (SSAP 12) and *Statement of Standard Accounting Practice 19: Accounting for Investment Properties* (SSAP 19) are available from Accounting Standards Board Publications at PO Box 939, Central Milton Keynes MK9 2HT (Tel: 01908 230344). An alternative source is the Institute of Chartered Accountants Accountancy Bookshop (Tel: 01908 248000).

The current annual reports and accounts for most major companies are available direct from the companies or from the *Financial Times* (order details inside back page of the second section, 'Companies and Markets').

Microfiches of the deposited annual reports and other company returns can be purchased from the regional offices of Companies House, where there are also facilities for making photocopies. This is time-consuming, and printed accounts can be ordered direct from the main Companies House in Cardiff, which provides a full information pack of services (Tel: 01222 380801; Fax: 01222 380900). The whole process can be outsourced to company search agents.

Information about the Investment Property Databank Ltd and the services it offers are available directly from IPD at 7/8 Greenland Place, London NW1 0AP (Tel: 0171 482 5149).

Part 3:
Real Estate Ownership Choices

8 Own or Rent?

8.1 Introduction

Nearly all business managers face a choice between owning and renting real estate. In the past, many did not give it much thought as long as they had buildings from which to run the business. Now that the value and potential of real estate to enhance the business's success have been appreciated such decisions are rather more significant – they can generate the most productive use of this important resource.

8.2 Financial implications of owning or renting

The business manager has a choice between owning or renting the real estate needed for the business. Real estate appears in the balance sheet if it is an asset which is not all consumed within the accounting period, normally a year.

Freehold operational real estate will be included in the fixed assets of the business. Leasehold interests in real estate may have rents below market levels because a payment, or premium, was paid up-front in consideration for the lease. It can also happen because inflation has caused market rent levels to rise while the rent fixed by the lease agreement remains the same. In these circumstances a financially valuable interest will remain at the end of each year. This will be an asset for the business, recorded as a fixed asset in the accounts.

A business which agreed a rent during a boom in property values can find itself paying rents above the market level during a subsequent property slump. Such a leasehold interest is not an asset for a business! However, it would be contrary to the managers' fiduciary duty to enter deliberately into such an unsatisfactory situation. Therefore the assumption must be that this would never be an intentional decision of a business's managers unless the risk of over-renting was offset by the potential gains of occupying the particular property.

The business manager deciding whether to own or rent real estate operational assets will be choosing between obtaining a freehold building, which will be a substantial fixed asset on the balance sheet, or a lease, which means paying rent – a cost against profits deducted before taxable profits are calculated.

An important influence on the choice can be capital allowances, as mentioned in Chapter 7. The possible relief from taxation can be substantial in some circumstances. An arrangement to divide the methods of occupation between both renting and owning can bring the lessee of a building the addition of the tax allowances for the plant and equipment (e.g. lifts, air-conditioning) when the tenant becomes the owner of these. As explained previously, there are various opportunities, but it is important to ensure that the overall package, if available, suits the business in the long term as well as in the short term.

8.3   Hedge against inflation

Many businesses have held freehold real estate as a hedge against inflation. As discussed in Chapter 2, the UK economy is now in a period of low inflation, which negates fear of inflation as a reason to own rather than rent.

Nevertheless, many business managers are still far from confident that low inflation will be maintained, and they are balancing their decisions when trying to decide what may happen. In this situation it is still relevant to consider attitudes to real estate under conditions of high inflation. It helps establish to the whole panoply of possibilities which warrant consideration when developing strategy.

While it is not difficult to appreciate the attraction for a business to own real estate and be protected from rising rent levels, there must be sufficient capital available for its purchase. It must be remembered that property values that rise with inflation are not adding to the real value of the business. A business may be much better off not spending money on a freehold interest but renting accommodation and using capital to invest instead in other factors of production, such as plant or IT. It would be hoped that these factors of production will create value for the business much faster than the rate of inflation. Then, in later years, paying a rent that has increased only by the rate of inflation will be no problem.

Sometimes property values rise faster than inflation. For example, businesses may have purchased real estate in relatively cheap locations and the success of those businesses, together with improved infrastructure and a skilled workforce, might cause local land values to rise faster than any prevailing inflation. If the increase has been greater than that which a business could have generated through its own operations, then to have purchased a freehold would have been advantageous. Owning a freehold could be almost essential for a business that wants to remain in the locality after the next rent review.

When an area becomes very popular and property is in short supply, rents and freehold values will rise. The corporate real estate manager has to consider the factors that can cause this situation and judge whether they are likely to arise in locations in which the business needs to locate. Some, such as population growth, can be predicted from published data; other aspects, such as the decline of key industries and changing transport links, cannot be predicted over the long term. Normally some warning is available, and real estate managers should be seeking suitable data and interpreting how political and economic changes at international, EU, national and local government levels will affect the real estate aspects of their corporation's operations.

The converse of deciding that it would be better to own a freehold is to be aware of factors that may cause property values to fall in a particular area and to decide to off-load freeholds facing this risk from the estate. The real estate manager needs to be proactive and to promote policies relevant to the current situation in each location.

From this it follows that the current value recorded in the fixed assets need not be an indication of initial purchase price. The business may well have made the decision to buy freehold property because land values at the time were relatively low and it was not a major expenditure. Asset strippers are always interested in companies that have not revalued their property interests and are unwittingly sitting on substantial assets that can be easily realised.

8.4   Return on investment

Most start-up businesses find it difficult to raise finance to cover the non-real estate fixed asset and cash flow requirements. Their owners have little choice other than to rent accommodation. The argument is, of course, different for a business that needs a particular building in order to operate – for example a geographically based tourist attraction.

More to the point, investors in equities are not seeking just an inflation-proof investment, but one that will bring a real return above inflation. Indeed, given the higher risk attached to this type of investment, many are seeking returns well above the level of inflation.

The difficulty of raising capital for new ventures limits most businesses' investment in fixed real estate assets. There is also the overriding fact that those who are investing in new ventures bear the high risk because of the opportunity for high returns.

If a management team predict a return of 50% on the funds invested by venture capitalists, the latter will immediately question the team's ability to achieve these returns if freehold real estate is to be purchased. If the returns can be achieved despite the purchase of freeholds, then the question must be 'how much better could the returns be if no freeholds are purchased?'. Unless there are strong business reasons for owning a particular building, venture capitalists will not favour this use of their funds.

When a management buyout (MBO) is being funded the venture capitalists will normally require the original company, or some other body, to retain the freehold of any operational property. A lease will then be organised so that the MBO company can pay rent for its accommodation.

For the mature company the issues are similar. If purchasing real estate brings lower returns than the main business of the company the shareholders will question why it happened. If there is no obvious reason, they will want to know why accommodation was not rented and the excess profits invested in high-value projects or paid out as dividends. Such situations can give rise to takeovers.

Property companies are a different proposition. The managements of these businesses are focusing their attention on one aspect of the property market where they believe they can make profits well above inflation. They often do this through meeting market demand by developing and supplying a type of property in short supply, by applying economies of scale to the property management process or by exploiting changing legislation or fashion.

Other investors in property, such as pension funds and insurance companies, are attracted to it in part because they believe that they can purchase real estate interests that will bring in returns above inflation. Secondly, property investments diversify their exposure to risk, as they are in a different market from equities or gilts.

8.5   Owning freehold real estate

The ownership of freehold property should be justified by sound business reasons, be they strategic or economic. These reasons will have to counter the argument that the capital tied up in property could make better returns elsewhere.

Strategic reasons to own real estate will include:

- security
- unique location
- transport links
- unique design for building
- safeguarding location for plant that cannot be moved
- ensuring space for expansion
- freedom of choice over property management
- desire to establish community links that will aid business
- supply of suitably educated or trained labour
- no suitable property available to rent

If the site is to be used for an unusual and potentially unneighbourly development, such as a chemical works, oil refinery or other specialised properties, its uniqueness and probable isolation will make it unattractive to financial institutions, and the business will have no choice but to own the freehold. This is often not a difficulty, because the business will want to be freeholders for sound business reasons, such as security of use.

The ownership of real estate can be part of a complex strategy to gain competitive advantage, as illustrated by the strategies of the Conrad Ritblat Group (see Chapter 19).

Economic reasons to own real estate will include:

- avoidance of rent rises
- avoidance of long-term commitments to lease conditions
- control over management costs
- protection of expensive investment in plant or local facilities
- potential for particular capital gain above level of inflation
- potential for long-term development opportunities
- contribution to joint venture programmes
- availability of grants
- capital allowances

Large, well-regarded corporations can usually obtain finance at very favourable rates which will make it easier for them to raise the finance to purchase, whereas this will not apply to smaller companies. A finance lease for the plant and machinery linked to the future capital allowances is another source of finance (see Chapter 7).

The ultimate real estate flexibility that has traditionally been linked to ownership of freehold property exists only if others are willing to purchase the property when the owner wishes to sell. As will be shown in Chapter 9, building obsolescence can mean that a desirable asset loses value almost overnight.

8.6 Renting real estate

As previously discussed, greater returns are normally expected from a capital investment in a business than can be achieved from investment in run-of-the-mill real estate. This reason for favouring renting may also be supported by other business factors, which will vary according to the length and terms of the lease but which may again can be divided into strategic and economic factors.

Strategic factors in favour of renting tend to be more significant the shorter the lease, and can include:

- freedom to move, especially if expansion is predicted
- less risk of being tied to an obsolete building

- freedom to reduce the size of the estate if floor space needs to be reduced
- opportunity to test locality without long-term commitment
- flexibility of size of letting
- availability of additional services
- accommodation included in outsourcing contract

Economic factors in favour of renting include:

- demands less capital
- desire to limit the size of non-liquid capital assets
- freedom to choose cheaper, or more expensive, locations

Obviously, the decision that real estate will be needed is a precursor to these arguments becoming relevant. This decision will be based on the net present value of the proposed investment. This will involve all aspects of the operation, such as the value of the business that will be generated, all the costs involved and the profitability.

The decision between renting and purchase may follow the investment decision or can be an integral part of the decision-making process, because real estate considerations are strategic to the success of the investment.

Issues that may make real estate a strategic part of the initial investment decision include:

- suitability of existing real estate within the business
- technological development changing operational needs
- availability in the market of suitable real estate
- time taken to gain planning and other approvals
- time taken to commission the building
- legislative changes that affect real estate
- subsidies, tax allowances and other government intervention
- long-term real estate policies for the overall business
- current state of the property cycle

8.7   Long leasehold interests

The owner of a long leasehold interest may gain some of the benefits normally enjoyed by freeholders, such as having an asset against which debt finance can be organised and security of occupation. If rents are low the long leasehold may well also be a hedge against inflation, if that is a likely problem. As both land and buildings of a leasehold interest are depreciated (amortised), the occupier has planned for its value reducing to nil, so loss of value through building obsolescence, unless early in the lease, is less likely to undermine the financial status of the business.

However, because there is less incentive to invest in the refurbishment of a leasehold interest, the business may still be burdened by attempting to operate from an inefficient building or having to pay rent for something that it abandons.

In the future it will be easier to completely dispose of unwanted leased buildings, and this will affect the balance between the various options available to the business managers as they plan their strategies. The changes are discussed in Section 8.10.

8.8 Sale and leaseback

Where there is no suitable property to rent it may be possible to arrange a sale and leaseback with a property investor, such as a financial institution, once the required premises have been constructed and occupied.

The onward sale of office buildings to institutional investors after development has long been a feature of the speculative office market, but now occupiers are using it for their bespoke buildings. It is a valuable way of releasing the capital needed to construct such buildings and often essential if a rapid expansion programme requires a constant supply of new buildings. The burden of finding sites and achieving planning permission lies with the future occupier or a developer partner – these are the best people to make a case for development, especially for difficult sites. Institutional investors would not want to take the risk at this stage.

The initial owner, who is the eventual occupier, will work in conjunction with the intended institutional investor so that the building will meet the investor's standards. While construction and other standards matter, the institutional investor's willingness to purchase a bespoke building will be due as much to the quality of the tenant as the building. The income is assured, not because the building could be re-let, but because of the expectation that the tenant will continue to run a successful business.

Sale and leaseback is also used by freeholders who have been owner occupiers for some time as a way of releasing the capital tied up in their real estate. The deal that can be achieved will depend on the quality of the business and the buildings. Businesses that have been successful and have strategies for the future which would suggest that success will continue are innately attractive to institutional investors, even before the real estate is considered. The funds released to the business can be used for future growth.

As tax accountants, lawyers and property specialists seek to produce the best arrangements for their clients, more sophisticated arrangements than sale and leaseback are being developed, including the use of joint venture companies (Catalano, 1996).

The time when it was felt essential to own real estate to support borrowing requirements is fading. The changing role of real estate in the accounts of the business will not be the only factor considered by credit rating agencies. Lenders and investors tend these days to look much more at the business's intrinsic value as a going concern that produces a certain cash flow than just its assets. Consequently, reducing assets by the sale and leaseback of real estate and investing the proceeds in operations that improve the cash flow may even enhance rather than restrict future loan finance.

8.9 The choice

As shown above, the choice between owning and renting will be complex and depend on the factors in each case, but it can be summarised as shown in Table 8.1.

Marks & Spencer plc owns nearly all of its retail stores but rents most of its distribution centres. The balance between owning and renting works out differently for different parts of the business, and as a consequence it has a variety of real estate interests. This is discussed further in Chapter 16, where Table 16.1 illustrates these choices using the same framework as Table 8.1.

8.10 Lease requirements

Arguments for or against buying or renting become much more specific when actual lease requirements are considered. There are no standard leases in the UK, and terms are agreed according to a general legal framework and the balance between supply and demand in the various property markets.

For many years the property world referred to 'the standard institutional 25 year lease for offices', but each was drawn up separately and contained its own mix of requirements. Even developments with a variety of tenants tend to have as many different leases as occupants, with each tenant securing slightly different terms according to circumstances at the time of the letting.

Table 8.1 The choice between owning and renting

Own	Business factor	Rent
if		*if*
Stable	OPERATION	*Changing*
Unique	ACCOMMODATION NEEDS	*Ordinary*
Control	MANAGEMENT	*Flexibility*
High	INFLATION	*Low*
Available	CAPITAL	*Restricted*

Alternatively, these variations are agreed as personal covenants so that the lease documents held by each tenant are the same.

Privity of contract has been a feature of leases. This is slowly passing into history, but as it affects all leases commencing before the implementation of the Landlord and Tenants (Covenants) Act 1995 (HMSO, 1995), it will affect the decisions of real estate managers in England and Wales for many years to come (Scottish property law has never incorporated privity of contract).

The tradition of 'privity of contract' is a complex issue, the detail of which is beyond this book but which can be found in land law textbooks, such as the fifth edition of *A Practical Approach to Land Law* (Mackenzie and Phillips, 1994). The arrangement bound the original parties to a lease for the length of the lease. Over the years it has been modified by various statutes, but in simple terms the original tenant of a commercial building, who undertook to pay rent and accepted other obligations (such as repairs and insurance) for 25 years, could be bound to that agreement for 25 years even though the interest was assigned after say, five years. Similar obligations fell on the original landlord, but because most commercial leases put the heaviest obligations on the tenant, it was tenants who found the provisions most objectionable.

If both the original landlord and tenant assigned their interests so that neither had an interest in the property then the privity of contract between them ceased to exist, but in many cases this break has not happened.

During the last economic recession tenants who had assigned leases many years earlier found that when assignees went into liquidation landlords were suing them for rents, etc. for buildings in which they thought they no longer had an interest. Further, having paid arrears they had no right to retake the lease. The situation was exacerbated because the economic recession coincided with a property slump.

One of the companies acquired by The Boots Company plc had owned subsidiary companies which had gone into liquidation. The real estate they had occupied was assigned to third parties, who eventually also ceased to be able to pay the rent. The vacant properties reverted to the previous owner, now part of Boots, who tried unsuccessfully to find new tenants to help with the rent payments. It was unsuccessful, and the 1994 accounts include an exceptional item of £2.2 million to cover the likely costs arising from the default of the assignees. Boots can cope with this, but such a sum would cause severe financial difficulties for a smaller company.

Not surprisingly, would-be tenants became very wary of entering into long leases. They wanted to be able to make a clean break from lease obligations if they left a building.

The depth of the recession and the consequent difficulty that landlords had in finding tenants resulted in representatives from all aspects of the property world supporting change and eventually accepting the terms of the Landlord and Tenants (Covenants) Act 1995 (HMSO, 1995), so that it was eventually enacted swiftly without serious objections.

The new Act is complex, but the core provision excludes the principle of privity of contract from new leases. However, it will be possible for parties to a lease to specify conditions that must be satisfied before a tenant may assign a lease – an 'alienation clause'. The aim of landlords will be to ensure that the assignee will be as satisfactory as a tenant as the assignor. Tenants may find the restrictions even more onerous than under the previous statute law; it will depend on knowledge and negotiation strength.

The Act also makes it possible for landlords to require an 'authorised guarantee agreement', to protect against the defaults of the immediate as- signee. A potential tenant will be able to resist, but negotiation of the terms will again depend on the relative strength of the parties in the market. The landlord is also likely to want the agreement to be backed by a surety.

Tenants may well pay more rent for a lease which is free of any restrictions; the landlord will of course have a higher income, but less security.

Further provisions are to restrict the ability of landlords to recover arrears and to allow those that have had to pay them to receive an overriding lease if they wish.

These are the key factors relevant to this discussion. There are other provisions and much detail in the Act which those undertaking lease nego- tiations will need to know. There are ways in which those taking on buildings between enactment and implementation will be able to use its terms, so for all practicable purposes deals since July 1995 will probably be under its provisions.

The law is new, the clauses are complex, the concepts innovative, and some existing legal provisions have been rewritten, although with no intention of changing them. The practical effects will only become clear as it is used and the wording interpreted by the courts and case law established. In the meantime, it is clear that it will allow market conditions to dominate would-be landlord and tenant negotiations rather more than in the past.

Even before the Landlord and Tenant (Covenants) Act 1995 there had been a noticeable change in leases. The 'standard institutional 25-year lease for offices' became very unpopular with tenants from the 1989 property slump onwards, and leases have become shorter with more option breaks for tenants.

8.11   Creating value from real estate

Some businesses create real estate value just by their presence. This is particularly true of popular shops, which are used by developers as 'anchors' for their shopping centre developments. A shopping centre is not seen as a viable development until certain key stores have agreed to take space. Such anchor businesses are in a strong position to gain an attractive deal from developers. Effectively, their real estate costs are reduced compared with their competitors who do not have quite the same pulling power. Their value as occupiers to developers and landlords gives them a considerable strategic advantage. This can be converted into gaining prime locations and excellent facilities, as well as good financial arrangements. Marks & Spencer plc, which is discussed in Chapter 16, is a good example of a business that creates value – just from its presence.

This concept of creating value occurs in other circumstances, such as when local authorities wish to encourage development. In these circumstances a would-be major employer can gain a number of advantages from the local authority, such as infrastructure development or provision of education facilities.

Conversely, local authorities can negotiate with keen would-be developers to get them to provide facilities for the local community as part of the process of considering and granting planning permission; this is known as planning gain.

These possibilities put the provision of real estate operational fixed assets in a very different situation from other fixed assets.

A further consideration for those that rent is that the leases' conditions are designed to provide a secure income for the landlords. The security of the income is a factor that will affect the capital value of the landlords' interest.

The 'institutional lease' has given landlords considerable security, as most of the risk has been borne by the tenant (who has to repair the premises, insure them and pay a rent revised to market levels every five years). If market rent levels fall, the tenants are not entitled to a reduction. The aim has been to reduce the risk attached to property investments so that they make a viable alternative to equity investments in institutional investment portfolios.

The one weakness is always that the corporate tenant may cease to exist. If business failure causes the tenant to become insolvent and go into liquidation, then the rent will not be paid. Hence the security of property investment is also driven by the factor of the tenant's financial status.

A 'good' tenant is very attractive. This works both ways. Corporations that are considered a good financial risk will be in a stronger bargaining position when entering into lease agreements. Conversely, if a 'good' tenant wants to give up a building by negotiating a lease surrender, then the landlord will be very resistant, because even if the tenant does not want to occupy the building, a 'good' corporate tenant will honour its obligations because it cannot easily avoid them! This has been one of the problems facing BT plc as it tries to dispose of unwanted premises (see Chapter 15).

A more recent development is the move to securitise debt. This can be undertaken in a number of ways. The aim is to be able to pass on the benefit of receiving the income in ways that allow entry to the real estate market by those investors whose capital is insufficient to purchase a whole building. The risk attached to the securitised product will be affected by the quality of the tenants who are paying the rent that provides the income. This has already been discussed at some length in Chapter 7.

All these developments are strengthening the desire of landlords to attract and keep 'good' tenants.

8.12   Current choice and predicted trends between owning and renting

Using information from the Investment Property Databank, Drivers Jonas researched market changes between 1989 and 1993 (Drivers Jonas and Investment Property Databank, 1995). They found that the average new commercial lease is now only nine years, compared with 20 years before the property slump. In central London it is lower, at seven years (compared with 16 years in 1989), while elsewhere in the south-east the average is only 5 years. The retail sector shows the same trend, with the average shop lease now only 11 years, compared with 22 years in 1989. Again London is now lower still at an average of just 8 years.

More valuable properties can attract tenants prepared to sign longer leases, but tenants break options, especially as five yearly intervals have become widespread for all types of property. They are significantly more common in London and the south-east, particularly for offices. Overall, Drivers Jonas concluded that there has been a fundamental change in leasing patterns driven by occupier demand.

In 1994, another survey, *Occupiers' Preferences*, for Richard Ellis (Richard Ellis/Harris Research Centre, 1995a) covered many of the same points. It found that 62% of respondents who were major users of office accommodation would favour a shorter lease with options to break every six, nine or 12 years. Respondents deemed shorter leases to be more expensive and 32% said that would prefer to lease for 20–25 years, presumably because they thought it would be cheaper – but this is not being reflected in their actions, except for the very best buildings.

The Harris Research Centre for Richard Ellis also asked occupiers whether they preferred to own or lease office space. With the exception of London and the south-east, on average two-thirds of users prefer to own rather than lease, but most reported a trend towards leasing. In London and the south-east a majority lease, and the expectation is that this will continue.

8.13   The end of the 25-year lease

In many Member States of the European Union lease terms are much shorter. In France, for example, most commercial leases have break clauses after three years. As with many aspects of UK life, the most likely scenario is a movement towards the main European position. This gives more freedom to businesses to readjust their business strategies so as to remain competitive.

The general feeling is that, even when the market picks up, owners of the mass of smaller and second-hand properties will not be able to secure leases of substantial length. Indeed, most go further and predict that the 25-year lease has gone, probably for good.

Hovering behind this situation is the future role of commercial property as an investment for fund managers. If the security of the investor is weakened too much there will be a marked lack of willingness by those seeking prime investment to choose property. The market is still weak from the recession, but it seems that would-be developers of large new schemes that address tenants' requirements are able to find tenants willing to take 15-year leases. This means that they can still attract investment funding.

If this fails to be the case then development funds will be more expensive, and only schemes with the prospect of high rents meeting the cost of the higher risk of voids will be built. There is a balance between length of leases and rent levels. Nevertheless, at the very top of the market, landlords of the few best properties can achieve both the highest rents and the longest leases.

8.14 Polarisation

It would seem that the result could be a polarisation of the real estate market and corporate structures. Institutional investors will be willing to invest in large real estate developments when the tenants are blue-chip companies who will take long (or relatively long) leases. Businesses that cannot offer this level of covenant as a tenant will find it harder to rent the best premises. Where having prime real estate makes a substantial difference to trading potential, lack of suitable premises will be either an entry barrier or (more likely) a barrier to growth.

At the other end will be small businesses, who will have to pay a proportionately higher rent, i.e. if the rent is the same, the premises will be worse than for the blue-chip company but will probably have a shorter lease commitment. A longer lease with the freedom for the tenant to break every three to five years has the attraction for tenants of reasonable flexibility accompanied by the security to be able to stay if the premises suit the business. A lease can contain break clauses for the landlord as well as the tenant, therefore not offering the tenant any guarantee of long-term security. UK leases generally allow a sitting commercial tenant to remain at the end of a lease and renegotiate new terms. There are circumstances where the landlord can reclaim the premises and, with a Court's approval, it is possible to contract out of these provisions before a lease is granted.

Moving can be very disturbing and adversely affect a business; consequently security of occupation is a serious consideration, even for those businesses that do not rate it so highly that they purchase real estate.

As the range of length of leases, lease conditions and the quality of buildings widens, it could be more difficult for growing businesses to jump the divide between second-rate and prime accommodation. Not only the rent, but also their inability to offer the security of a blue-chip company and their lack of willingness to commit to a long-term arrangement will be against them.

The blue-chip companies will need substantial market share, economies of scale and excellent strategies to maintain their ability to gain competitive advantage from prime real estate.

The greater the range of lease arrangements, the wider the choice when considering whether to own or rent.

No one knows what will happen. What is clear is that the economic recession, the property slump and the advent of the Landlord and Tenant (Covenants) Act 1995 have created a more dynamic commercial real estate market, where change is possible. Change means opportunities for those who seek them.

8.15 Summary

Clearly, the ground rules previously used by real estate managers when making recommendations about the strategic benefits of owning or renting are shifting. Economic factors have driven the changes, but within a very short period they have led to fundamental changes to English property law. As a consequence, there is greater freedom to react to the changes being brought about by new technologies. Now the choice between owning and renting is much more strategic than previously, and looks set to change further over the coming years. In addition to these changes, the main issues considered were:

- the need to consider future levels of inflation
- the likely rates of return on an 'investment' in owning operational real estate
- the tax implications
- the strategic considerations
- the possibility of changing tenure by sale and leaseback

9 Building Obsolescence

9.1 Introduction

Building obsolescence has a way of striking unsuspecting building owners, especially those who generally ignore the role of real estate in their business. It can be hidden by a variety of situations. In this chapter, ways of addressing the apparent unpredictability of the onslaught of building obsolescence are discussed.

9.2 Depreciation

Depreciation is defined by accountants as 'the measure of wearing out, consumption or other reduction in the useful economic life of a fixed asset, whether arising from use, effluxion of time or obsolescence through technological or market changes' (Accounting Standards Committee, 1987).

Depreciation of assets over time is understood by business managers, who are used to making annual charges for depreciation against the value of operational assets in their profit and loss accounts. The preciseness of accountants often clouds the fact that the allowances are a rough and ready way of addressing the issue – reality can be much more complex.

9.3 Obsolescence is one of the causes of depreciation

Obsolescence is one of the causes of depreciation, and is not the result of an asset wearing out, being consumed or the passage of time. It occurs for other reasons, such as changing technology or market requirements.

9.4 Characteristics of building obsolescence

In a search for a better understanding of building obsolescence, those writing on building depreciation and obsolescence in recent years have attempted various classification systems.

A good starting point is to consider the characteristics of building obsolescence – how do you recognise it? Jones Lang Wootton viewed this very pragmatically in their paper *Obsolescence: The Financial Impact on Property Performance* (1987). They highlighted two main characteristics which provide a useful basis for a study of the issues:

1. Building obsolescence cannot be rectified by the normal process of building maintenance, or repair, and therefore requires major capital expenditure.
2. The rental growth potential of the building is reduced in comparison with trends in full market rents.

This was published before the fall in real estate values and now the second characteristic might reasonably be expanded to read:

2. The rental growth potential of the building is reduced in comparison with trends in full market rents or, alternatively, in a period of falling real estate values, the fall in rental value is faster than the trend in the fall in full market rents.

9.5   Unexpected depreciation

Many corporate owners have found that the allowances made for depreciation of their building stock have been unrealistic because of unexpected obsolescence. Buildings which were physically sound, having been well maintained, have been found to be worth far less than expected. It was a shock when during the 1980s many owners found that the company assets were depleted – almost overnight.

Here, we are considering operational assets which are subject to depreciation allowances. In property circles the more dramatic problem has been with investment properties, which in the UK are shown in the accounts at open market value (see Chapter 7). When some of these buildings were found not to be worth what had been expected, the effect was dramatic – the buildings losing value were part of the very backbone of the company's activities. Investment surveyors began to rethink their methods of valuation, which previously had not included an explicit allowance for any form of depreciation.

As the problem first came to the fore and was being digested by the real estate profession during the 1980s, some valuers, most frequently in the large practices, developed very analytical approaches which involved calculating costs related to different causes of depreciation. These included building obsolescence, and used discounted cash flow techniques to capitalise the resulting income streams.

By 1988 it was suggested by Richard Lay, in an article on *Real Estate Portfolio Valuation* that building obsolescence had became a common factor that had to be allowed for in the valuation of offices. He said that valuers were giving up attempting to identify precise costs and were reverting to the old practice of adjusting the 'all-risks' yield on the current rental income.

The most comprehensive study was by Andrew Baum (1991), through a research project which classified the forces behind building depreciation and sought to model a framework for the 'depreciation sensitive analysis of real estate investment'. The work also included two empirical studies: one of offices and the other of industrial buildings. Baum's initial literature search included American sources. This resulted in his subsequent book introducing to the UK ideas developed in a market where depreciation of building assets held for investment has been understood for many years, as it is part of US accountancy practice.

As the major research project in the field of building obsolescence, Baum's work has been influential. It is valuable not only to investment surveyors but also to corporate real estate managers as a guide to matters that they should consider.

In 1991 Gerald Brown, in contrast to Lay, encouraged valuers to develop quantitative skills to justify investment decisions (Brown, 1991). He also pointed out that those who were skilful could manage depreciation and technical obsolescence to their advantage. This is important to corporate real estate managers; they need to be able to predict the unpredictable!

9.6 Land and buildings

Although valuation methodologies are beyond the scope of this book, there are some financial considerations which warrant inclusion. Real estate is made up of two components: the land and the buildings. Most of this chapter concentrates on buildings, but it is also possible for the site to lose or gain value quite independently of its building. Land can, for example, be affected by planning decisions or changes in the local economy.

Building obsolescence will be less obvious if the building represents only a small proportion of the total real estate value because it is small in relation to the site or the site has a high value.

An owner who sees real estate increase in value year by year may not be aware that other properties are increasing in value much faster. To gain this awareness the owner must make the effort to monitor the values of comparable buildings. It is easier now for real estate investors who can view comparable data from the Investment Property Databank, much of which is also useful to corporate real estate managers. Other indices are published by the major real estate consultants. Those corporate real estate managers who have properties affected by a variety of local real estate markets should be seeking local advice in each area on the performance of their real estate in comparison with others in the locality.

Even a building which in itself is serving the business well and is not obsolete for the required purposes may not be making full use of the site. If the location becomes more attractive, a higher return may be achievable from a different use or because the site is ripe for redevelopment. The result is that the building has a very high opportunity cost.

9.7   Building obsolescence hidden by inflation

The effect of building obsolescence can also be hidden by inflation. When all real estate values are rising because of inflation, it is easy not to appreciate that a particular real estate is not increasing in value as fast as the others. It was a particular problem for some property owners during the 1980s.

Newly created value from a business's trading activities may be lost if the real estate assets fail to keep pace with inflation. It can also be damaging to businesses who have used, or wish to use, real estate as collateral for debt finance.

9.8   Curable and incurable obsolescence

One widely used approach to understanding obsolescence is to divide it into curable and incurable, particularly when considering the qualities of a building that have caused it to become obsolescent. However, this is too simplistic and clouds the issues. For example, it is often possible to improve buildings and give them a useful life without completely curing the problem that caused the obsolescence.

If obsolescence is curable, can it really be obsolescence? Surely it is simply accrued lack of maintenance or repair that have depreciated the value of a building but which do not make it obsolescent. A better term would be 'curable depreciation'.

A building which has been deemed obsolete because of changing technical requirements can be rendered useful again by further technological development. An example is the classification in the 1980s of many 1960s buildings as obsolescent because floor to ceiling heights were inadequate for the services to support the computer technology of that decade. Support services, such as underfloor wiring and air-conditioning, are no longer needed to the same extent, so the buildings of the 1960s are once again suitable once refurbished (Spring, 1995).

Many older office blocks move from suffering incurable obsolescence to curable obsolescence. In central London alone it has been estimated that there is 1.1 million m^2 of old or redundant office space, and much of it could again become usable with cordless technology (Buchanan, 1995).

9.9 Unpredictability

The possibility that fast-changing technology would soon overcome the need for floor and ceiling voids was made by Hollington (1986). It started happening nine years later. The problem is that these predictions are not so difficult to make, but putting a date on them is rather more difficult!

Building depreciation does not occur at a steady rate, mainly due to the effect of building obsolescence, which in the recent years of fast technological change has begun to affect buildings very early in their lives. The empirical research undertaken by Baum (1991) showed that for offices the greatest rates of depreciation in capital value were in the period of 11 to 26 years after construction – a time when the original building should still be physically sound. These buildings were losing their value because of factors other than decay over the passing of time – particularly internal specification, external appearance and configuration.

Baum found that it was the failings that include an element of obsolescence that were significant in the depreciation of office buildings. Most important was internal specification, and this was mainly related to the provision of services. The second was external appearance and least important was configuration, which was a little surprising as it was also a predominant cause of incurable depreciation.

The second-fastest period of depreciation, although not as rapid as the later period, was early in the building's life, just two to seven years after completion. This situation probably equates to the rapid fall in value in new cars when they have been registered with their first owner; a second-hand building, like a car, is just less desirable than the new model.

Baum stresses that his conclusions should not be taken as a generalisation, and that different results might well arise with a different sample and at a different time. Nevertheless, they should cause the corporate real estate manager to think twice.

9.10 Overcoming unpredictability

Corporate real estate managers have some advantages over property companies and those who hold commercial real estate as an investment, and these will help their ability to plan for change, as follows.

● They know who will be occupying their buildings – they are not usually involved in speculative development for unknown users. They can be close to those who are at the vanguard of the specific changes in their company's industry that will affect real estate requirements, whether in design or location. They should be able to jump before they are pushed.

- They have a choice of tenure arrangements and can decide to rent and have only a short-term commitment to any particular building rather than owning or developing their own buildings. When entering new leases, tenants must ensure that the conditions give them the freedom they need (see Chapter 8).

- In companies that are freeholders who fund their own development, without any charge on the property, they can build to any standard to suit themselves, subject to current legislation. They can choose short-life materials at minimum cost and plan to demolish buildings that become obsolete. They can also decide not to maintain a building that is becoming obsolete, whereas a landlord has to meet specific repair obligations.

- Some occupiers spread the risk by occupying a variety of buildings with a variety of tenures. This is particularly the case for businesses that have a large, geographically widespread real estate acquired at different times. Businesses that are based in one location may be better served by having interlinking units that can be replaced individually rather than one massive construction.

- When new buildings are constructed, the real estate manager can select a design that will be more likely to remain attractive to others should the business wish to sell or lease out the building at a later date. It should be possible to avoid the limitations of idiosyncratic buildings.

- When building obsolescence is likely to be an obstacle to a particular objective, the real estate manager can bring it to the attention of the strategic planners before decisions are made.

- It may well be possible to make savings in the expenditure on real estate by deliberately seeking nearly new buildings or ones that are past their prime. Many businesses have are least some operations that have been unchanged by new technology.

- The real estate issue can be removed from operations that are subject to fast change by outsourcing the operation and shifting the burden of the real estate on the contractor.

- Those locations where real estate values and construction costs are low may be rather more attractive than those of highly developed densely populated locations with high land values – especially if there are government inducements to build. Governments still tend to see a new factory as a long-term contribution to economic growth, while in reality, if the costs of providing buildings are low, it gives the business greater flexibility – less capital has been invested, leaving greater freedom to develop in other locations. This is completely different from a real estate investor, will tend to avoid areas where demand is still to be proven.

- A business with a long-term interest in an estate can upgrade buildings on an ongoing basis to meet changing environmental and energy standards.

● This all builds up to the need for corporate real estate managers to be able to cope with the unpredictability of building obsolescence by ensuring flexibility, not only in the physical design of buildings but also in their management.

9.11   Classifying building obsolescence

In 1986, Salway produced a practical classification for building obsolescence which used the six headings of functional, aesthetic, legal, social, environmental and economic obsolescence. These are shown in Table 9.1 and are now discussed. Examples are included from a wide range of different commercial situations. These are given as a guide to real estate managers, as obviously each will have specific, and often unique issues to consider.

Functional obsolescence

Although designers are trying to make buildings more flexible, most of our existing stock was built with quite narrow perceptions of how it would be used. Even when the use is still required, the working methods may have

Table 9.1 Classification of the main causes of building obsolescence (Source: adapted from Salway, F. (1986) Depreciation of Commercial Property, *Centre for Advanced Land Use Studies, College of Estate Management, Reading)*

Type	Causes
Functional	Technological change resulting in changing occupiers' requirements. Inadequate floor plan configuration. Lack of modern services.
Aesthetic	Incompatibility with current images of architecture, fashion or corporate aspirations.
Legal	Changes in EU and national legislation and regulations plus local government decisions.
Social	Changing social patterns plus occupiers demanding a better quality environment.
Environmental	Global move to higher environmental standards. Also changing local environmental requirements.
Economic	Downward changes to the economic potential of the buildings which may be accompanied by the appreciation of the development potential of the underlying land.

changed. The changes may not be dramatic, but the new methods may well bring economies, resulting in lower prices to consumers than can be achieved by those using older methods. The margins in many industries are very low.

A warehouse with low eaves that cannot take full-height racking, or one with adequate racking but constricted by small bay sizes and intermediate columns will be usable but may make the business's operation uneconomic.

Likewise, an office building with slow lifts and inadequate goods and post distribution arrangements can function as an office but will slow down the output of the occupants compared with those in a new building.

Functional obsolescence can work in the opposite direction; some buildings are obsolete because they provide facilities that are no longer needed. For example, large cellular offices with plenty of space for filing cabinets are fast becoming redundant. Using them will mean wasted space and unnecessary heating and lighting bills.

Aesthetic obsolescence

Fashion has much to do with this type of obsolescence. Many buildings that are rejected at one stage of their lives as being 'old-fashioned' frequently find themselves back in favour a few decades later. What does not suit is the building which echoes the fashions that have just past. High-tech industries, for example, favour either new accommodation or something that can provide enough flexibility but also a contrasting historical image – an old Victorian mill building, for example. What a high-tech user will avoid is a 1960s office block – it just does not suit the corporate image!

Another aspect of aesthetic or visual obsolescence is the shabby building. This is more than needing a coat of paint – which is just poor maintenance – it is when the whole structure, the services and the individual components, although serviceable, are just dull and uninspiring.

Some corporations, for example wine merchants, find that they can operate very well from dilapidated (but secure!) buildings because they present an image of being the place to pick up a bargain. What matters to the business manager is having buildings that reflect the image of their products or services. In many cases, this means having an aesthetically fashionable building, and the real estate manager is going to have to plan ahead to ensure that this is maintained.

Legal obsolescence

Both Westminster and Brussels have legislators and administrators developing legislation with the judiciary of both systems interpreting its meaning. It means there is much that is new (and also uncertain) that will affect the business community's real estate requirements: health and safety; access for the

disabled; environmental impact; employment law; commercial drivers' regulations – the list is endless.

The real estate manager needs to be well briefed on what is being proposed
and be able to advise the corporate hierarchy when proposals look like
imposing heavy burdens on industry and commerce. It is easier to influence
legislation before enactment than to try to change it afterwards. This is not
an easy task for real estate managers, because much of the proposed legislation
will not be real estate-oriented. It helps if the real estate manager is backed
by a large corporation's specialist legislation monitor team.

Under the title of legal obsolescence will come decisions by local authorities
which can adversely affect real estate interests. In some cases, such as local
plans, where there is an opportunity to influence the outcome of the decisions,
the corporate real estate manager has to ensure that the necessary information
and dates for objections and making representations are not overlooked (see
Chapter 15).

The effect can be similar if planning permission is granted for uses on neigh-
bouring sites that are non-conforming to the area, and worse, just plain unneighbourly. The corporate real estate manager has to make sure that information is
received about the plans of each local authority and be alert to planning
applications submitted by others wherever the business has land or buildings.

Social obsolescence

Society changes, and this will affect the demands made upon buildings.
Businesses which wish to be seen as good employers or alive to the needs
of their customers find that they have to update their facilities. When John
Lewis, the department store in Oxford Street, provided a baby-changing area
it was one of the first available, and seen as an amazing improvement by
mothers with young children, but the original facility in the ladies toilet at
the top of a flight of stairs has long since been replaced – too many other
shops began to serve the needs of both parents much better.

In some areas, such as access for the disabled, legislation pushes social
change forward for new buildings and sometimes demands that older ones
are updated. However, whether affected by legislation or not, buildings which
fail to meet these sorts of standards are obsolescent, although the situation
may be curable.

Buildings with poor sanitary facilities, poor security, heavy traffic noise, and
which are reached via windy, desolate piazzas and underpasses will be prone
to social obsolescence – they just fail to meet the quality of life that users expect.

Environmental obsolescence

Environmental issues are of particular importance to industrialists who find
that buildings and sites have been contaminated by earlier processes or that

the built part of plant, such as chimneys, is no longer adequate to meet modern standards, such as for gas emissions.

A difficult area for hospitals, hotels and other institutional buildings is contamination in the air-conditioning and hot-water systems, giving rise to the risk of legionnaires' and other diseases.

Likewise, businesses can find that they receive unwelcome publicity if processes are considered to be environmentally weak or unneighbourly, even though legal. Again, it is a field where the corporate real estate manager needs to be well briefed, this time keeping up with the vanguard of public opinion.

Within individual buildings there is much that can be done to avoid environmental obsolescence, by updating facilities regularly so that premises do not fall way behind current standards. There are official research and government-sponsored publications which offer advice. Valuable information is to be found in the Building Research Establishment Environmental Assessment Method (BREEAM) publications, which are available for existing as well as new buildings (BRE, 1990, 1991, 1993a,b). The Energy Efficiency Office publications provide case studies as well as guidance (BRE, 1995a,b).

Economic obsolescence

This occurs where there is a downward change to the economic potential of buildings; for example, shoppers choosing to use out-of-town retail warehouse sites or shopping centres rather than a high street.

Also under this heading is the situation where the site has increased in value but this cannot be realised by the existing building. The building is then obsolete for its location. Redevelopment will release the value in the site.

9.12   Post-modernism

It may be helpful at this point to reflect on the ways that other aspects of our society have handled change. We live in what is called post-modern society, a phase coined to reflect the pluralism, variety, contingency and ambivalence that have replaced all-embracing solutions of modernism. Post-modernism has been described as 'an incessant flow reflexivity' (Bauman, 1991), a phrase which must feel particularly relevant to corporate real estate managers who are forever looking at what is happening and trying to decide the best way to react.

Post-modernists see our habitat as a complex system which differs from the mechanical systems of modernism in two respects – it is unpredictable and is not controlled by statistically significant factors – i.e. it is argued that we are free of deterministic logic, so that statistical analysis is of no use in evaluating the probabilities of future development. This idea will ring true to corporate real estate managers trying to predict the future. This can seem a somewhat heavy approach for managing real estate but as chaos theory has featured on the pages of the *Estates Gazette*, it is not very outrageous (Mills, 1994)!

From this point, it is interesting to look at how architecture has developed from modernism to post-modernism. Modernism in architecture is well reflected by the 1924 thesis that 'form follows function' (Sullivan, 1956). It is the concept that a building should be designed so that it is itself an art form, a tectonic, composed from materials needed and used for its construction and rejecting applied decoration and mannerisms – the perfect one-off solution to an occupier's needs.

Post-modern architecture, on the other hand, seeks no such unity. The structure and the outer appearance rarely reflect each other, and they are visually often unrelated. The difference is so great that it has been called a schism (Frampton, 1985). Consequently, post-modern architecture should, and probably does, reflect the need of corporate clients for flexible buildings.

The problem seems to be that post-modernism in the construction process has not moved beyond the architect, who in Britain is not usually a powerful management force in the construction team. Post-modernism has not permeated to the financial advisers in the construction team. While there is a schism between the structure and the outer finishes, many of those finishes are specified by those who believe that the tenets of life-cycle costing – long life and low maintenance – are relevant even when the building will be obsolete long before maintenance is needed.

The importance of materials and components working together to form an integral whole must not be overlooked, but it might be that buildings would prove to be more adaptable to serving the corporate client's changing needs if greater emphasis were placed on the ability and economies of renewing various layers according to changing needs.

The latest ideas circulating in the real estate world may be showing a move to this approach. Leisure industry operators and their advisers are now promoting 'leisure boxes' (Thame, 1995a). These are enclosed spaces, well served by car parking, that can be adapted to serve the public's changing leisure needs – an ever-changing mix of bingo, cinema, pubs and restaurants, or whatever else becomes fashionable. It is, in reality, little more than a shed to be divided up and finished as the leisure market demands.

9.13 Specification

For those corporate businesses that build their own (possibly idiosyncratic) premises, studying the latest output from the speculative developers gives an indication of what may prove more generally acceptable should they later wish to sell. Another source of information is the research into tenant needs undertaken by teams from surveying practices, firms of architects and the academic and professional institutions.

In 1994 the British Council for Offices published *Specification for Urban Offices*. This document sprang from the question asked at their 1992 conference: 'Why do office buildings cost so much?'. The immediate answer from delegates was that it was due to over-specification. Consequently, the Council set up an expert panel who investigated this aspect, and *Specification for Urban Offices* was the result.

An initial finding was that the aim to achieve flexibility had given rise to over-specification because developers had sought to provide for too wide a range of possible requirements. The result had been excessive specifications and expense.

They found that even with expensive specifications flexibility has not always been achieved, and often the result was wasteful. They proposed that developers should focus on the normal demands of the majority of occupiers but make designs adaptable to occupiers' changing requirements throughout the life of the building.

The specification promoted the shell and core level of finish as standard unless an occupier has been identified. It would include fully finishing only the entrance hall, staircases, common parts, toilets and core, and for office space would exclude suspended ceilings, lighting, raised floor, wiring, air-conditioning ductwork, and terminal boxes and decoration.

Controversial proposals included a recommendation to reduce floor loadings to match the lower needs of most tenants. It has been argued since that, as the cost savings would be small, it is not worth the developer taking this risk.

Interestingly the specification did not include air-conditioning as standard, and included proposals for natural or mechanical ventilation as well as air-conditioning. Although air-conditioning is typically provided by developers it is not popular with occupiers. A survey for Richard Ellis (Richard Ellis/Harris Research Centre, 1995b) revealed that only 9% of occupiers had a preference for air-conditioning, whereas 89% did not want it and 2% did not know.

9.14   The role of refurbishment

It is worth remembering that there are many buildings from the 1960s and earlier that are still in occupation with contented occupants. The more prominent have been refurbished and updated on a regular basis. They may not have the value of newer buildings, but if the owners, whether landlords or owner-occupiers, have been constantly aware of their market value, and their value to their own operations, there have been no nasty surprises.

Hollington, writing in 1986, argued that the death of the older office building was much exaggerated, and that many 1960s buildings were providing satisfactory office space. Baum's research found that original buildings seem to be more flexible than already refurbished buildings in terms of the ability to refurbish to cure depreciation (Baum, 1991). As far as the corporate real estate manager is concerned, the acid test will be the ability of the building to provide for the needs of the occupants at an economic cost.

9.15 Flexible lease terms

This chapter is closely linked to the previous one, which considered the choice of owning or renting real estate. For the occupier, one of the easiest ways of avoiding the problems of building obsolescence is not to own real estate. The move to shorter leases, or including tenants' break clauses in longer leases, brings the flexibility to move out of buildings that suffer from obsolescence. The only disadvantage then is the disturbance of moving, which is easier with some business operations than others.

9.16 Summary

Actively managing real estate needs will leave less scope for unexpected building obsolescence. The key points introduced were that building obsolescence:

- is just one of the causes of real estate depreciation (land as well as buildings)
- cannot be rectified by normal maintenance and can seriously affect the value of real estate
- can be delayed or avoided by ongoing programmes of constant improvement, especially for environmental and energy efficiency matters
- can be hidden by inflation
- can be highlighted by monitoring an estate's value against real estate price indices, as this will reveal falling real values
- can be classified according to the causes which assist identification
- may be avoided by adopting the greater flexibility of post-modernism, which should apply to construction as well as design
- may be avoided by designing new buildings that will be attractive to other users as well as meeting specific operational needs

9.17 Further reading

The main text on the effect of building obsolescence is Andrew Baum's book, *Property Investment Depreciation and Obsolescence*. David Isaac and Terry Steley's book *Property Valuation Techniques* is an easy to read source of discounted cash flow and other newer valuation methods designed to overcome some of the difficulties presented by the risk of building obsolescence.

9.18   Sources of information

Published information on rental values is available from Richard Ellis, DTZ Debenham Thorpe, Jones Lang Wootton and Hillier Parker. Details about Investment Property Databank (IPD), who also produce real estate market indices, are given at the end of Chapter 7. Some of the indices overlap each other, but each uses different sample properties, so results can vary. The details are given below.

Richard Ellis Monthly Index (REMI)

The Richard Ellis Monthly Index is the earliest published index showing changes in the direct property investment market. It measures changes in capital values, rental values and total performance for each of the office, shop, retail warehouse and industrial markets back to 1979. An index of rental values is also given for the London office market. REMI also measures average initial yields and average equivalent yields. This is the longest set of actual market yield data available in the UK property market. The index is also published in the following subsets:

- *Richard Ellis Short Term Indicator (RESTI)*: a three-month annualized average of returns on the index which provides a 'leading indicator' for property
- *Richard Ellis Scottish Monthly Index (RESMI)*: records performance for Scottish office, retail and industrial properties
- *Industrial Quarterly*: looks in more depth at performance in the industrial sector
- *Richard Ellis Retail*: examines the high street shop and retail warehouse property markets

These are available on subscription from Richard Ellis Research Consultancy, Berkeley Square House, London W1X 6AN (Tel: 0171 629 6290).

Hillier Parker Indices

Hillier Parker produce a wide range of indices. The Rent Index and Property Market Values Index give quarterly information that covers much the same ground as Richard Ellis. There is a separate half-yearly index for High Bay Warehouses: Rents, Land Values and Yields. Other indices published by Hillier Parker focus on the needs of real estate investors and developers. Any may be of use to business managers who hold investment as well as operational properties or who feel that their real estate could become obsolescent because of action elsewhere in the market, for example a sudden increase in stock due to new speculative building. The other indices are:

Shopping Centres in the Pipeline
Shop Expansion Plans
Scheduled Shopping Scheme Openings
Shopping Centre Vacancies
Shopping Centre Investment Activity
Retail Warehouse Parks in the Pipeline
Average Yields
Secondary Property
Specialised Property
Property Investment
High Bay Warehouses: Occupiers and Investors

All are available (for various prices) from Hillier Parker, 77 Grosvenor Street, London W1A 2BT (Tel: 0171 629 7666; Fax: 0171 409 3016).

DTZ Debenham Thorpe/PMA (Property Managers Association)

Index of Retail Trading Locations: this annual report is available from DTZ Debenham Thorpe, 44 Brook Street, London W1A 4AG (Tel: 0171 408 1161; Fax: 0171 491 4593).

Jones Lang Wootton UK Property Index

This quarterly index, produced by JLW Fund Management, is aimed at the real estate investment market. This is the sector most concerned with obsolescence, and they consider this from time to time in the accompanying text. This is available from Jones Lang Wootton Information Centre, 22 Hanover Square, London W1A 2BN (Tel: 0171 493 6040; Fax: 0171 306 1818).

Information on environmental improvements and energy efficiency is available from HMSO and government departments and agencies such as the Department of the Environment, the Department of Trade and Industry, the Harwell Laboratory in Oxfordshire, and the Building Research Establishment, whose publications are published by CRC Ltd, 151 Rosebury Avenue, London EC1R 4QX (Tel: 0171 505 6622; Fax: 0171 505 6606).

Part 4:
Development and
Implementation

10 Strategy Presentation and Implementation

10.1 Introduction

To successfully activate the use of real estate resources in order to improve business performance, the presentation of the strategy and its successful implementation are essential. The contents of this chapter are generic and apply whether the real estate strategy is presented as part of the overall corporate business strategy or separately.

It is important that strategy is presented in a clear way which highlights the main aims and objectives. The strategic plans must be relevant, usable and adaptable to changing circumstances.

The documents that circulate among board members will be very different from those circulated to promote and implement the policy. This chapter focuses mainly on the presentation of the content of strategy proposals throughout the business – the process of ensuring commitment to the proposals and their implementation.

10.2 Boardroom documentation

At the highest level there is a need for much more detail to be available. Board members who are being asked to accept responsibility for changing the company's methods must be able to see how the strategy will change the financial state of the business, whether directly in the accounts or by creating options for future developments.

Nevertheless, all that is written in this chapter about keeping the message clear and simple still applies. A clear executive summary, good referencing and supporting detail in supplementary papers or appendices will make it much easier for busy people to follow the main arguments and check the detail, including any necessary financial analysis.

10.3 The vision

The key to any strategic plan is the vision, the strategic intent, that it promotes. This must be presented very clearly and not be buried in a long 'wish list'.

The vision should be a simple statement or mission that is achievable, with an obvious target. Examples could be:

- In the next three years rationalise space allocation to ensure that at the end of this period all staff have adequate low-cost but high-quality accommodation without any wasted space.
- Introduce workflow methods with rationalisation of staff and accommodation requirements. Debt finance will be used to fund the technology and re-engineering, and the debt will be repaid from real estate and staff budget savings.
- Staff restaurants and works canteens will be combined in each of our plants on a rolling programme timed to coincide with the normal re-decoration schedule.

All are clear. The first would be more precise if space standards or occupancy cost guidelines were given together with quality measures. Even so, it is easily possible to measure current standards and plot progress.

The second is ambitious and would be backed by detailed financial calculations, but the key points are easy to express. The staff reductions would be handled more sympathetically below board level.

The third is much more specific, but still straightforward and easy to measure. Depending on the size of the businesses, the first two examples may be part of overall corporate strategies agreed at main board level, with the third being part of the strategy of a subsidiary company.

The vision should also explain briefly why the strategy is to be followed and how it fits into the business strategy. For example:

- The strategy is needed because our staff are poorly housed but the real estate budget is 50% higher than the industry average.
- The introduction of workflow will enable the company to restructure the business so that it can gain competitive advantage from new technology now and in the future. The process will focus on customer service. We will be able to despatch all orders within two days of receipt rather than 10 days, which is the industry norm.
- Staff restaurants and works canteens will be combined in each of our plants on a rolling programme timed to coincide with the normal re-decoration schedule. This will:
  - reflect the new flatter organisational structure
  - reduce space requirements and costs
  - enable a wide choice of eating environments for all

The key targets should also be clear. Where a programme extends over several years, the targets for each year should be included, so that success can be measured during the programme. For example:

- The re-engineering will start on site next year.
- After a six-month pilot the re-engineering will proceed throughout the organisation and should be complete in two years.
- Disposal of surplus real estate will start next year.
- The cash flow proposals, including reductions in the staffing budget, show that the debt should be cleared within three years.
- Running costs will have been reduced by x%.

10.4   Supporting information

Snappy vision statements will encapsulate the strategy and make it easy to communicate, but the people who are to implement the proposals need to know more. They will appreciate some of the background information, such as why the changes are necessary and also what research or experimentation has been undertaken to support the changes. The circumstances will be different in each case. It may be that some aspects remain confidential, but this can be counter-productive if it means that the staff implementing it do not understand what is required and why.

Some aspects of the supporting information may well lend themselves to articles in the company's staff newsletter: for example, an interview with those who took part in a trial experiment or a message from the chairman as to why the change is needed.

Just as with boardroom papers, detailed supporting information may be better placed in the appendices of the strategy plan, so that it is available but does not break up the key components of the message.

10.5   Implementation methodologies

Implementation will require quite precise programming, otherwise it loses its strategic value. Some timings may be dependent on the state of the real estate market and other uncertainties, which become less precise the longer the programme period. Nevertheless, it should be possible to project reasonably realistic targets. There may be a need for some overarching policies to change responsibilities; for example, a strategy to rationalise accommodation may be accompanied by a policy that all future real estate decisions will be removed from the regions to the centre.

It is normally not feasible to develop detailed implementation methods ahead of presenting the strategy, because it will involve inputs from so many people that it will probably be impracticable. This does not mean that development of strategy need only be a top-down process. Management styles vary, and many strategic reviews will include inputs from staff that are incorporated into the final proposals. Whatever the system of creating the strategy, getting into the details of the full implementation before it is published will mean risking the loss of the main strategic thrust in a mass of detail. All that is needed prior to the presentation stage is sufficient investigation of implementation options to ensure that the strategy is viable.

The development of detailed implementation arrangements needs to involve those who will be responsible for the tasks, some of whom will be members of staff, although others may need to be appointed to provide the skills needed for implementing new ideas. It is possible that implementation methods will change over time to meet new situations.

10.6   Monitoring

Strategy is about the future of a business. If well conceived its implementation will be vital for the future of the business. It cannot be left to chance. The implementation process should be monitored to find out whether it is going as planned. Alongside this, the success of the policy must also be monitored.

Part of an implementation policy may be to rationalise the use of three existing buildings so that only two will be needed in the future. The first success is physically achieving the change. But this is not all – success depends on this process producing the savings expected, and this may not happen; for example, removal costs may be higher than expected and disposal of the surplus building may not be possible.

Failure to dispose of a building is obvious. The monitoring process needs to be sufficiently sophisticated to pick up the small items that could mean not meeting targets; for example, small slippages in the programme and lower selling prices than expected.

Intangible consequences should also be monitored – they need not come as a surprise. For example, bringing staff together could be expected to result in a measure of greater awareness about each other's contribution to the business, and although this is not easy to quantify, it should not be ignored. Some intangible consequences can be completely unexpected. If not sought out, they can easily be unwisely overlooked. If detrimental to the business, they need to be overcome; if beneficial, it may be possible to replicate them.

Monitoring should go deeper, and as well as measuring the progress and success of the individual objectives, it should also monitor the success of the strategy in supporting the overall business strategy. If attempting to cut real estate costs means being so restrictive that it hampers business expansion it could all be counter-productive. Monitoring should also include the external environment – indeed, any factors that were influential in designing strategy but may change over time. The reaction of the competition to the strategy should also be carefully monitored.

Frequently, the monitoring process will reveal a need to adjust the implementation process or fine tune the strategy. The strategy and the implementation processes should be designed to allow such changes to take place. The business needs to remain responsive to its environment and customer demands.

10.7 Review

A strategy does not last for ever, even when regularly refined and updated. Eventually the process needs to start again. The fundamental assumptions on which the strategy was based have to be reconsidered.

The process is much the same as the process of creating the initial strategy. The exception is that the effectiveness of the existing strategy must be assessed.

If the existing strategy has been highly successful, it is not sufficient to do nothing. The world changes. There will have been changes in the external environment and competitors will have changed their strategies. Consequently, even a successful strategy will need to be revised. Success needs to be enhanced.

The key success factor, as initially, is to research the business's market and understand the changes that have taken place and will occur.

When it comes to the real estate aspects, the real estate manager must review how the estate has performed and how cost-effective it has been compared with competitors, and must understand how organisational developments are changing the demand for real estate. All new and impending legal changes must be considered; changes in the finance market as it affects real estate may also be important, as will any technical, cultural and social shifts which influence expectation of real estate provision.

It is clear that, as business managers begin to realise the importance of real estate strategies to the success of their operations, the competitive advantages gained by the first movers will be eroded. The forerunners will be looking to further their lead. The gains will be smaller and the leaders will be those who are completely in control, knowing exactly what constitutes their estate, how each property performs and how capable each building is of meeting future demands.

It is impossible to say now what may be important in five or ten years' time, but it could well be heating costs, ease of maintenance and multifunctional use. All these are areas where the difference between the adequate and the cost-effective may not be large but may be sufficient to make a difference – a difference that could well depend on the skills and abilities of the real estate manager rather than the real estate.

10.8 Summary

This chapter has explained how to sell a new corporate strategy within the business and uses examples related to real estate. It emphasises:

- the importance of catching the main board's interest with an easy-to-digest report
- the need for a vision that gives the purpose of the strategy, shows how it fits into the overall business plan, sets a target and shows how success will be measured
- the value of supporting information that addresses the need of each target audience, such as financial models at one level and personal interest stories about a pilot study for others
- a viable implementation programme to change the vision to reality, including scope for input by all who will be involved
- the evaluation and fine tuning of the implementation by a structured monitoring programme
- the eventual need for a review, not just of the strategy's success, but also a consideration of the continued relevance of the assumptions that supported the original proposal

11 Management Information

11.1 Introduction

This chapter is about obtaining the management information necessary to make the strategic decisions and supporting day-to-day policies to ensure that real estate resources are contributing to business effectively. It is additional to the ideas in specialist texts on the preparation of corporate strategy (e.g. Reading, 1993).

11.2 Data for strategic objectives

As the purpose is to produce strategic policy, data focused on that aim must be extracted from the mass of general data available in many organisations.

The emphasis of the company's management style will have a bearing on the management of real estate; as explained in Chapter 3, some business managers tend to focus more closely on long-term strategies, while others aim at current financial performance. Nevertheless, all managements need reliable information on which to develop their ideas.

Given that a key success in business is to set the best objectives and achieve them efficiently, this should also be the aim of the corporate real estate manager. Superb records and well-maintained buildings are of little use if the business is failing; they will not save the business, and the cost will probably hasten its decline. Even reasonably priced accommodation, efficiently maintained, will be a drain on a business if competitors are managing with only half the space, or space in much cheaper locations. This is why it is essential to think beyond facilities management.

As explained in Chapter 3, if a business is growing rapidly the real estate costs are probably insignificant, although location could be vital. They can normally be covered by high earnings and good profit levels. Management of the rapidly growing business needs to ensure that there is provision for expansion when required but that long-term real estate commitments will not over-burden the business in future years. Otherwise energy spent on real estate by the management of a fast-growing business could well be misplaced, unless real estate is an essential component of the product or service, such as in the hotel industry.

When the aim is to be profitable, the key components of the management system are financial, but they must be backed with systems that ensure that the non-financial objectives are also being achieved. As an obvious example, there is no gain, and probably a great deal to lose, if the maintenance costs of a food factory are reduced but dirt then contaminates the products.

While the focus of this chapter is on real estate information, the importance of normal corporate financial data should not be overlooked. If a business is making a poor return on net assets, or if sales per square metre or sales per employee are lower than competitors there may be real estate changes that will help overcome these difficulties. Strategy related to real estate needs to focus on contributions to all aspects (and measures) of a business's success.

Real estate, whether used for retail operations, offices, distribution or manufacturing, is under pressure from changing technology. At a strategic level the competitive decision could be very dramatic, such as, switch from high street to mail order, but for most businesses more gradual change will require appraisal of individual buildings and their contribution to the business. This means that information on each real estate holding and its locality will be needed. The questions that need to be asked are usually simple and are shown in Figure 11.1. Finding the answers can be much more difficult! First it is important to have the right information to analyse.

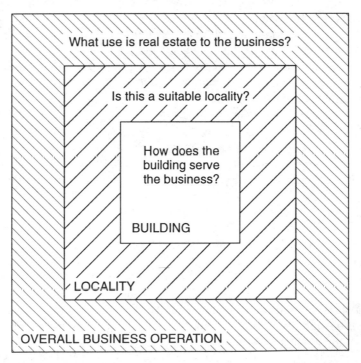

Figure 11.1 Questioning the use of real estate.

11.3 Getting it right

The data used should be as accurate as possible. Basic mistakes, such as muddling gross and net floor areas or imperial and metric measurements, must be avoided. Obviously, well-programmed computerised systems help.

It is amazing how frequently large organisations will under-resource their real estate management and its strategic development. The cost of adequate resources would be minuscule compared with the waste from inefficiency in the use of the real estate assets. A young surveyor explained recently that he was meant to produce a real estate strategy for a national business which had recently been restructured. He had problems – there were few records, he was working alone, the computer facilities were inadequate and he had no contact at board level. Not surprisingly, he had achieved little after a year on the task. He was fed up – especially as he could see the potential for using real estate constructively to support the organisation. It can only be a matter of time before he takes his knowledge to a competitor!

Conversely it is worth remembering that dotting 'i's and crossing 't's often does not greatly influence the result, especially when all that is needed is an overall trend. Once a trend is established, the effort to get better information can be concentrated in the areas which look most likely to be relevant to the objectives of the business.

11.4 Information systems

In recent years many businesses have installed custom-made real estate management software and made significant changes to the storage of real estate information. Even so, most do not have full property management information systems (Avis and Gibson, 1995).

The momentum for computerisation should gather speed. Better dedicated software to support the real estate function has come on the market, and this is coupled with falling hardware prices. Additionally, business managers are becoming more comfortable with new technology and are more willing to use it as a tool to implement their management objectives.

There is not one ideal solution because there are many different needs, depending on the size of the estate, the number of separate holdings, the tenure and maintenance responsibilities, and whether the costs are borne by others who have to be charged for services. Those organisations that also invest in real estate will have further requirements. However, many software programs are modular and allow units covering different aspects of real estate management to be used as necessary.

The growth of the annual Property Computer Show, the subsidiary Property Computer Show North and the ever thicker *PCS Property Software Directory* provide a clear indication of the growing market and success of the products (Cash and Taylor, 1995).

The choice is wide: there are mainframe systems, PC-based programs, and possibilities for online links and for using groupware. Some systems include links into other open systems and for using geographical information systems; some systems are little more than computerised land terriers; and others will handle a full facilities management service.

There is also software available for those who want to link into general property data for comparison information, to search for development opportunities, to check on the rating list or even gain market information from databases. Each business needs to assess its requirements and investigate the suitable systems and reappraise them and new products on a regular basis.

As with most computer installations and software purchases, the process is most likely to be successful if:

● top management and users (real estate managers and staff) are committed and involved in the selection and installation
● a pilot scheme is fully tested
● progress is in stages rather than all at once
● backup data is held in secure conditions

An interesting finding in the USA during research for MIT was that the mere presence of computers in a real estate organisation is no guarantee of good management (Veale, 1988). It was found that those who under-managed their real estate assets were just as likely to use computers as those who managed their real estate well. It acts as a reminder of the old adage of 'garbage in, garbage out'.

11.5   Management information

Real estate middle managers will need to focus on individual buildings and the local property market and planning details. These can then be combined with the financial information already produced by the business to produce financial performance analysis. Marketing and employment data can be obtained from the specialist departments of the business or from various outside sources according to the business's needs (Figure 11.2).

Building data

Most businesses keep basic terrier information, such as location (address and local authority area); gross and net floor areas; and age and construction details, including, where available, plans. It is important to ensure that the information is constantly updated.

Financial performance

Number of occupants
Floor area per occupant
Cost of accommodation per
    occupant
Earnings/profi t from occupancy
Profit per member of staff in
    each building
Suitability for modern industry
    and business

Property and planning

Lease obligations and
    conditions
Rent reviews and break clauses
Local market conditions for
    disposal
Transport connections and
    road network
Any special economic status
Local plan inquiries

Building data

Location
Floor areas
Number of storeys
Age
Construction & condition
Use
Suitability for current use
Better uses
Rent & service charges
Capital value
Rates
Utility charges
Occupancy costs

Marketing data

Local population
Status of population
Age of population
Wealth of population
Car ownership
Leisure interests
Purchasing habits
Newspaper readership
Housing type and value
Industry/ services

Employment data

Wage and salary levels
Skills base
Academic achievements
Unemployment levels
School and college leavers
Student population

Figure 11.2 Information for strategic planning.

Capital values, rent, rates and service charges should not be very controversial, but all these monetary sums should be up-to-date. Valuations undertaken on the basis of the RICS *Appraisal and Valuation Manual* (Royal Institution of Chartered Surveyors, 1995) will be needed for company accounts. For management purposes, the current value of real estate must be known for good decision-making. As mentioned in Chapter 7, it helps to understand the full potential of the real estate by having information such as open market valuations and valuations based on 'what if?' scenarios whenever these are relevant.

Utility charges have been reasonably uncontentious, but, as the privatisation process moves on to allow greater competition and regional variations, utility charges such as business rates may vary significantly from locality to locality.

More subjective decisions have to be taken to decide on the building's suitability for current use, other uses and development potential.

Occupancy costs, other than real estate costs, will come from the facilities management system and are considered further later in this chapter.

Financial performance

How much a building costs to operate is only one side of the equation. To be able to make a judgement about whether this is satisfactory, it is necessary to compare the costs of providing the building with the profitability that can be achieved from its use.

The results may not provide guidance for simple solutions. Given that real estate has been a 'free resource' in many businesses, it will not be surprising to find operating units that cannot make sufficient from their operation to justify the cost of the accommodation they occupy. Even if a unit can cover expensive accommodation costs, it is only one aspect of a justification for an expense that the business may be able to avoid. Some very unsuitable and expensive real estate is kept by businesses for historical and marketing reasons, because it provides good facilities for senior staff to use for influencing politicians or foreign visitors (which are not measured directly by financial targets) or because disposal could prove even more expensive. The aim is not to create turmoil, but to ensure that strategic planning of the business is based on sound financial and other accepted criteria.

The finance department should be able to provide the latest business operating statistics. The quality of the business's ordinary management accounts will be an indication of its ability to address the issues raised when investigating the contribution of real estate to the business operation. If there is compatibility between the computer systems used by the real estate department and the finance department, the transfer of information will be easier to organise.

To be worthwhile, the strategic planners need up-to-date ongoing financial information that is compiled so that it can relate to individual real estate holdings. Where operational units do not match up exactly with individual buildings, the allocation of real estate costs and contribution to profits will have to be calculated individually. Formulae can be developed which will cope with this.

Property and planning data

It is not easy to abbreviate lease details so that they can be fed into spreadsheets or other analytical tools. Brief management information should have details of times when notice can be given to break a lease and information on rent reviews, together with responsibility for repairs, insurance, etc. Ease of disposal can be an important consideration.

Transport and communication links are frequently important for staff and clients and for distribution. Information should be up-to-date, which is more difficult when privatised services respond rapidly to changing demand. GIS, tracking services and road condition surveys may also be useful.

Any special economic status that will bring grants from local authorities, central government or the European Union should be noted, together with the time-scale for applications.

An aspect that many businesses overlook is local authority local and unitary development plans. These plans are developed by local authorities and sent out for consultation, and then public inquiries are held to deal with acknowledged disagreements. Local real estate owners should take an opportunity to influence development proposals to include future uses that they may require. If this is overlooked it will be much more difficult later to obtain planning permission for development which does not conform with the plan. Of course, making a proposal that a possible change should be included in a plan does not mean that it will be agreed (see Chapter 15).

Marketing and employment data

The examples given in Figure 11.2 are just an indication of the issues that can be important when considering locations.

The marketing department of a business is the most likely source of most of this information. Marketing data is now available on GISs and can be used with GIS property-based information, making possible a closer interface between real estate and marketing departments (Baker and Baker, 1993).

For operations that involve complex distribution arrangements, transportation and logistics data, together with future government infrastructure plans, may be influential, as will experience of routes by delivery drivers.

The cost of a particular building needs to be appraised, not only in comparison with other suitable buildings, but in relation to the suitability of the location for the product or service market. This is very normal for leading retailers, but can be relevant to others. Suitable labour, at reasonable wage rates, has long been an important cost consideration. Nowadays, regional accents can influence the location of telephone-based services.

11.6   Occupancy costs

Occupancy costs is a term that can be used to include rent and capital costs of occupation plus operational costs, which will extend beyond maintenance to matters such as furnishings and insurance. There have been no clear definitions, and the real estate manager contributing information for corporate strategy will have to decide about the components and measurement criteria for each cost figure produced.

Section 11.10, on comparison and benchmarking, highlights some of the variations that occur in published and privately circulated data. There are moves to try to overcome these difficulties.

The important consideration is to realise that, for most buildings, property costs will be responsible for 80% of occupancy costs and operational costs for the remaining 20% (Bernard Williams Associates, 1994). Although they are the smaller part of the occupancy cost, operational costs can still add up to very significant sums and need to be a focus of attention, usually by facilities managers. However, it is important to remember the relationship and not to become overwhelmed by the detail of operational costs, which offer only proportionately small opportunities for cost savings and overlook the larger real estate costs.

There will be a relationship between real estate costs and occupancy costs. It is not fixed or predetermined, but each building will have in-built factors that will affect operational costs. Such matters include ease of access for cleaning and maintenance, the life expectancy of the materials, the quality of the design, the choice of services, security requirements and the space planning options.

Occupiers will want to achieve the lowest costs for the level of service they require. This can be a balancing act, as, for example, one building may be easy to clean but lack the preferred services. To some extent, the occupancy costs of a leased building will be governed by the lease conditions.

The Building Research Establishment's *Office Toolkit* (1995b) has been devised to help occupiers to analyse their use of resources, particularly in matters of environmental concern. It includes a computer spreadsheet to assist calculation of the impact of office activities and a manual to suggest how savings can be made. Designed to assist small and medium-sized organisations, it will be too restrictive for larger, complex companies, but can be used for their individual buildings (Morgan, 1996).

Increasing the number of people in a building will increase some of the operational costs for the building, but as these will be much less than the real estate costs, the overall cost per person for accommodation normally falls as density of occupation increases. Obviously the point will be reached where overcrowding will cause other aspects of the business to work less efficiently. Hot-desking can be a way of gaining the cost savings of higher occupancy without the disadvantages of overcrowding.

Detail on occupancy costs and their make-up is beyond the scope of this book. A good general introduction to a wide range of financial and economic matters is given in *Building Economics* (Seeley, 1996) A more focused introduction has been produced by Bernard Williams Associates in *Facilities Economics* (1994), but there are limitations to this text because it is based on the methods used by one consultancy only.

It is important not to overlook the opportunities to include repairs in revenue expenditure for tax efficiency. Some other costs may be within the terms of the various capital allowances. These allowances were discussed in greater depth in Chapter 7.

11.7   Data analysis

The following sections aim to indicate ways in which quantitative information related to real estate can be presented and analysed to provide data to assist the preparation of the overall business strategy or specific real estate strategies.

It is impossible and irrelevant to suggest detailed ways of approach; the successful strategies will be ones that are appropriate but also different. To do that they will probably link aspects of the business which have previously been seen as independent of each other.

As well as gaining information on the current situation, the analysis and recording methods should build up statistics on a regular basis which can be monitored over time. The frequency of entries will vary between the different sources of information and the use to which they are put.

11.8   The real estate overview

The global view

A first step forward is to present information about the real estate in global terms:

- freehold value (now and as recorded in the accounts)
- freehold value of any investment properties
- annual rent and rates bill
- occupancy costs
- length of leases and commitments
- net income from investment properties

● future expensive maintenance, repair or lease obligations

When this is used with the normal financial records, it is easy to calculate:

● total value of the real estate
● total annual expenditure on real estate and occupancy costs
● time-scale of existing commitments
● extent of future real estate liabilities
● real estate costs as a percentage of total costs
● value of real estate holdings as a percentage of total assets
● return on real estate investment compared with business overall

Once this global overview has been performed, the strategists will begin to understand the role of real estate in the business's financial affairs.

Investment properties

The business managers will also be able to calculate whether the returns from investment properties are adequate to warrant the business being a landlord in addition to its other operations.

Costs influenced by real estate

Another real estate-focused analysis is to investigate all costs that are in some way influenced by the location of real estate or the use of particular buildings (see Chapter 2).

11.9   Contribution of individual real estate holdings

Once the broad brush approach has shown that real estate should be considered as a strategic issue in its own right, or could make a major contribution to the total business strategy, the contribution of the various parts of the real estate to the business objectives should be considered in detail. Again, the relationship of just a few figures will draw attention to key issues.

The following data will make it easy to compare individual buildings.

● total occupancy costs (including rent or equivalent and rates)
● earnings
● floor area in square metres
● number of employees

Ideally, the earnings should be related to the individual operating unit or cost centre relevant for each building. A building used by different cost centres should be included for each unit, with the percentage use recorded. The costs must include all related usable floor space in a building. Unoccupied space should be noted, whether partial or whole buildings.

Comparison of data – costs by area

Earnings less occupancy costs divided by the amount of usable floor area for each individual building will give figures in units that can be compared across the real estate, i.e.

$$\frac{\text{earnings} - \text{occupancy costs}}{\text{floor area}}$$

It will directly relate the cost of real estate to earnings and is not related to any other consideration such as intensity of use.

Comparison of data – costs per employee

Where buildings are used for similar purposes, such as office use, comparing the earnings less occupancy costs divided by the number of employees will produce another range of figures that will warrant comparison. Under-occupancy will directly create high real estate costs. In factories and warehouses the use of space for unused machinery or storing excessive inventory is a cause of high real estate costs.

Other breakdowns

Breaking down the figures further may produce a better indication of precise excessive costs. Considering occupancy and rent (or allowance for the opportunity cost of using freehold real estate) separately will show up buildings that are expensive to finance separately from those that are expensive to maintain and service.

An organisation can build up a very complex analysis if it is felt that it will add to its understanding and if it has sufficiently detailed information. As already discussed, leading retail organisations are undertaking very complex analysis of the shopping centres in which they trade (see Chapters 6 and 18).

Further investigations

Any of these calculations carried out on a spreadsheet can be sorted to rank the buildings on the basis of the results. The ordering will probably change depending on whether floor area or numbers of employees are used for the divisor.

It can be that shops in popular locations will have the highest takings per square metre, but when high rents and occupancy costs are taken into account they are not as profitable as locations which have lower takings but much lower total costs.

Once the expensive sites have been isolated, reasons for the expense can be sought. It may be that a building is in an expensive location, but it could also be that it is under-utilised – one or both could apply. It could also be due to expensive repairs or refurbishment.

If all business overheads are taken into account, other factors, such as local salaries or wage rates, could be influential. Likewise, if staff numbers vary from location to location a better comparison may come from including all outgoings, i.e.

$$\frac{\text{earnings} - (\text{occupancy costs} + \text{all other overheads (salaries etc.)}}{\text{floor area}}$$

It is open to an organisation to build up a very complex analysis if it is felt that it will add to its understanding, or if it has sufficiently detailed information. For organisations with large real estate holdings, multi-regression analysis makes it possible to look for correlations across a range of independent variables.

When real estate is spread nationwide or further across international boundaries, real estate costs may be only one of a very diversified range of issues to be considered, such as local employment legislation, social security costs, political stability, distance to raw materials and tax regimes.

11.10   Comparison and benchmarking

Many businesses have buildings of different types – factory, warehouse, office, shop – that together provide the accommodation to house the processes that create and market the finished product or service. Annual occupancy costs for the whole estate must be broken down to separate buildings to aid understanding of the make-up of the costs. This helps to indicate where it may be most valuable to concentrate attention on cost-reducing measures.

Some items of expenditure may well stand out as excessive, and these can be addressed. More frequently, the areas of excessive cost only become apparent when compared with the costs of other businesses. This is problematic because there is no standard method for content, measurement of occupational costs or statistical presentation arrangements.

Avis and Gibson (1995) found that the most common measures are:

● return on assets

- costs per unit of area
- property costs as a percentage of turnover or profit

In the USA, recent research has revealed much the same approach (Lambert *et al.*, 1995). The most frequently used measures there are:

- costs per unit of area
- area per employee
- costs per employee
- employee satisfaction with work environment
- costs as percentage of operating expenses

Lambert *et al.* found that 61% of respondents tracked performance measures over time.

Interestingly, whereas several corporate real estate departments in the UK are keen to emphasis their reductions in space per office-based employee, Lambert mentions that space per employee is a less common measure for offices and retail space in the USA.

She also reports that in the USA the companies with the most consistent profits focused much more on sales per unit of area rather than occupancy (property) costs. Could this be because, in much of the USA, land is not in as short supply as in the UK? The concern about costs expressed by the companies interviewed for Chapters 14–20 suggests that reducing these costs is important to UK companies who actively manage corporate real estate and focus on corporate strategies.

Standards for comparison

Standard methods of measurement are needed. In 1995 the British Institute of Facilities Management published a Measurement Protocol which sets a framework for measuring costs and for collecting data to help ascertain any special features. Concerns have been expressed that the Measurement Protocol's focus on costs for internal areas focuses on tenants' requirements, rather than those of landlords, and therefore limits its value (Lowe, 1995). It is too early to ascertain its acceptability and whether it will be adopted by any of the services that offer to compare occupancy costs.

A project partly funded by government through its research grant to the Centre for Facilities Management at the University of Strathclyde and supported by industrial partners resulted in the development of a 'Performance and Cost Management System' to assist building owners and their advisers to make decisions about the initial and ongoing costs of building ownership and usage. The first report (Clift and Butler, 1995) is being followed by computer software to implement the system. Funding arrangements for the final stages are holding up progress.

Benchmarking

There has been a tendency to call cost comparison 'benchmarking', but simple comparison of data lacks the depth of proper benchmarking. This normally involves focusing on a business process which gives cause for concern. The process can be an aspect of facilities provision and management.

To start with, the whole process is scrutinised as it is currently being undertaken – a full analysis of all aspects of techniques and communications is made.

The next step is to look for a company undertaking similar tasks more successfully – a company that can do more for less. As it is the process that is under scrutiny, any business with a similar process may be used for benchmarking the techniques and methods. For example, the process of reporting failures in the facilities management service may gain from bench-marking against any efficiently run complaints service, as well as against another facilities management service.

The company to be benchmarked is visited and its process studied, espe-cially any areas of excellence. The initial survey of the existing process will provide a framework to guide the study. The search is to discover working methods and practices that will make a difference when implemented in the initiating company. The research needs to be wide-ranging around the process. For example, a component of improving a complaints service may be more closely connected to the supply of spare parts than the work of those initially receiving the complaint. An example for services that are subcontracted, could reveal that the detail of the contract is as important as the work actually undertaken.

The people involved need to be able to get beyond fixed mind-sets and look to the future. They will need to have problem-solving skills, be able to exchange ideas freely in brainstorming sessions, have the statistical and other analytical skills to be able to seek out cause and effect relationships, and be able to manage the project.

Proposals are then made for changing the process in the initiating company. The acceptance of these new methods will be easier if top management has been supporting the benchmarking process and if explanations are provided.

Benchmarking is a process that is much more complex than just comparing cost data. Experience has shown that businesses are willing to be benchmarked for the gain of others. Normally this is because they are offered the opportunity to look at processes in the other company   a quid pro quo. Benchmarking clubs are groups who work together to exchange information in more detail than is available from published surveys. They know who is receiving their data and who they are benchmarking against.

Benchmarking is a complex and expensive process. Selecting the more suitable processes to benchmark is as important as thorough implementation. The expected gains must be sufficient to warrant the time and effort involved.

Available services

In 1994, SJT Associates Ltd, together with the Centre for Facilities Management at the University of Strathclyde, produced a report of the sources of occupancy cost data, some of which offer some forms of benchmarking. Some of the companies listed provide consultancy services, which enables a more precise identification of specific problem areas. The report was included in the Centre's own annual publication called *Facilities Costs and Trends Survey (FACTS '94)*.

A common problem for all the services is the limited amount of information available to each one. Data is difficult to collect, and those who contribute often supply incomplete returns. Even when data is supplied the impact of periodic costs, such as decoration and replacement of mechanical plant, will skew the figures from year to year for individual buildings. The best that is generally achieved is only adequate to provide an indication of the range or trend of occupancy costs. Among the companies listed were the following (contact details are at the end of the chapter):

- *Building Maintenance Information*
  Within the sphere of building maintenance many have used data produced by Building Maintenance Information (BMI) to attempt to judge
  their own success in achieving reasonable costs.

  Its main publications are the annual BMI *Building Maintenance Price
  Book*, supported by quarterly cost briefings which include cost indices.
  These indices track trends in building maintenance costs for specific
  sectors (including one on private sector buildings); they are also produced
  for different services, such as redecoration costs and for items that make
  up total costs, such as labour, materials and energy. BMI also undertakes
  special surveys, producing reports on building occupancy-related issues
  which help to keep readers abreast of cost-related issues.

  Among BMI's special reports are the Building Owners' Reports, which
  cover property occupancy costs. The reports give annual expenditure
  on individual buildings broken down into elements and sub-elements.
  They is supported by data solely on building maintenance costs and
  another set on energy costs. The building maintenance costings cover
  180 buildings, property occupancy costs cover 80 buildings and energy
  costs are given for 40 buildings. It is hard to match like with like, especially
  given the wide range of users and their different quality standards, but
  this should not discourage the use of BMI's main building maintenance
  pricing products.

- *The Premises and Facilities Audit*
  This occupancy cost database has also built up over a number of years
  and is run by Bernard Williams and Associates. It uses the methodology

explained in their book on *Facilities Economics* (1994), but is only available to clients.

● *Workplace Benchmarking Group*
  This was formed by a consultancy, Advanced Workplace Associates Ltd (AWA), in conjunction with *Facilities Management Journal*. It is interactive and workshop-based, with face-to-face discussions between facilities management and property professionals, the aim being to improve workplace and business performance. Bespoke reports are available. Study groups of at least five members are set up, based on an industry, function or topic.

● *JLW OSCAR: Office Service Charge Analysis*
  For 10 years property consultants Jones Lang Wootton (JLW) have been publishing an analysis of audited service charges. It is now based on details from 225 buildings owned by JLW's clients. The greatest concentration is in London and the south-east. It is only a guide, as the buildings differ substantially in terms of standards, layout, age, structure, net to gross size and staffing.

● *IPD Operational Property Databank (OPD) and Retailers' Property Databank (RPD)*
  These independent databanks were launched early in 1996 by Investment Property Databank as an extension of their property investment index services. The aim is to achieve the high standards set by these existing services and hence produce valuable occupancy cost and benchmarking data on a true like-for-like basis. Both will be confidential to users.

11.11   Real estate and new opportunities

This section considers some of the opportunities for businesses and suggests the information that may help to relate the real estate aspects to overall strategy.

New markets and overseas

The attitude has often been that operating locations would be based on an analysis of all factors, except real estate, and when the decision had been taken on location the business would just have to buy into the local real estate market – as best it could. This is very naïve when, in retailing for example, real estate accounts for 20% of the costs. The development of business in any location should consider the real estate costs and other real estate risks, which can be complex in difficult markets such as the emerging economies. If an issue is complex it does not mean that it should be ignored.

New operations

Understanding how much a particular operation contributes to a company when real estate costs are considered will help decide which aspects of the business should be expanded.

For example, a retail company could decide to switch to a direct mail service – the cost of shop premises would be saved, but the set-up costs for offices, automated warehousing and distribution systems can be expensive and capital-intensive. If this means that the business becomes highly geared, risks are further increased, particularly if the economic climate is unstable. An alternative route to greater profitability, without high gearing, may be to off-load shop premises where the contribution to profits is low even if turnover is high. Expansion could then take place, selecting premises that analysis has shown will be profitable – a mixture of market knowledge and appreciation of real estate and other location-related expenses.

Breaking a stranglehold

The clearing house banks branch network involves high real estate costs. Direct banking using the telephone for communication is a competitive operation with lower real estate costs. Amalgamations and mergers among the branch bank networks and building societies allow real estate and other costs to be reduced by closing redundant branches. The result is more customers per branch and a reduction in real estate costs per customer. All banks seem to be following the same course. Those that fall behind will become weaker and will probably be acquired – if the price takes a realistic view of surplus real estate.

Trying to stay out in front in a strategy that is being used by all in the industry is hard work, not very inspiring and probably dulls the thinking about alternatives. Real estate costs are clearly an important factor, and it is unlikely that all banks will close all their branches and only offer a telephone/online service, as there is a client base of those who want face-to-face banking in a branch. Will the competitive advantage be gained by the banking business that addresses the real estate cost issue by a different strategy? Realising the information that will help the decision process is an important first step.

Options

Owning real estate as a freeholder, or long leaseholder, gives a business a physical presence in a locationally based market-place; keeping currently uneconomic real estate could be an inexpensive way of maintaining an option.

Data which relates the business to economic, political, infrastructure and any other relevant forecasts will give the business greater opportunity to consider the real estate options.

Exit barriers

Business strategies for mature industries should involve exit strategies from markets in which the business cannot trade profitably. Matching units with limited futures within the business with short-life real estate and placing the growing businesses in better accommodation is a possible strategy. Alternatively, starting a new business in a short-life property because it will expand and move on if successful could also be successful. If data about the real estate is available to the strategists they have the option of making these choices – they can attempt to match business 'horses' with real estate 'courses'. Well-developed strategies should limit the possibility of real estate commitments being an exit barrier.

Competitor analysis

Looking for real estate (and other development potential) has long been an occupation of the asset-stripping conglomerates. As technological developments make it possible to reorganise businesses and to be more effective in the use of real estate, there are opportunities for those who understand the competition more fully by undertaking a strategic appraisal of their competitors' use of real estate.

11.12   A more comprehensive model

This chapter focuses on the basic statistical information that will help corporate planners make better use of real estate. In the companies where this is already happening managers and their advisers are moving on to build more comprehensive statistical models with the aim of incorporating more breadth and depth into the mental pictures real estate decision makers hold in their heads as they consider their future strategies.

The idea involves a matrix of information – most of it not difficult to obtain – which is monitored using statistical quality control techniques to produce a feedback loop between managerial action and real estate performance. Duckworth (1993), who presented these ideas in his prizewinning paper, worked with the real estate and strategic decision-makers at the Digital Equipment Corporation to develop the process for their use.

11.13   Summary

For many organisations actively including real estate within corporate strategy is a new experience. Methodologies are still developing. This chapter has been more about suggesting ways forward than making prescriptive approaches. The key points have been:

- the data and matters considered need to be of strategic importance
- both financial data and non-financial issues will be relevant
- computerised real estate management systems are fast being introduced
- valid data will be wide-ranging including much from beyond the business
- corporate financial information may indicate a need for real estate action
- operational costs are important but of limited value strategically
- inaccuracy from changing units of measure should be avoided...
- ...but identifying and monitoring trends can be more important than accuracy
- start with a strategic overview of real estate and its influence on other costs
- consider the contribution of individual real estate holdings
- focus on aspects which show strategic potential
- new opportunities will require consideration of new factors and new data
- until standardised approaches are agreed businesses will probably gain most by focusing on their own situation rather than attempting comparisons

11.14   Further reading

The *PCS Property Software Directory*, compiled by Henri Cash and Gail Taylor, is published by Property Computer Show Ltd and given to those who attend the annual show. It is also sold via RICS Books (Tel: 0171 222 7000).

This chapter is only about the data required to consider real estate issues. For a corporation-wide overview of data collection and analysis and the development of corporate strategy, *Strategic Business Planning* by Clive Reading is very straightforward and extremely helpful, especially for those who do not revel in figures, accounts and statistics (Reading, 1993).

GISs are used to link locational data on real estate with market information, but it is beyond the scope of this book to go into a great deal of detail. Those who want to know more will find that *Market Mapping* by Sunny and Kim Baker is a comprehensive introduction (Baker and Baker, 1993). Sources of actual data are very varied and more the province of a marketing department, especially when relating to specific industries. Census and other government statistics, which in some cases are available for areas as small as a local authority ward or civil parish, are readily available.

Facilities management is fast becoming a major area of professional and managerial expertise. Two books that will provide more information are *Facilities Management: An Explanation* by Alan Park (1994) and *Facilities Economics Incorporating Premises Audits* by Bernard Williams Associates (1994).

11.15   Sources of information

BMI, an RICS Business Service subsidiary, can be contacted at Building Maintenance Information, 85–87 Clarence Street, Kingston upon Thames, Surrey KT1 1RB (Tel: 0181 546 7555; Fax: 0181 547 1238). They offer a subscription service and some items can be purchased individually.

The annual *Facilities Costs and Trends Survey* by the Centre for Facilities Management at the University of Strathclyde together with SJT Associates Ltd is available from SJT Associates Ltd, 4a West Point, 39–40 Warple Way, London W3 0RG (Tel: 0181 749 7557; Fax: 0181 749 7507). The survey of occupancy cost services was in the 1994 edition. It was reported in *Property Week* on 26 January 1995 in an article called 'Benchmarking: Taken to the Cleaners?' by Peter Holdsworth.

The Centre for Facilities Management at the University of Strathclyde can be contacted at University of Strathclyde, Graham Hills Building, 50 George Street, Glasgow G1 1QE (Tel: 0141 553 4165; Fax: 0141 552 7299).

Information on the Measurement Protocol is available from the British Institute of Facilities Managers (Tel: 01799 508608; Fax: 01799 513237).

Information on the progress of the 'Performance and Cost Management System' should be available from Michael Clift at the Building Research Establishment, Garston, Watford, Herts WD2 7JR (Tel: 01923 664122).

The Premises and Facilities Audit is run by Bernard Williams Associates, Kings House, 32–40 Widmore Road, Bromley, Kent BR1 1RY (Tel: 0181 460 1111; Fax: 0181 464 1167).

The Workplace Benchmarking Group can be contacted at Advanced Workplace Associates Ltd, Magdalen House, 136 Tooley Street, London SE1 2TU (Tel: 0171 378 7655; Fax: 0171 378 1834).

Copies of the JLW *OSCAR: Office Service Charge Analysis* are available from Jones Lang Wootton, 22 Hanover Square, London (Tel: 0171 493 6040; Fax: 0171 408 0220 and 0171 409 3440).

The IPD Operational Property Databank (OPD) and Retailers' Property Databank (RPD) can be obtained from Investment Property Databank, 7–8 Greenland Place, London NW1 0AP (Tel: 0171 482 5149; Fax: 0171 267 0208).

12 Managing Real Estate

12.1 Introduction

This chapter covers an important consideration when seeking to make the best of real estate – its management in the context of its contribution to corporate strategy.

With so many different styles of corporate management and businesses varying so greatly in size and in their use of real estate, there could never be one 'correct' way. Nevertheless, certain practices seem to be more relevant to those who want to make active use of real estate for corporate gain.

12.2 Anything goes

There is no research published in the UK on the day-to-day management methods for corporate real estate. Research undertaken in the USA has found that corporate real estate is organised in every conceivable way (Lambert et al., 1995). It is not unreasonable to assume that in the UK almost anything that can be done in the name of corporate real estate management is being done – ranging from effective to unmitigated disaster!

Lambert et al.'s Generating High Performance Corporate Real Estate Service included the results of focus groups with corporate real estate executives, company case studies, telephone interviews and a survey of corporate executives from five main industry groups. It was an extension of the work undertaken by Joroff and his team in the early 1990s.

Lambert and her team found that corporate real estate managers who wanted to contribute to higher levels of corporate management found it difficult to develop, and were facing extraordinary challenges as they succeeded in becoming a new resource to internal customers or in contributing to corporate strategy.

12.3 Real estate management choices

Links between day-to-day real estate management and overall corporate strategy are usually only a very small part of any real estate organisation

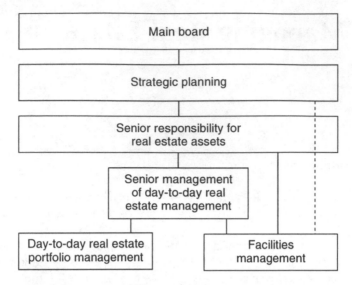

Figure 12.1 Real estate management choices.

undertaken by senior management. For example, although Railtrack's property directorate has 1100 people, most are engaged in mundane tasks (London, 1996). Ideally, the corporate needs should be understood by and motivate all the workforce.

Between the main board and the day-to-day real estate teams are a number of different managerial possibilities. A simplified diagram of these levels is shown in Figure 12.1. In a retail organisation such as Marks & Spencer or Sainsbury's, where the importance of real estate is acknowledged, the most senior real estate appointment is at main board level.

In many organisations the most senior real estate appointment is the manager of day-to-day real estate matters, who will then report to the financial director or a deputy. This director needs to have a very close relationship with the real estates department, receiving regular and frequent reports.

When the reporting line is to the operations director, real estate tends to be even further away from the corporate heart of the business.

The model includes facilities management, as this service is often interwoven with the real estate management provision, but it may have its own reporting structure, especially if non-property facilities, such as computing, are part of the facilities management organisation. Sometimes facilities management may be split, so that real estate issues are the responsibility of the real estate manager and the responsibility for other aspects of facilities management reside elsewhere.

New construction may well come under the estate management department and building maintenance under facilities management. Where construction is constant and ongoing there may well be an architects', building or project management department which encompasses these services.

When real estate is of limited importance or is undervalued the pecking order can be reversed and real estate can become the responsibility of the facilities manager. The more dispersed within the management structure the responsibility for real estate and associate issues, the less likely it is that a coherent corporate approach will be achieved.

There also appears to be an advantage from centralising the day-to-day management of real estate. This is the view of many of the real estate directors and managers who have instigated the programmes that have revealed the strategic importance of real estate in the UK. They have found that when real estate management was decentralised there had been a lack of appreciation of the overall spend on real estate, both as annual expenditure and on real estate fixed assets.

When real estate management is decentralised it also seems that issues related to personal or departmental grandiosity play a greater role in the real estate decision-making process than is in the overall interest of the business. This is especially the case if there is no internal rent or other charging or if the unit is very profitable and can afford to pay for excessive space.

Naturally, the organisation of the management of real estate is affected by the size of the company. If the business owns very few buildings it will not require teams of people to care for them; indeed, there could even be insufficient work to warrant the employment of any in-house professional managers.

12.4 The main board

For real estate issues to be included in main board decision-making the facts must be known and the issues understood by those who prepare proposed corporate strategic planning policies. If not, it can almost guarantee that the real estate strategic perspective will be absent from all major decisions – even those directly related to real estate!

Very few real estate managers have main board seats. There are very strong arguments that this should change, especially for businesses that have both a high value and a high percentage of real estate among their fixed assets. The same applies if, due to a policy of leasing rather than owning, they have high real estate costs.

There are problems – not least the shortage of experienced real estate professionals who have the understanding, experience and knowledge to contribute to corporate management. The situation is gradually changing as senior real estate employees complete executive management courses and younger ones gain MBAs. At board level, directors need to be able to take a wide-ranging overview, understanding corporate finance, strategic planning and global issues. A boardroom place given to a person with a narrow focus will weaken, not enrich, the ability of the board to lead the company.

The second consideration is custom and practice. There is no tradition of real estate professionals contributing directly to the main boards of major corporations. Businesses should be flexible and change to meet new circumstances. Some have, but others, while quite innovative in many of their business practices, seem to be far less flexible higher up the organisation.

Thirdly, main boards are run very differently from business to business, and some are much smaller than others. BT plc, the UK's largest company, has just six executive main board directors, whereas Marks & Spencer has 17. BT, with its small board, does not have a real estate main board director, while Marks & Spencer, with its larger board, does. Where the main board is small the value placed on the real estate within the business must be judged by other criteria. In BT very few aspects of the business, including its major subsidiaries, are directly represented at main board level. The appointment of a Director Group Property is one indication that real estate is considered to be important, and this is backed by the support shown by the main board for the work of the real estate team (see Chapter 15).

A fourth consideration is the ability of the real estate manager to research, develop and present a case that will attract the attention of the existing main board members and convince them that they need a stronger real estate input at their main board meetings.

An alternative to an executive real estate director is to include a real estate professional among the non-executive directors of the firm. Again, such a person will need a wider viewpoint than an excellent understanding of real estate issues. A real estate non-executive director would normally be expected to be able to contribute a wide understanding of other corporate business issues.

For a company with major real estate holdings, it will strengthen the understanding of the varied issues, even when an executive real estate director already reports to the main board. This of course is not uncommon among property companies and major institutional investors, such as insurance companies and pension funds.

12.5   Strategic planning

To successfully incorporate real estate into strategic planning will need commitment from all involved. The process may start with the corporate strategic planning team requesting an input from the real estate team. However, in many businesses strategic planning is not undertaken in such a formalised way and ideas may be developed within the real estate team or be driven by others in the business, such as the marketing, sales or distribution teams, in which case the real estate team will need to liaise with them.

Realistically, the real estate team must be able to be, or become, effective from within the existing organisation. A proposal to improve the real estate input which starts with proposals to reorganise the whole company must have little hope of success. Pragmatic proposals are vital.

The level of involvement from the real estate team will, to a large extent, depend on the ability of the team to understand corporate business decision-making and strategic planning skills. It is not just a matter of learning about the processes, but also the ability to be visionary – to be able to see beyond a real estate professional background. However, as the decision-making process must be based on facts and not fantasies, those involved must have the foresight to initiate the research and analysis to draw out the relationships and trends that underlie serious forecasts.

Combining this mix of skills with real estate market and professional skills means that rarely will all the contributors to real estate strategy be real estate professionals. It will need a mixed team which brings various specialist skills – strategic thinking, corporate finance, economic forecasting etc. – to the group but which has the capacity to take an overall view of the work in progress. Some of those contributing will probably have other roles within the real estate team, if only because a 'hands-on' feel for the real estate market is essential knowledge for such a team.

To switch from being a company that ignores real estate to one with the drive and vision to consider and act on the strategic considerations will need some sort of a catalyst. It could be acute financial problems; the appointment of new managers (either a new chief executive officer or a new head of the real estate team); the realisation by existing staff that real estate has become important in other businesses; a strategic review; or the result of attending a strategic management education programme.

12.6 The strategic management of the real estate team

As well as contributing upwards to the overall corporate strategy, the real estate manager has to plan to ensure that the real estate team implements the corporate strategy and especially its real estate aspects. It will mean policies on matters such as staffing, operations and computerisation. Much of this is normal business management.

The most comprehensive text on the specifics of the organisation of the corporate real estate department is a US publication, *Managing Corporate Real Estate* (Brown, 1993). It contains an immense amount of detail which links into strategic objectives and is a valuable source of information, but it is very focused on US practice and law and predates Lambert *et al.*'s work, published in 1995.

On a day-to-day basis there seems to be a general consensus that the contribution from the real estate team to the preparation of corporate strategy requires directly employed staff – an in-house team who know the corporate business and the real estate market. Success depends on a close working relationship where confidential information can be exchanged and market-sensitive ideas formulated. While technical qualifications and abilities are clearly essential, more and more real estate professionals are finding that the challenges lie much more with management and leadership issues, including corporate politics (Rondeau, 1988). This is not an area which can easily be delegated to external experts, although an external consultant seconded to BT began their inclusion of real estate into strategic planning (see Chapter 15).

Many real estate directors employ their own staff to head specific aspects of real estate services, but for day-to-day tasks they employ consultants. Consultants should be able to charge fees that are competitive with directly employed staff because they are employing people who can undertake work for other clients to keep them fully employed.

Some businesses favour using just one or two consultancies with whom they build a close relationship, while others switch about, selecting the consultants that they feel are best suited to a task and who offer competitive fees. Savage fee-cutting is not normally encouraged by the corporate real estate managers of the leading businesses – they want a quality of service which they know they cannot receive if fees remain too low for too long – which is not to say that some have not placed some commissions with consultants who offer loss leader fees!

Corporate real estate managers, especially in retailing, are in businesses that face severe competition. Costs matter. They are looking to save money. It is part of the strategy for the survival of the business – even when profits are high. This need to cut costs is leading these corporate real estate managers to seek out the most cost-effective way of delivering the real estate service. When they feel that consultants are not doing this they turn back to their own organisations to look for alternative approaches(see Chapter 18).

12.7 The in-house property company

For companies where real estate holdings are large, an option is to set up a separate real estate company that holds all or most of the real estate interests. This company then focuses on real estate as a core business, but will have a special, but nevertheless commercial, relationship with the main company. Figure 12.2 illustrates the basic model. If the property company is to maximise the use of its resources to support profitable operations then it will probably also seek tenants from outside its own parent company. This is an attraction for a retailer that can use its own property company to undertake retail developments and can select tenants who will support its operation by providing other goods and services and attracting shoppers to the site (see Chapter 18).

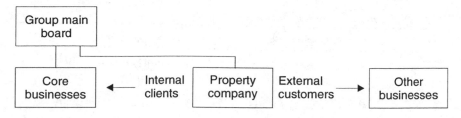

Figure 12.2 In-house property company.

This type of operation does not take the real estate off the group balance sheet, but does separate it from the core business, enabling a clearer picture of the success or otherwise of the core operations to emerge.

12.8 Facilities management

Some businesses have their own in-house facilities services which employ all necessary labour and management, but most real estate departments seem to be at least at arm's length from the day-to-day management of directly employed labour. When there is no in-house organisation, these services are outsourced to specialist facilities management companies. These contracts seem to fall more frequently under the responsibility of the real estate manager, although it is hard to be precise as facilities management is a fast-changing world.

Some facilities management companies are subsidiaries of or joint ventures with surveying consultancies and will offer to undertake real estate management functions as well as clean the toilets. Some have entered into outsourcing contracts where they have employed the client's previous staff, causing a quantum leap in the size of the organisation they manage.

Surveys by 3i (1994) and SJT Associates/University of Strathclyde (FACTS '94, 1994) have looked at the issues of client satisfaction with outsourced facilities management. As shown in Table 12.1, the service provided, as with most industries, does not always match what is wanted. Nevertheless, a survey published early in 1996 by Asset Information found that 80% of clients who have outsourced facilities management are happy with the standard of service they have received.

The 3i survey published in 1994 also showed that when it came to outsourcing services, IT/facilities management and property which were listed separately were not a particularly popular choice. Software development, pensions, security, car fleet, public relations and travel services were just a few of the services more likely to be outsourced.

However, in 1996 Asset Information noted that the UK facilities management market is at the beginning of a growth curve. Progress along the curve

Table 12.1 Outsourcing facilities management

	Clients' demands	Clients' problems
3i report	● Free management time	● Maintaining quality of service
	● Reduce staff costs	● Communication with service suppliers
FACTS '94	● Make financial and operational savings	● Slow reaction time
		● Future cost rises

has been sufficient for competition to be increasing, attracted by the growing size of the market and its profitability. Costs per customer are decreasing, and service differentiation has started. In the UK, facilities management has become a lucrative but competitive market-place.

One of the strengths of the facilities management industry is that its clients are not just corporate businesses but property investment companies, who as landlords are looking to pass on all the responsibilities of management and just enjoy the rental income. It encourages the service providers to ensure that they provide a comprehensive and easy-to-use service.

It is a market that is being driven by companies that have American parents. These companies are able to draw on their experience across the Atlantic, where facilities management has a longer history.

12.9   Property and facilities management in the USA

It is the property management side of facilities management that seems to have been the driver of change in the USA. The US market is breaking into two sectors, the large national providers serving major property owners and the small local or regional property managers offering a personal service and acting quickly in niche markets.

According to Jane Alder (1995) the driver is computerisation. Companies that have real estate across the USA want to be able to access data on their buildings that will slot into their own computer systems. If they use different property management companies for different buildings they will find that each is using different software and that they are faced with an unnecessarily complex (and expensive) task when they prepare their own financial management records. As the large companies emerge from both consolidation through mergers and acquisitions and from internal growth the market is becoming very competitive and fees are falling.

At the same time as being the cause of rationalisation, computerisation is helping to provide a more cost-effective service and reduce the labour levels and wage costs. For example, clients want to be able to access their property managers' computers directly to download management data as they need it – this cuts out handling in both companies.

Alder (1995) also reports that not only are the leading US property management companies expanding from the limited services of traditional property management into a full range of facilities management services, they are also moving into asset management, providing hold/sell analyses, valuations, capital expenditure forecasts and cash flow projection. Some property management companies are now linked to equity asset management companies to broaden yet further their role in the financial aspects of business through offering leasing and investment services.

Services now include advising clients on how to differentiate their buildings and put them in a position to capture a disproportionate increase in occupancy, rent or both. To meet these demands, leading property/facilities management companies are investing heavily in the education and training of their staff in everything from indoor air quality regulations and life safety codes to financial and strategic planning.

The US corporate real estate market has proved very attractive to the property management companies because the corporate clients keep their buildings longer than the property investors. This brings the property managers more stability as they can enter long-term contracts and then make long-term operational plans.

Alder (1995) reports that, having brought together all this expertise to sell services to clients, some property management companies are becoming real estate owners in their own right, especially through joint venture partnerships with institutional property investors. The property management company contributes only a small share of the purchase price/development costs but fulfils its part of the joint venture contract by providing the long-term property management service.

Many of the clients of the US property management companies have real estate all round the world. Partly to serve these clients, and partly to enter markets where fee levels are not so low, the US property management companies have developed businesses outside the US. This is especially true in the UK, where they have frequently acquired local businesses that continue to trade under the original names. An example is the US company Johnson Controls, which is the parent of one of the leading UK facilities management companies – Procord.

Another management option popular in the USA is for companies to occupy buildings on lease terms that put all the management responsibility on the landlord. In these circumstances there is little need for corporate real estate management. The in-house need is for someone who can monitor the services provided. Such a person will also be required to examine the track record, experience and financial viability of the proposed landlord. UK leases have generally not provided such comprehensive services for tenants, but there are signs of change.

12.10   The future of property management in the UK

The UK tends to lag a year or two behind the USA when leading edge ideas are first developed on the west side of the Atlantic. The changes reported by Alder are already being felt in the UK. There is overstaffing at all levels of the UK property and construction industries, and rationalisation and consolidation are under way. It would seem that this will continue, and one of the outcomes will be the formation of some very large property/facilities management firms.

The choice between in-house staff, short-term consultancies/contracts and outsourcing will perhaps become harder as facilities management contractors offer services increasingly focused on customer needs. The factors influencing the selection will vary, and in part it will be a strategic matter reflecting the nature of the business, geographical location and future plans. The service levels that can be provided and the cost will be important.

Just as in the USA, no doubt many large companies with geographically widespread accommodation will be looking for a comprehensive service that can serve all sites equally. Levels of sophistication, especially with IT support, will be guiding factors. For companies whose operations span Europe or the world, a large company that can provide a regional or global service will be attractive. Even if different companies are used in different continents, there are benefits in being able to contact them easily from any part of the world.

A note of caution has been expressed by Avis and Gibson (1995), who noted that one-fifth of the organisations that they studied (both public and private) had no one in-house undertaking any professional property management work. They also found that 40% of private sector organisations had outsourced a significant proportion of property management activities, which they inferred was mostly facilities management. Altogether this caused them to doubt that consultants and outsourcing contractors would be properly briefed or their performance monitored.

12.11   Postgraduate education

Reports from the USA and the UK are continually emphasising the need for a higher level of business and finance education among the property professionals engaged in corporate real estate and facilities management. The lack of knowledge of real estate issues by UK corporate business managers and finance officers suggests that there is also scope for the higher education they undertake to include more on real estate issues, a view echoed in the USA by Rodriguez and Sirmans (1996).

A telling comment by one corporate real estate manager was that the staff in a company's real estate team were among the best and excellent at their work, but in this large team there were only two or three who had the potential to undertake the development of strategic policy. There is no reason to believe that it is very different elsewhere. People involved in this field need to be able to add value – this may be clearer for consultants or outsourcing contractors to appreciate, as they are always selling their services.

Many of the people who are now leading the corporate real estate teams, and the senior consultants who serve them, received their initial higher education before most of the current management theories and techniques were formulated! They passed through university without touching a computer, yet now a knowledge of spreadsheets and databases is essential – double entry book-keeping is not a sufficient foundation for advising on the financial aspects of real estate ownership in a global or even just a national context. A relevant postgraduate education is vital, and it needs to span beyond the local market and introduce real estate personnel to the global issues that now affect all businesses.

Writing of the needs of all real estate professionals in the USA, whether advising corporate or investment clients or marketing real estate, Nass (1995) wrote of the need for a basic MBA education, international awareness, management and leadership skills, financial skills, banking and investment knowledge, marketing skills and experience of realising profit potential, and the ability to deal with environmental issues, public affairs and politics, all of these together developing the ability to address new challenges. All this applies equally in the UK. Nass also focused on the importance of real estate managers being able to work together as a team, to be solidly aligned behind a clearly defined vision.

It also follows that to run a successful consultancy or outsourcing business will also require astute business management skills. The UK contractors and consultants with American parent companies are already recruiting people with these skills. As the industry consolidates it would seem most likely that the most successful companies will be those that are best managed – probably by those who are well-educated with business skills to support their professional expertise.

Few UK business schools run any courses that introduce business managers to the importance of real estate and its interrelationship with business operations. Furthermore, the specialist real estate programmes (with just two exceptions) are not based in business schools. This chasm between two vital areas of business is not beneficial for the future of British business.

12.12   More for less – a challenge for all

The pressure for corporate real estate teams in the USA is to do more for less and at the same time to do it better, faster and cheaper. Chalk (1994) tells how this is being achieved in a number of companies. These businesses are seeking to identify issues that hinder efficiency and customer satisfaction by defining current processes, discussing needs with clients and then brainstorming between members of the real estate team to find ways of improving the process. Chalk tells how the object of the process, which is fundamentally a Total Quality Management exercise, is to eliminate errors, maximise the use of assets, provide for easy customer interface, adapt to customers' changing needs and provide the organisation with a competitive advantage.

Gordon Edington, Group Property Director at BAA plc, has for some years been keeping a close watch on changes in the USA. He has now introduced similar process analysis and redesign to the operation of BAA's real estate operation. The aim was to improve the service that the company provides to its many tenants, and the positive effect was soon noticeable; this is expected to continue (see Chapter 13).

Corporate real estate teams in businesses that have focused on quality management are among the first real estate organisations to gain BS EN ISO 9000 accreditation. Sadly, many of the consultants they wish to commission cannot offer this accreditation.

The need is for consultants to be more focused on the needs of their clients. This requires a change from the mind-set that produced the proposal that there should be an agreed specification of property-related services from which clients could select the services they need from a standard breakdown of agents' functions (Carpenter, 1996). While there is clearly some merit in the proposal, the idea that the corporate real estate team should choose from a predesignated menu is very presumptuous.

Those real estate consultants who can break out of this straitjacket and reorganise themselves to address the needs of their major corporate clients with efficient and effective services geared to the changing market-place are going to be the ones to survive in the consolidation process which is gathering pace in the industry.

It has already been pointed out that, if they do not, the facilities management contractors will take all or part of their business (Carpenter, 1996). This seems no idle threat when the wide-ranging services offered by property/facilities management companies in the USA are considered.

Another challenge comes from the real estate consultancies managed by management consultants who aim to overcome the criticism that 'Surveying firms are notoriously bad at managing themselves, often relying far too heavily on a reactive approach to the state of the market' (Whitmore, 1996).

An annual property fair is organised by the UK chapter of the American corporate real estate professional grouping NACORE. Here, in London each

November, business users can deal direct with each other. The development is a clear indication that when a market does not provide the required service the users will create a new market-place. The leading corporate real estate users, finding that the recession has given them a stronger bargaining position in the market-place, are clearly turning the tables to ensure that their needs are met – not only in management but also by by-passing the need for agency services.

Brown (1987) put it very succinctly when he wrote that the professional real estate consultant firm 'must be every bit as professional, sophisticated and knowledgeable as its clients'. Those that succeed in this very competitive world will either offer a better service or find a way of offering new services that meet a need, or more likely will do both.

12.13   Summary

While there has been no in-depth research in the UK into the best ways to manage corporate real estate, some practices seem to be more successful and indicate principles to be followed when activating the management of real estate resources. The main points highlighted in the chapter are:

- the seniority and responsibilities of the real estate manager vary from business to business
- if the reporting structure between the senior professional real estate manager and the main board is complex the main board will overlook real estate issues
- for a business with considerable real estate interests, a real estate manager with corporate business skills sitting on the main board is the most affective arrangement
- alternatively, a non-real estate main board director must have a clear responsibility for real estate, be well briefed and involved in strategic contributions
- another possibility is to appoint a non-executive director with real estate expertise
- an in-house property company has proved attractive to some businesses
- the success of incorporating real estate into the development of strategic policy will depend on the expertise, experience and commitment of the real estate team, and this is probably best undertaken by in-house staff
- within the real estate strategy should be policies for the team's own management (including the use of consultants and contractors), development of new services and success in serving corporate needs
- consolidation in the property/facilities management market in the USA is producing some large contractors with comprehensive and technologically advanced services which they are now beginning to offer in the UK

- consolidation in the UK seems set to follow and will create a very competitive industry focused on serving the needs of corporate business
- there is concern that inadequate in-house real estate expertise in many businesses will mean that consultants and outsourcing contractors will not be properly briefed or their performance adequately monitored
- corporate real estate professionals and business managers will need to improve their intellectual and practical business and real estate skills through postgraduate education and global experience
- the traditional real estate consultants will have to match the business management skills among corporate professionals and focus on clients' needs if they are to continue to find profitable commissions from corporate clients.

12.14   Further reading

The report by Sandra Lambert, Jean Poteete and Alison Waltch of MIT called *Generating High-Performance Corporate Real Estate* is an invaluable source of information on the recent developments in the USA. It contains five case studies. While there are differences between practice in the USA and the UK, much that happens within corporate America is relevant to corporate UK. The report is available from the International Development Research Council (IDRC) at 35 Technology Parkway/Atlanta, Suite 150, Norcross, GA 30092, USA (Tel: 00 1 770 446 8955; Fax: 00 1 770 263 8825). The earlier report by Michael Joroff, called *Strategic Management of the Fifth Resource: Corporate Real Estate*, is available from the same source.

Facilities Management, a bi-monthly journal, and the quarterly *Management Guide* provide articles on current FM theory and practice. Both are available from Facilities Management, The Eclipse Group, 18–20 Highbury Place, London N5 1QP (Tel: 0171 354 5858; Fax: 0171 226 8618).

12.15   Sources of information

Details of the Annual NACORE UK Chapter Property Fair in London is available from NACORE at the address given at the end of Chapter 1.

Part 5:
Implementation in Practice

13 The Front-Runners

Each of the following seven chapters is about a company that has included real estate as a component of corporate strategy. The companies have been selected for this book because they illustrate ways in which real estate can contribute to business success. Each makes a different contribution and each shows the value of strategic vision.

All of the companies have been very supportive by contributing to interviews, arranging site visits, providing papers and commenting on drafts. Without this support it would have been impossible to have compiled this part of the book.

Sadly, there is not a history or ethos of research into the real estate operations of UK companies. There are no full real estate case studies that follow the development of new policies and their implementation. Our understanding would be stronger if this had been undertaken and we could now review the process of devising, adopting and implementing real estate policy. Hopefully, this will happen in the future, and real estate strategy case studies will sit alongside those of other aspects of business operations and become core components of MBA and similar courses.

In the meantime, the best that can be made available are studies undertaken after the event. Not unnaturally, it is the successful companies that come to our attention and the processes that took place are inevitably viewed in the light of the final success. Nevertheless, the following chapters are as objective as possible, identifying the learning experiences and passing on ideas that will be helpful.

The main lesson from all these businesses is that their gains came from incorporating real estate issues into their strategic planning. This is more important in some ways than how the strategy was implemented. For long-term success businesses need to constantly review both their strategy and tactics; in some cases strategy can remain stable, while in other cases market conditions change and new approaches are needed.

Some successful businesses in the same sector have very different strategies; in part, the differentiation is a positive benefit – there are fewer head-on clashes or neck-and-neck races, so that each gains different advantages over the other. Very often, historical developments have brought companies into the same market from different routes and they become competitors, but with operations that are very different – a single strategy could not be devised to suit both companies even if their analysis of the future of their market was the same.

There are also fashions. The companies selected for closer study in this book are the front-runners. They devised their strategies to suit their needs and by and large they have worked; the companies feel that they have succeeded or can measure the success after implementation. Other businesses are following them by implementing similar management changes. If these followers do not undertake the same rigorous development programmes to ensure that the processes are both right for them and, importantly, that the market conditions are appropriate, what was successful for A can be a disaster for B.

The aim is not that corporate real estate managers should focus on the actions illustrated in the following chapters. It is important that they seek to achieve the most suitable solution for their business. The following chapters are included in this book:

- to show that real estate has been an important consideration for many leading businesses
- to provide some information on the practical issues of devising and implementing policy, particularly when it involves changing attitudes throughout an organisation
- to trigger ideas and help those who realise that real estate has become a moribund asset that is not making its full contribution to the business

Of the seven companies, six are major and well-known corporations. The seventh, Z/Yen Ltd, is a much smaller and newer company. It has been included as a working example of how many predict businesses will operate in the future. Whether Z/Yen's style of operation is appropriate for the organisation of a major corporation must be open to question, but it is clearly an example of an operating method that is viable and will, at the very least, affect the future real estate needs of larger businesses.

There are chapters on three major retail groups – Marks & Spencer plc, J Sainsbury plc and The Boots Company plc – who have a long history of appreciating the importance of property to their operations. They have been chosen because each has different real estate policies and has undertaken new real estate management developments in recent years. Some of these differences are reflected by almost exactly opposite strategies; for example, Marks & Spencer would like to hold the freehold interest of all its stores, while J Sainsbury evolved a strategy specifically to retain 40% of its accommodation as leasehold.

IBM UK Ltd, a leading high-tech business, is very well known as a front-runner that has initiated new ideas on how business could radically improve the contribution of real estate to the success of the business. BT plc, another high-tech business, illustrates how real estate change can be undertaken in support of cultural change and be part of a long-term strategy stretching into the next millennium.

The Conrad Ritblat Group plc has real estate management and professional services as its core business. It has used these core skills in a different form of operation to strengthen its ability to undertake and grow its main core operations.

At least some aspects of the real estate operations of the six major companies featured in this book have been covered by the press, often on more than one occasion. Many of the generalities will not be new to readers. What has been missing has been the detail of each operation, and often little has been written on its effect on the overall operation of the business. Often, strategic change is a component of a long-term policy that may not immediately be reflected in the financial performance of a business. However, as the focus of corporate success in the UK is normally measured in financial terms, many of these changes can be followed through to changes in the financial success of the business. Several of the chapters include information from company annual reports which illustrate this process.

These chapters cover most of the new developments in using real estate within a corporate strategy. Issues relating real estate to environmental issues have been excluded as, although they can be of strategic importance (especially with regard to image and marketing), they are just too wide-ranging to fit into this book. *Greener Buildings: Environmental Impact of Property* covers some of the issues (Johnson, 1993).

It has also not been possible to include a full chapter on the development at BAA plc of strategies of customer care and greater efficiency. The reason for this omission is that BAA's Group Property Director, Gordon Edington, is writing a book, together with members of his staff, about real estate management. It will contain information on the use of customer care strategies and other aspects of real estate changes at BAA in recent years and will shortly be published by Macmillan Press.

This focus on customer care is important, but does not feature strongly as a component of real estate strategy in companies studied in the following chapters. In place of a full chapter, the following brief synopsis includes the main points about BAA plc's real estate customer care and greater efficiency strategies.

BAA's real estate strategy

BAA's primary purpose is to run the main UK airports to provide a service for airlines and passengers. It has developed what was a secondary function – being a landlord – into a major income-earning component of the business. In doing so it has made real estate fundamental to corporate strategy.

BAA is now very determined to attract users, especially major space users such as airline maintenance, to their airports rather than see them sited overseas. Airports, both landside and airside, offer comprehensive shopping opportunities. They are landlords to most of the major shopping chains in the country and several specialist luxury stores. BAA is still an airport operating company but it is also very much a property company – not a vision promoted at privatisation.

BAA decided to change its relationship with tenants from one of conflict to one of customer care – to treat tenants as valued customers. This was in line with the main corporate policy of focusing on customer need. It was appreciated that this would be very different from the traditional culture of real estate services, which has been based on conflict – not giving anything away in making the deal. It would clearly be a new development in the property world, which BAA felt was not user-friendly; there was not a culture of client service or total quality management.

The focus of BAA's real estate strategy became to make money from satisfied customers. Six steps were identified as necessary for success. They were:

- researching what customers (tenants) want
- implementing it
- measuring success
- aiming for continuous improvement by providing more for less
- benchmarking
- training

Although BAA has succeeded, implementing change to address the issues raised by the research proved much harder than expected. Edington now realises that he underestimated the extent of the change needed and the time it would take. The basic problem was that the real estate team did not believe it was possible or would happen. They did not have the resources and did not believe that they would get more resources because they had not had them in the past.

The first attempt to implement change ended up in a false start. The second attempt was presented in much more detail to staff. It was backed by more training, milestones were identified and people were empowered to take action to meet them. Once the leaders were moving in the right direction the rest followed much more easily. To speed up change, some new managers who had experience of change management in other companies were employed.

The real estate team at BAA are not providing better customer care with no thought for cost, as the other aspect of their strategy is great efficiency – doing more for less. To help them to achieve this they have reviewed process management. BAA are seeking to gain from experience beyond the property world. The performance targets that BAA set themselves as landlords and which staff implement include five key targets for service to tenants. Rent increases will not be invoiced unless all five targets are met.

BAA real estate team have sought to attract tenants and keep them. Along the way they have learned a lot, and their book should be a very useful addition to the understanding of the role of real estate in corporate strategy.

The companies studied in the following chapters offer many experiences that will be directly relevant to corporate real estate users. The important point is for corporate real estate and business managers to make sure that their real estate assets meet their needs and make a strong contribution to corporate success. It will need vision. The following chapters provide ideas – not off-the-shelf solutions.

14 IBM UK Ltd

14.1 Introduction

IBM UK Ltd was one of the first UK companies to make significant real estate savings. It did so as part of a corporate strategy which turned the business round following a drop in sales and declining profitability. Had the market for mainframe computers not declined, or had the decline been forecast in time for new products to have seamlessly taken their place, the real estate team at IBM UK would not have been at the vanguard of change.

An important factor in the changes at IBM UK was that Michael Brooks, the Property Director, did not lose sight of the real estate team's role as a support service. He realised that the retrenching process had to take place without unduly disturbing profit-making activities. This does not mean that staff were not disturbed – some in the South Bank offices in London moved three times – but the focus was on providing accommodation that reflected and supported the way staff worked.

The main trading company IBM UK Ltd was selected because it records most of IBM's activity in the UK. The real estate team is based in this company. The ultimate parent company is International Business Machines Corporation (IBM Corp.), which is based in the USA. Its accounts have been used for comparative purposes in this chapter.

14.2 Catalyst for change

It is well known that IBM Corp., the star of the 1980s stock market, hit hard times in the early 1990s. Much has been written about the company's misplaced confidence in long-term profitability from their leadership in the mainframe computer market, their inability to predict the importance of the PC market and the stiff competition they faced from rival manufacturers. Changing demand left IBM with falling sales and, as initially its cost base had not changed, there was falling profitability. Terminal decline did not look impossible.

The problems did not affect all parts of this global company in the same way or at the same time. In the UK, turnover failed to grow in 1990 and when it fell during 1991 the organisation was still growing and profitable across the rest of Europe. The slump was felt first in the UK because the UK economy experienced a sharp decline at the same time as UK industry began moving away from mainframe computers and into networked personal computers (PCs) together with laptop PCs. This was ahead of the industry elsewhere.

Figures 14.1(a) and (b) show the turnover for the UK company, IBM UK Ltd, and for the parent global company based in the USA, IBM Corp., from

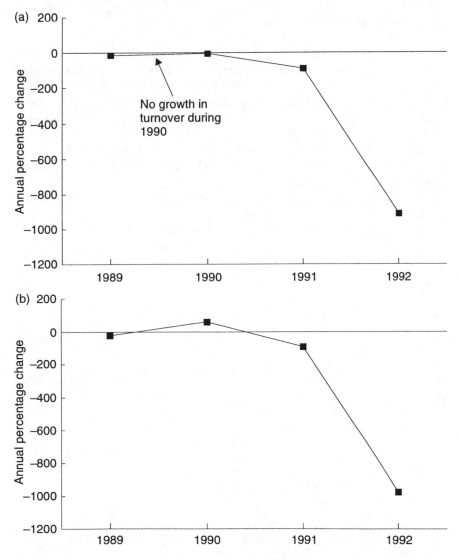

Figure 14.1 Percentage change in turnover for (a) IBM UK Ltd and (b) IBM Corp.

1989 until the end of 1992. It shows how the fall-off in sales was experienced in the UK during 1990, a full year ahead of the overall global business, which had growing sales during 1990.

The earlier decline suffered in the UK caused local management to realise sooner than in other parts of the company that action would be needed immediately if their business was to survive.

14.3   Turnover and costs

As discussed in Chapter 2, profitability is not just related to the level of sales or turnover – the level of costs is also important. When turnover falls without matching cuts in costs, the business rapidly becomes unprofitable. As shown in Figure 14.2, during the late 1980s costs had been under 90% of turnover. In 1990, while they fell to only 84% for IBM Corp., they rose to just over 90% of turnover for IBM UK.

As soon as IBM UK's turnover began to fall in 1991 this level of expenditure was unsustainable, and by the end of 1991 expenditure (costs) was almost at the same level as sales, as shown in Figure 14.3.

The graph in Figure 14.3 well illustrates the difficulty facing IBM UK. Sales can fall very quickly, and it is almost impossible to remain in operation and cut costs to match such a severe drop in sales. Although this chapter is very much about IBM UK cutting costs, all that the company actually managed to achieve was a decline in the rate at which costs rose. It was essential for IBM

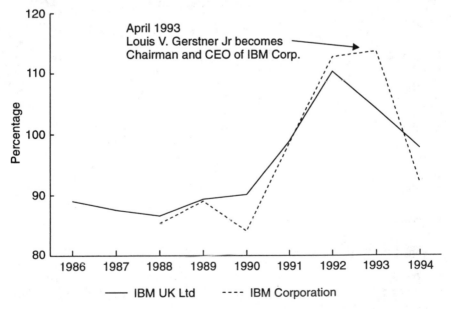

Figure 14.2 Costs as a percentage of turnover for IBM UK Ltd and IBM Corp.

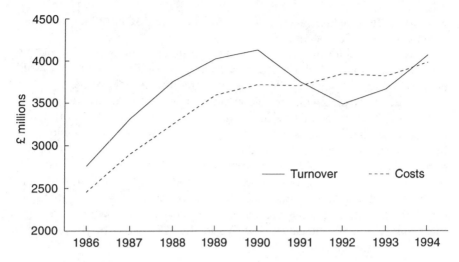

Figure 14.3 Turnover and costs: IBM UK Ltd. (Source: IBM UK Ltd annual reports)

UK's future that sales increased – rapidly. Hence the importance of ensuring that cost-cutting measures did not hinder the productivity of revenue earners. Indeed, it was important that everything possible was done to make their task easier.

Although moves were made almost immediately in the UK to introduce cost-saving changes, the situation did not really begin to improve until sales began to pick up after the end of 1992. IBM Corp., the ultimate parent company, continued to have costs rising as a percentage of turnover until a new Chief Executive Officer, Louis Gerstner, was appointed in 1993 (see Figure 14.2).

14.4   Realisation of the importance of real estate

Before the slump in sales hit the company, it was clear that costs would become more important. Michael Brooks described the sense of foreboding at the time as 'the fog was on the horizon'. During the late 1980s staff at IBM had studied developments in Japanese office layout, where shared desks had been introduced. As many of those working in sales and marketing are not in the office very frequently, the idea of sharing desks seemed worthy of further consideration.

An experiment during 1990, called BOOT 90, sought greater efficiency in the use of space. Small experiments in Richmond and Glasgow with staff space-sharing, but with everyone having an individual computer screen, were successful. They acknowledged 'common tools' (e.g. computers and tele-phones) for all office occupants.

In order to save further space a feature of a similar scheme in Birmingham was an arrangement for three people to share two computer screens. It failed because it had not acknowledged the way in which people worked.

IBM UK had been uncomfortable with the out-of-date, expensive buildings used to provide customer services in west London. They did not portray the desired image and there was no space for expansion. The management of IBM Corp. had been attracted by the real estate profits enjoyed by property entrepreneurs like Donald Trump. Joint ventures (JVs) with property compa-nies were seen as a way to leverage IBM's need for office accommodation. Feltham, west of London, was selected for a European JV with a leading UK developer to build the new customer service offices, which were to become the productive Bedfont Lakes. The JVs in the USA were to prove mostly financially unsuccessful.

14.5   The real estate target

When the severity of the slump in sales become clear in 1991, the role of real estate in the business's finances was already at the forefront of managers' minds. Unlike many business managers who turn a blind eye to real estate, those in IBM UK included it immediately in the cost-cutting exercise. The initial target agreed was to save £10m per annum in real estate costs.

14.6   Implementation

Space savings

In many people's minds, the key feature of IBM's real estate strategy in the early 1990s was the introduction of shared desks, or hot-desking, but this is only one part of the story. The real estate team were responsible for intro-ducing, together with other managers in the business, much more compre-hensive real estate changes. In doing so IBM UK developed the tactics needed to achieve their real estate targets. Understanding the underlying factors, including the difficulties encountered, is probably more valuable to corporate real estate managers than focusing on the final results – especially just the one highly publicised tactic of hot-desking.

The uncertain future meant that IBM UK were fighting for survival. As he planned to attack the first tranche of cost savings, Brooks was confident that they could succeed. During the time of super profits, accommodation requests had been met from central resources in a fairly generous manner, so that staff at all levels had more space than they needed.

Even so it is not easy to cut back on the use of space. Declaring space standards for specific grades of staff often bears no relationship to operational needs. Nevertheless, it was reassuring to calculate that implementing not unreasonable space standards would bring in the £10m savings. On paper, the reduction was possible.

Cutting the amount of space used is only the first stage of achieving a reduction in real estate expenditure. It must be matched by an equally rapid disposal programme.

It was important not to lose sight of the real estate department's role as a support service. The retrenching process had to take place without unduly disturbing profit-making activities.

Staff reductions

A significant contribution to the cost saving came because the business was contracting to become a leaner operation. Soon the senior management was reduced from 300 to 65. Staff numbers also declined. At the peak of the business in the late 1980s, IBM UK had employed over 18 500 people, including 12 500 in the headquarters offices and marketing. The remainder had been in manufacture. The 12 500 had been supported by about another 2000 people working on contracts, via agencies or occupying a small number of part-time posts.

The 12 500 members of staff had been reduced to 6500 by 1996, but were supported by more people working on contracts, via agencies or part-time: 6000 rather than the pre-slump 2000. Figure 14.4 shows the changes. Again they show how difficult it is to reduce costs. While staff numbers almost halved, to fall well below the levels in the 1980s, the result in costs was less dramatic, and they fell back only to the levels of the late 1980s. Of course, if inflation is taken into account the improvement will be greater.

On the surface, cutting staff numbers would suggest that space should become redundant, but when a few people go from here, and a few from there, it is very easy for the remaining staff to spread out to fill the space available. The downsizing must be managed if real estate requirements are also to fall.

Moving fast

At the time of tackling the savings to achieve the first tranche, there was an urgent need to move fast. Decisions were made quickly. They were based as much on experience as research. For example, the decision on which buildings to keep was based on their intrinsic value to the various IBM businesses.

The human factor

Trying to squeeze more people into existing office layouts without adversely disrupting their work and working relationships is difficult. IBM UK overcame

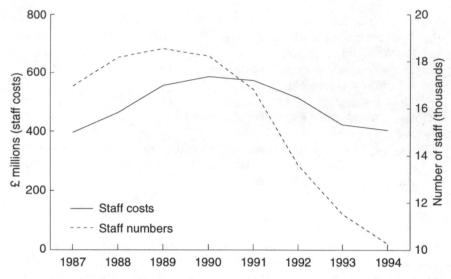

Figure 14.4 Staff numbers and staff costs: IBM UK Ltd. (Source: IBM UK Ltd annual reports)

many of the complications by achieving most space savings at the same time as staff were relocated. Having networked PCs and begun the installation of comprehensive databases, the need to store paper documents in filing cabinets and cupboards diminished. New space requirements did not have to provide for endless filing cabinets and cupboards, although some still exist. Open plan arrangements predominated, but those who managed people still had their own offices. Space was allocated for a work-unit to be managed as needed, rather than per individual. In 1991/92 across-the-board evaluations in size and efficiency of the workstation footprint and the size of individual offices were introduced and implemented in new layouts.

The easiest way of achieving the reduction was to allow staff to leave behind all unwanted furniture and papers when they moved to new offices. Sorting out and packing for a move is a tiring business, and rather than complain many are grateful to be able to walk away from papers that they have not used in years!

Space not occupied by people

Space savings have not just been focused on the space occupied by individual members of staff. Some fairly simple research showed that people space accounted for less than half of most offices, as shown in Table 14.1.

There has been a concerted effort to be restrained in the use of special space. Most of this space is not used for the intended purpose all day. For example, during the 1980s restaurants would only have been used for about

Table 14.1 The use of office space by
IBM UK prior to reorganisation in the
early 1990s

People space	35–40%
Special space restaurant data centre meeting education customer space	25–30%
Support space circulation post room print storage workshop	>25%

two hours per day, and there would normally have been meeting rooms sufficient to satisfy peak demand plus a 15% margin. Now the policy has changed. The number of meeting rooms has been reduced to below the peak demand level. Those needing space have to match their meetings to the times when the rooms are free or use another option – they can meet in a restaurant. These are open for long hours, with tea and coffee available. Facilities are varied and staff are encouraged to meet over coffee or round a lunch table. At the same time as remaining open longer, the restaurant space has been reduced so that staff who wish to miss the crush can dine early or late.

The same philosophy is spreading to all sorts of facilities, and has resulted in fewer print rooms and stationery stores. When it is just that little bit less convenient to copy, staff are more likely to go electronic.

Ambience

The new facilities are to a high standard. Walking round the offices it is clear that considerable thought has been given to design. Some aspects are exciting and others restful (but never dull) – the impression is of being in buildings where things are meant to happen and do happen.

Internal rents

Another prong in the attack on space was the introduction of internal rents. Business units began to pay rent for the space occupied and facilities used.

Charges for normal office space were agreed and then included automatically in the accounts.

Introducing internal rents had its problems, especially when charges were calculated for occasional use of space, such as meeting rooms. All business units had sufficient rooms for normal use, but all occasionally needed more rooms. One part of IBM allowed the businesses to hire or rent meeting space. This inevitably led to arguments over the price level, but after real comparisons with external costs the internal opportunities gained in attractiveness, which met with the approval of the businesses.

Now that charging for space has served the purpose of making managers more aware of the cost of the facility, there is a debate within IBM UK as to whether internal rents should be continued. The concern is that business units remain in control of space, preventing its use by others, just because their business unit has paid for it. The aim would be to replace internal rents with a culture which frowns on any space being under-utilised. Already some senior managers are making their individual offices available for general use when they are out. Some, including Brooks, are dispensing with private offices in exchange for the use of a range of facilities which are available when needed but are not dedicated to individual use.

There are now fewer and fewer individual offices in IBM buildings. The focus is on teamwork, which is not easily promoted by individual offices.

Bedfont Lakes

Against this environment, the design and layout for the new Bedfont Lakes building in Feltham to house the national marketing centre was developed. It incorporated all the new ideas and the lessons from the Glasgow, Richmond and Birmingham pilots (BOOT 90 experiment). The aim was to provide space that served the way people worked.

In 1992, when it opened, Bedfont Lakes was at the vanguard of business flexibility and shared space. The offices achieved up to 30% space-saving compared with traditionally arranged offices. Four years later these offices are still seen as revolutionary by many, although several other UK firms have similar accommodation.

It seems a little strange now to learn that during one of the pilot projects IBM, a computer manufacturer, tried to reduce space requirements by reducing access to PCs! IBM UK now works very differently, and staff all have their own PCs, with many having laptops which they can use anywhere. Within company buildings they either use their laptops (on their own or in docking stations) or may switch to a PC. Some staff now have desks with as many as three PCs and terminals. It is clear that IT connectivity is a key driver in the business.

The offices at Bedfont Lakes are divided between the various work units. Banners mark the doorways leading off the balcony atrium walkways into each different unit. Between the atrium and the external walls a further corridor/walkway links all the different units, making informal contact between business units easy.

The accommodation consists of individual workstations and banks of personal cupboards and filing cabinets, plus further cabinets and cupboards to hold business papers. Individual offices take up some of the external window space. Some of the workstations are occupied by staff who are permanently based at Bedfont Lakes. Others are used by more than one person – the shared desk arrangement (see Chapter 6). The number who share a desk or a group of desks depends on the frequency with which they use the office. Although now widely called 'hot-desking', at IBM UK the term used is 'shared desk space'. Each individual has a cupboard and cabinet to store personal belongings when not at a desk.

The restaurant is at the centre of Bedfont Lakes. Situated on the ground floor of the atrium, it is open to provide drinks and snacks all day, plus a full service for main meals. It is a hub, with many meetings being held around its tables. It is a restaurant where mobile phones are not banned!

The restaurant leads into the main foyer and into the corporate entertainment space in front of the main client presentation lecture room. Additionally, the company defrays part of its costs by charging some of the other tenants on the Bedfont Lakes Park who do not have their own full restaurant facilities and need somewhere for staff to eat.

Touchdown facilities

A further innovation was the introduction of touchdown facilities, which were fully incorporated into the initial provision at Bedfont Lakes. These facilities provided for those who, although not based at Bedfont Lakes, need to work from the building. Facilities, many of which can be booked, range from lockers and wall-mounted telephones to individual quiet rooms with a PC. There are docking stations for laptops and PCs linked to the main company databases. Full printing and copying facilities are provided, together with official stationery. The range and design of facilities has been reviewed and updated since the initial installation.

Since IBM purchased Lotus Development Corporation, the company has started to standardise on Lotus products, including Lotus Notes groupware (see Chapter 5). This is making it easier to serve all staff needs at each touchdown PC. Staff can draw down their own specific information from the networked servers. The touchdown facility is well managed so that all facilities are kept operational with adequate paper supplies. Information is provided on where to gain help and details of all other support facilities, including the times of meals.

Touchdown facilities are now available in most IBM buildings – they have become part of the business culture. The space available at each facility is adequate but certainly not generous, as they are not designed for permanent use. The touchdown rooms have the ambience of a university computer laboratory. This analogy is further enhanced by the intensity of concentration on the faces of those working on the PCs!

Touchdown facilities are often vital for capturing business. Staff can leave a client, make for the nearest touchdown and be able prepare a detailed proposal exactly suited to the client's needs using information that in earlier times would only have been available in their own office. They can also print it out on official stationery and fax it to the client. It is a more attractive option than crouching over a laptop in a car or hotel bedroom.

IBM is a global company with global clients. However IBM organises its national and regional marketing and sales personnel, it can never match the organisational and physical location of all of its clients. There are always going to be staff with clients a long way from their base office. The touchdown facilities are vital, especially for those on the move. Bedfont Lakes is close to Heathrow Airport, and IBM's London South Bank offices at Waterloo are near the Eurostar terminal.

It is now some years since the offices at Bedfont Lakes opened. The methods tried there and at other key sites have now been incorporated throughout the IBM UK estate. Sometimes the layout of existing buildings means that space standards cannot be so efficient. Nevertheless, the benefits to the company of being efficient and (most importantly) effective in the use of space are well appreciated by those now enjoying the renewed profitability of the company.

Success and new targets for the real estate team

The real estate team is a lean organisation of 12 people, and most of the professional and facilities management needs are commissioned or outsourced, which is seen to bring greater flexibility while retaining management control through contract conditions. Importantly, the real estate team has the support of IBM UK's senior managers. This is based on their early recognition of the importance of real estate and also on the ability of the real estate team to deliver the requested savings. Since 1991 new targets are set each year. The real estate team are constantly addressing the conflicts that arise from cutting costs and assets at the same time as the business is growing.

IBM UK averaged 22 m^2 (245 ft^2) per office-based employee in 1991, but by 1995 was using only 17 m^2 (185 ft^2) per person; the comparable figures for their USA operation are 28 m^2 (300 ft^2) in 1991 down to 25 m^2 (250 ft^2) in 1995. This is an overall measurement identifying the amount of space used in the business rather than the amount of space occupied by an individual employee.

The Glasgow experience

An example of the changes within IBM UK and the subsequent use of real estate is illustrated by the provision of offices in Glasgow. In 1989 new offices were occupied providing 3500 m^2 (38 000 ft^2) of office space – 3000 m^2 (33 000 ft^2) for the current needs of the local marketing department and the remainder to provide for expansion. Using shared desks it was expected to house 130 people using 95 workstations. This was one of the successful ventures under the BOOT 90 experiment.

In 1994 the office was closed and the marketing department moved into 420 m^2 (4500 ft^2) at the company's nearby Greenock factory, with 95 m^2 (1000 ft^2) of serviced office space in the Glasgow city centre being used to meet customers. For a number of reasons this arrangement proved unpopular with staff and customers.

Early in 1996, to achieve more efficient and effective accommodation, the ground floor of the Glasgow building was brought back into use for the local marketing department as a new-style business centre. Now 45–50 people have use of 375 m^2 (4000 ft^2), of which one third is laid out for customer use. There are 25 workstations with just one individual office and one meeting room for staff use. No staff have their own workstation or office – this is a system which has been called 'hotelling'. The Glasgow office is the first IBM location to be totally without 'owned' space. Even the location manager does not have sole right to the individual office. The upper floors of the building have been sublet.

The asset base

The value of real estate fixed assets has not changed significantly during the 1990s. Figure 14.5(a) shows how the value of land and buildings within the balance sheet assets has remained fairly stable, despite the pressures on the company.

Change has come where the effect directly affects the bottom line in the commitments for rent – a cost charged directly to the profit and loss account. Figure 14.5(b) shows how the value of lease commitments has fallen since the end of 1991. Although the real estate rent costs fell from the end of 1991 onwards, as shown in Figure 14.2 the overall reduction of costs in the UK was not significant until a year later.

Figures 14.5(a) and (b) are based on the IBM UK Ltd annual accounts, so while they clearly show the overall position of real estate within the company with regard to value, they are not necessarily a perfect indication of the amount being used or owned because property values have been changing over time and from region to region. It has been the role of the real estate team to work with the changing real estate market to achieve the best for IBM UK.

14.7   A fundamental conclusion

It is easy to focus on hot-desking and cost savings and miss what is probably much more important for IBM UK, which is that the real estate changes have

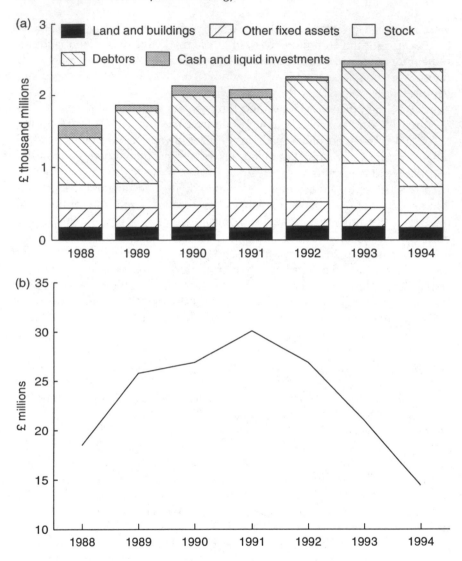

Figure 14.5 IBM UK Ltd: (a) balance sheet assets and (b) lease obligations for land and buildings. (Source: IBM UK Ltd annual reports)

been part of a process that focused not only on savings but on supporting those getting the business – the people making the sales of PCs and software in new markets. Cutting costs was important, but without the new sales the business would have collapsed. After all, while saving £10 million per annum in real estate costs is impressive, especially over such a short period, it hardly makes an impression on the thousands of millions of pounds per annum spent by IBM UK.

Nevertheless, even five years earlier these savings in real estate would been difficult or impossible. They were only possible because of IT developments – databases, servers and groupware that have replaced the filing cabinets brimming with papers.

The real estate changes at IBM have had a clear focus on providing what the staff really needed. This has been the physical support for their PC connectivity systems, locations where teams could meet and work and places where they could go to link up with their colleagues wherever they happened to be. The savings have come from taking out of the real estate provision that which was not needed – the over-spacious offices, stores of paper, space for expansion, empty restaurants and redundant copying and printing facilities.

The business has turned round in part because the real estate team provided what was needed. As the new facilities are changed, upgraded and fine tuned, it is clear that the real estate team did not get everything right first time – no one can. What they did was keep in mind the purpose of the provision (the vision), and if it was not perfect they tried try again.

Unlike cost savings there are no figures that can be quoted to illustrate the benefits of providing the right facilities, except to point out that every time an IBM employee gained a sale from responding faster than the competition, the real estate facilities probably had a part to play.

14.8 Transferable experience

The key points that can be implemented by other companies are:

- the importance of senior management appreciating the role of real estate
- incorporating real estate into the main business strategy
- remembering that real estate is a service supporting profit-making activities
- ensuring that real estate provision meets business needs
- making IT and connectivity facilities available to staff wherever they are working
- using shared desk space (hot-desking)
- easing out of surplus real estate facilities without excessive disturbance
- not providing excessive facilities to allow for undetermined growth
- combining downsizing with moving
- providing all special and support facilities for average and not peak demand
- gain advantage from studying businesses operations elsewhere, even overseas
- internal rents can help promote change but may not be a long-term solution

15 BT plc

15.1 Time for change

BT is one of the largest companies in Europe. Not surprisingly, although not a property company, it has one of the largest commercial property holdings in the UK. During the period from 1990 to 1995, real estate operating costs began at around £1.2 billion per annum and reduced to £980 million per annum – amounts larger than the turnover of many businesses. But this is in the context of a turnover for BT of £13.67 billion in 1994, which dwarfs most businesses.

Privatisation, when BT stopped being a state monopoly, was the biggest catalyst for change. From then on it had to make profits for its shareholders. Following privatisation came deregulation of the telecoms sector, which has made the UK market the freest telecommunications market in the world. Even so, the market regulation through Oftel limited the prices that BT could charge and the services it could sell in the UK. To retain its pre-eminent position BT had both to compete successfully with global operators allowed to enter the UK market and to take advantage of profitable opportunities overseas.

All round, the pressure mounted to become cost-competitive and at the same time to gear the business to meet the demands of being a lead player in the 'information revolution' in all its markets.

Not only did BT have too much space, it also had poor quality accommodation, with inefficient usage of space and excessive operating costs. Change was essential, but the role that real estate was to play was not obvious. Indeed, in the years immediately following privatisation BT's capital spend on real estate had increased, as shown in Figure 15.1.

15.2 Real estate reorganisation

Realisation of the strategic importance of real estate

The strategic importance of real estate to BT became apparent when Michael Dow, a consultant from Jones Lang Wootton, was called upon in 1990 to

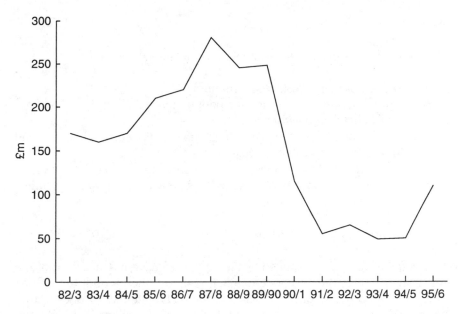

Figure 15.1 Capital spend on land and buildings by BT plc. (Source: BT plc Group Property 1996)

run the BT Group's real estate office during an interregnum. He was joined by Alan White from the TSB Group in 1991.

Together they began to draw together the facts of the BT real estate operation, which could not be ignored. They drew figures from all the disparate estate operations and found that the total running cost was £1.2 billion per annum and rising by at least the rate of inflation. As the property boom switched to slump, many of the offices were 'over-rented', i.e. the rents being paid were much higher than market levels, and with upward only rent review clauses reductions were unlikely. The situation was much worse in London. As a stopgap measure the Group Finance Director's approval was needed before any new space could be acquired, and all lease ends and lease breaks were operated, *even* on those buildings not immediately on the disposal schedules.

Real estate was now on the main board agenda, and the first move was to centralise the group's real estate operation under Dow and White. Soon the 24 district estate management posts were history. A real estate team of 200 was based in London. No one else in BT could deal with property or the strategic investment in new and refurbished buildings. The days (real or apocryphal) when two BT businesses would outbid each other for the same building passed into history. In 1993 White was appointed Director Group Property, while Dow continued to be retained as a consultant and subsequently moved back to the JLW business.

New policy

The policy for the use of real estate was formulated:

- to reduce property costs to a minimum
- to provide appropriate space for people and equipment in a technologically changing environment
- to provide buildings and space which enhance the corporate image and
  help to attract and retain people
- to ensure that real estate does not tie up corporate resources unnecessarily
- to ensure that a global real estate service is available to support expanding
  overseas business

Audit and strategy plan preparation

Four imperatives were identified as the key to effective management of the
portfolio. The first, the corporate commitment, and the second, the linkage
between the corporate business plan and the real estate plan, work together
almost as one. The third is the powerful IT infrastructure and network. The
fourth makes use of the IT infrastructure.

A complete computerised portfolio audit was undertaken using a system
that is now online to over 200 locations. This has become an ongoing activity
and gives the real estate team a detailed understanding of the physical
attributes and condition of each property in the estate. It also contains details
of ownership, occupation and, where appropriate, leases. Figure 15.2 shows how
the audit assesses a variety of detailed areas under the four main criteria of:

- costs
- value
- efficiency
- quality

This audit fed back into the corporate and real estate plans, and a very
detailed assessment of space and costs was produced for the whole portfolio.
Using the business plan as a guide, it was then projected over time. Divisional
business plans and unit plans were incorporated to assist long-term planning.
At times this has required a corporate willingness to champion integrated
business/real estate plans, even when involving painful decisions resented by
those in operational divisions.

Internal rents

The Director Group Property has also needed the full support of senior
management to implement the introduction of charging business units a

Figure 15.2 Portfolio audit: seeks to identify information in the cost, value, efficiency and quality sectors. (Source: D. A. White)

market rent and utility and other occupational costs. He sees this as essential for bringing discipline into space use efficiency and sensible parameters into overall business/property decision-making. As in other organisations, there has been considerable resistance ('a lot of grief') from those who have grown used to accommodation being a free resource and who fear that occupation charges will make their division unprofitable.

The introduction of internal charging was allied to the strict control of departmental budgets so that, although business units may choose to spend more on increased office specification or a slightly more generous space allocation, it has to be at the expense of other operational costs, such as labour or equipment.

The disposal programme

Seventy-five per cent of the estate is freehold. These are mainly operational buildings, purpose-built for the original analogue telephony system. The remainder, mainly office accommodation, warehouse and industrial units and retail outlets, is leased. Landlords do not want to lose BT, a highly rated tenant with an AAA cash flow. This has made it difficult for the company to unburden itself from expensive leases.

Although BT has made dynamic changes to its estate, its sheer size, the lack of flexibility and BT's good financial standing have been obstacles to speedy change. At any time, BT has a number of empty buildings on the estate which are awaiting disposal but which still require security, minimal maintenance and possibly rent payments. The process of change on this scale takes time.

BT, as a major property owner, finds that its actions can be sufficient to change local markets. It has to move carefully. To some extent, it needs to manage the real estate market-place: BT's real estate team may need to hold surplus space off the market because of pre-existing oversupply or introduce new stock to take advantage of undersupply. Different policies are needed for the leased and freehold premises.

Vacating leased buildings held on long leases without break clauses has proved difficult. Where landlords have been willing to consider releasing the company from lease commitments or shortening the lease, the price of a one-off payment of advance rent and amelioration of accrued repairs liability has been high. It can, however, still be attractive to BT, because rent is sometimes only 40% of annual outgoings for some of their buildings.

Other landlords, especially those with well sited buildings which BT had occupied for a number of years, have been keener to allow BT to give up its leases, as they were able to relet at higher rents. The slump in property values and rents restricted landlords' opportunities for more recently let properties, where BT's rent was at or above current market levels.

In some cases BT sublet the redundant accommodation. Owners of buildings on sites with development potential have also been keener to agree to BT vacating. For example, in Birmingham, BT worked with an existing landlord and came to an arrangement to give up its lease on an unsuitable office block in exchange for a new building, built to its specification, in the new nearby central office, entertainment and residential district of Brindley Place. The vacated building will be redeveloped by the landlord, who will capitalise on the general improvement to the area brought about by the Brindley Place development and nearby urban improvements. It is one of the 'win–win' scenarios that BT has tried to find as it seeks solutions to its real estate problems.

BT's real estate team are proud of their success in selling surplus land and buildings for conversion to alternative uses, including student accommodation, hotel, residential conversion and development, retail warehouse, fast food, religious, light industrial and leisure uses. Developers and adjoining owners wishing to expand have been keen purchasers. BT has also established an in-house real estate development company, Southgate Developments Ltd, to redevelop its surplus operational sites and buildings, mostly as joint ventures.

BT's retail premises are mostly in main shopping locations, as this serves customer needs. This is also seen as a good real estate policy, because should they become redundant there will be a good demand from retailers.

The freehold properties, which were mostly designed specifically for analogue telephone services, present another range of problems, because there is no obvious need for the redundant switching centres and other specialist operational buildings. New uses are needed if they are to find new owners.

With so much accommodation becoming redundant, protecting its value and maximising development potential is essential for the realisation of assets to produce new resources for the business. BT is monitoring local government planning policies across the UK, especially the production of local and unitary development plans, to influence policies and proposals which might encourage or inhibit profitable redevelopment (White and Taylor, 1995). By 1995 its fees to consultants for undertaking this work had exceeded £1 million (see Chapter 11).

Overall, the disposal programme has concentrated on getting rid of high-cost units and looking for the quick routes out. It has meant finding the most marketable units, not just the ones that were currently surplus. The downsizing exercise is so large that both good and bad buildings have been vacated and sold. It has proved invaluable to BT not only to know its own portfolio and its potential but also to know its landlords' circumstances, portfolios and liquidity levels.

The size of the task was so large that three parts of the policy were identified as of key importance:

- the UK office plan
- the London and home counties office plan
- flexible working – Workstyle 2000

A Senior Steering Group headed by the Director Group Property was established, with teams responsible for each of the three activities meeting monthly and reporting to it. These teams are formed by staff from different parts of BT according to need, but particularly including members of the real estate team and from the personnel department.

Action to implement the overall real estate strategy is being taken with regard to other properties, such as switching centres, and other functions, such as refurbishment, but the amount of energy required and its importance to the success of the overall strategy is not seen as being as great as those matters highlighted for the attention of the Senior Steering Group.

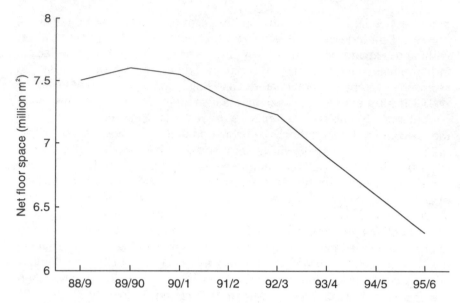

Figure 15.3 Total net floor space for BT plc. (Source: BT plc Group Property 1996)

The first achievements

The result has been a reduction in the size of BT's estate since 1992 of 250 000 to 300 000 m^2 per annum (Figure 15.3), and this is expected to continue at this rate until 2000. The difficulties of disposing of all properties immediately they become redundant means that the estate has been carrying on average 150 000–200 000 m^2 of excess space each year.

Real estate expenditure fell by £220 million between 1990/91 – when real estate became part of the corporate strategy – and 1994/95. The capital spend on real estate fell dramatically in 1990 and remained low in the following years (see Figure 15.1). A recent increase reflects programmes aimed at adapting the estate to meet the need for quality improvements. This is the result of the implementation of the third of the key components of the policy, as is now discussed.

15.3   Flexible offices

The aim in BT for all accommodation is to match people with technology and workplace to bring out the best in all three. There is a strong belief among senior management that real estate is a powerful tool in the challenge to change culture and optimise efficiency and productivity.

A specific project, known as Workstyle 2000, is the innovative strategy to implement these ideas by creating new working environments. The aim is to meet BT's business needs in the new millennium with quality offices which enable staff to make best use of BT's technology to meet customers' requirements efficiently. This includes the flexibility to adapt to new technology as it is developed and the freedom to change work processes, including work away from the office.

BT's real estate team market their success by saying that they provide 'the office you wish you had'. Creating a cultural change is as important to BT as embracing new technology. Workstyle 2000 is being designed to:

- stimulate team and project work
- maximise people's potential
- maximise technological advantage
- project the image of a world-class organisation
- reduce operating costs
- support flexible and home working
- support relocation to London's periphery and the provinces

The drivers

Frank Duffy's architectural practice DEGW published *The Intelligent Building in Europe* (DEGW and Tecnibank, 1992), which introduced the concept of the computer-integrated building being the norm from 1995. The opening of IBM's new office in 1992 at Bedfont Lakes was well reported and influenced the thinking of many involved in office layouts. These showed what was possible – especially for a high-tech company.

Important as these were, the existence of change elsewhere does not make it happen in another business without a great deal of effort. A key driver for BT was Neil McLocklin, a member of the real estate department, who, for an MBA dissertation (McLocklin, 1993), studied the creation of office working environments most suitable for the 2000s. His thesis 'Flexible Working Practices' arrived on White's desk just as he was pondering the problems faced by BT.

McLocklin had studied the concepts and practical implementation issues faced by those who had already implemented some of these practices in the UK, and was to become a driving force for turning the ideas into reality for BT. He was appointed project manager of an implementation team reporting via the multidisciplinary control board of personnel staff to the Senior Steering Committee.

Another key driver was the then Group Managing Director of BT, Michael Hepher, who was horrified by the large, fragmented, inefficient and expensive real estate occupied by BT in central London. He saw the need to do something – and fast. Commitment at the highest level always helps move projects forward!

Workstyle 2000

The project gained the name Workstyle 2000 to reflect the changing style of work which would be needed in the future. It focuses on interlinking four systems – IT, management, working practices and built environment – through an iterative process, as shown in Figure 15.4.

Without the changes in technology, much of the rest would not have been possible. The IT network, with its supporting management and systems processes, is the primary form of communications and the means to select the information, build systems and documents to support customer services. The aim is for buildings within the Workstyle 2000 concept to be comfortable and efficient environments in which staff can access and use the network and facilitate the other main form of communication – face-to-face contact between members of staff and with customers. They form communication hubs supporting a wide and disparate population.

To establish Workstyle 2000 the BT team questioned everything – all processes and, importantly, all the assumptions on which they were based. Recognising a need and developing proposals to address it is only the start; senior management support is vital. In BT, senior management realised that the use of information and not the performance of set activities would drive

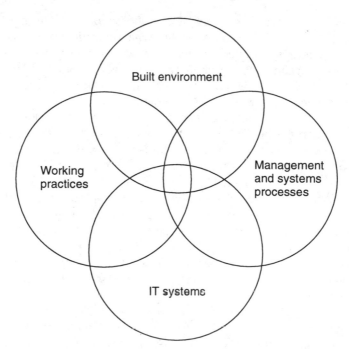

Figure 15.4 Workstyle 2000: IT systems are an integral part of the whole. (Source: BT Property Group)

the business forward in the future. They accepted and supported the new concepts and then supported the strategy through the most costly and time-consuming stage – making it happen. It is change management on a grand scale, and much of the process is beyond the discussion of the real estate issues.

In a global business, BT faces constant pressure from all sides to offer more for less – it has to be able to move fast and operate around the clock. Workstyle 2000 has been designed to make this possible. It is easy to move, to create new teams and to work wherever necessary.

The key features of the new facilities are:

- workstation flexibility
- staff can access their personal work from any PC
- powerful email
- 'friendly' video-conferencing
- staff can relocate for £150 rather than £2000 per person
- single filing facility – working towards the paperless office
- voice recognition software
- flexible, non-specialist, open-plan layout
- sensitively located offices
- environmentally friendly
- specification at least to British Council of Offices standards
- project work rooms
- quiet rooms (no communications!) for report writing etc.
- meeting rooms
- shared workstations (hot-desking)
- 'touchdown' workstations for visiting staff
- flexible, attractive staff facilities, such as a 'Parisian café'

Unrolling the real estate

BT began the search for suitable out-of-London premises. Westside, near Apsley, Hertfordshire, close to the M25, was leased. It had been speculatively built three years earlier and was highly suitable for the planned flexible working methods. This extended to the lease terms: 15 years with a tenant's break clause after 10 years.

Westside was fitted out in 1994. Two buildings at the award-winning Stockley Park, in London's western corridor to the UK silicon valley, are being fitted out for occupation in 1996. The next stage will be a building to the north-east or south-east of London.

Locations are being chosen to be within reasonable travelling distances for staff and to put BT in areas where suitable future staff will reside. A mapping exercise revealed that of the 17 500 staff currently working in London 70% live within the M25. By the financial year 1999/2000 only 6000–7000 will remain in central London.

In the three years from 1995 BT can vacate nearly 100 000 m² of accommodation in central London by invoking lease end or break clauses. Over the same period, 11 250 will move – mostly to the new Workstyle 2000 sites, where, for many, the journey to work will be counter to the rush hour flows.

Workstyle 2000 will be implemented in other BT offices, especially the new offices in Birmingham and Northern Ireland. Those staff remaining in London will eventually have similar facilities, restricted only by the constraints of older buildings, although the aim is to keep only those buildings that will generally meet BT's needs. The London office estate will have been reduced from 64 to six buildings.

Westside – the first Workstyle 2000 building

New Workstyle 2000 buildings are intelligent buildings with the flexibility to support changing communications technology. The core of the IT structure is the multi-mode fibre vertical spines up the building, with horizontal flood wiring using Ethernet cabling and power supplies direct to each desk through raised floor grommets. The furniture is designed with channels for the cables within its structure.

At Westside work areas are divided into 3 m × 7.5 m deep spaces. Lightly fritted glass panels are used for internal partitions to cellular offices, meeting rooms etc. so that daylight from the external walls and the atria filters through the building. The 3 m high ceiling enhances the light quality in the deep plan spaces. The building has a variable air volume control-activated system with recessed perimeter radiant heating.

There is a strong sense of space when walking round Westside. The offices are very clear, with wide spaces between groups or lines of workstations. The spaces are broken up by groups of filing cabinets that provide two wide drawers per person and cupboards for team papers and equipment. Occasional round tables with four chairs have been provided for informal meetings. Each workstation has a set of small drawers and connections for the user's PC.

Staff were asked not to bring more than four crates and their PC to the building. This is the maximum that is moved when staff change desks/offices. In fact, 20% of the people moving in did not need a removal service – all they brought was a briefcase!

The office spaces are almost clear of papers, without even illicit stores in the only cupboards – wardrobes provided for coats. Most information that the staff working at Westside require is available on the BT network. It seems that staff simply do not need extra piles of paper. Laser printers are provided at the rate of one per 50 people and sited in bays alongside photocopying facilities, and even these are little used. While not a paperless office, Westside has much less paper than most offices. Consequently less floor space is needed for printing facilities and for storage.

Senior staff have individual offices, but there are only a few of these, with just 4% cellularisation. Some special arrangements apply where security is a consideration: for example, some personnel staff have dedicated laser printers by their workstations.

Sixty bookable meeting rooms are sized to take four, eight, 12 and 20 people. For those that find the open plan space and telephone calls too disruptive there are quiet desks, mostly six in a room, but also some singles; quiet rooms do not have telephone connections.

Project rooms

Project rooms have eight desks supported by IT and communication connections. These can be booked for one week or up to three months. The teams use their own PCs and printers, and request any specialised furniture. The flexibility of bookable project rooms enables the salespeople to come together to work on specific tenders with very little trouble – the logistics are as simple as making a phone call.

Hot-desking

Three hundred and fifty people, about 24% of the people working at Westside, are hot-desking. They share desks with others in their team. Mostly these are sales and marketing staff who only rarely visit the building, with the most intensive use of desks being 40 people sharing 10 desks. The hot desks are smaller than the normal workstations, with just a straight desk and no return. Some have docking stations for laptop PCs.

Additionally, there is a 'touchdown' facility where staff based in other buildings can work. Set in separate rooms, this service is similar to the hot-desking facility. Staff can use the PCs provided and call up their own email and other work on the BT network. These bookable facilities are only in the early stages of use within BT, and parallel facilities now exist in London, Edinburgh, Ipswich and Cardiff, with another planned for the new offices at Stockley Park. It is planned to replicate them throughout the UK office portfolio.

Facilities support

Westside is run by a facilities management office, and one internal telephone extension number is used to report all problems, from building defects to software difficulties. When staff move from one team to another, their crates and their PC are moved overnight, the telephone number and other communications links are rerouted and the cost is only £150 per person. The low cost of 'churn' encourages flexibility within the business operation. The building even has a page on the World-Wide Web to which BT staff and visitors can turn for information.

The ground floor is the meeting place for this 'mini-town'. There are no walls between the three atria which house the Parisian café, the restaurant, a shop and the marketing and conference centre – it forms one large social centre. The spaces are vast, with the glass-sided lifts taking the eye up to the glass atria roof 20 m above.

A corporate centre

The managing director of one of the BT businesses, BT Personal Communications, has made Westside his base, together with the 10 directors of that business. There is a boardroom for his use, but unlike previous BT practice this can also be booked for use by others. There are also two directors from other parts of BT in the building. The willingness of senior management to work from the building has ensured that it is not seen by others as a backwater.

BT has clearly put a lot of effort and expense into making Westside and Workstyle 2000 work. The quality of the accommodation, the staff facilities and the support services are first-class.

Adjustments to Workstyle 2000

Over the short period that Westside has been in use there have been remarkably few changes. It has been found that little use is made of the round tables and chairs for informal meetings. The four-person meeting rooms are unpopular. The quiet rooms have been little used, and some have already been converted into further touchdown facilities. The building is eerily free of signs, and desks have been numbered to provide location guides.

If people miss things about their old offices or have more difficult journeys these disadvantages seem, at least in part, to be offset by some aspects of the new offices. People are using the Parisian café throughout the day, not just to snack and chat but to hold meetings and to work on papers and laptops. The new facility at Stockley Park will be very similar, but will have fewer round tables for informal meetings, fewer four-person meeting rooms and quiet rooms, and the desks will be numbered as a matter of course. The touchdown facilities will be more comprehensive.

BT is now seeking to find out whether Workstyle 2000 really works. The overall impression within the real estate team is that the managers of teams based at Westside are pleased with the work environment and the flexible working possibilities, and feel that they are gaining greater productivity. In response to a simple questionnaire circulated about nine months after initial occupation, 75% of occupants said that they were generally happy with their work environment. It was a slow process to get managers to agree to move their staff into Westside. Clearly there must be good messages coming out of the building – the real estate team have had no problem filling the spaces at the next Workstyle 2000 building at Stockley Park.

It is not an easy task to measure increases in productivity when there have been such extensive changes, but surveys are being undertaken. Even if productivity changes can be quantified the reasons may not be clear. External matters, such as improved or worse journeys to work will influence replies. The policy is to move ahead slowly, tackling each problem that arises.

The Workstyle 2000 team are becoming more ambitious and are seeking greater refinements. The aim is to set internal environmental control standards that give individuals much greater control of their environment especially with regard to heat and light. Since Westside was open Becker and Steele's book *Workplace by Design* (1995) has been published, providing further stimulus towards creating the ideal working environment.

The requirements for Stockley Park are being implemented by a team that has cross-company multi-disciplinary support from all divisions, whether or not they will be using the building in the initial occupation. Experts include building facilities managers, real estate professionals, human resource managers, industrial relations specialists, communication and IT engineers and, on occasions, union representatives. When the planning was in hand for Westside, many of these representatives only became involved on an *ad hoc* basis. Now all are showing greater commitment. Resources were provided to support a two-day exhibition in London for staff to see how Westside operated and the facilities planned for Stockley Park. Marketing of Workstyle 2000 is becoming much more proactive.

Density of occupation

The 17 500 m^2 of Westside currently contains 1150 workstations and is used by 1500 IT account-holders. Each member of the BT staff has an account and can only be registered at one building. The aim is to increase the number of account-holders based at Westside by increasing the use of hot-desking and touchdown facilities. It is being done on a trial-and-error basis, with the numbers being increased slowly and then waiting to see if the concept still works.

Work patterns are becoming more flexible as people absorb the changes and consider how to adapt to the new possibilities. Already more work is being undertaken at home and while travelling. In a recent survey, 89% of the people at Westside said that they would like to be able work at home some of the time. There are no plans to move workstations closer together, although it feels spacious now. If the desks come closer together there is a concern that the system would not work – it would be noisier and it would begin to feel congested. It is expected that, by 1997, up to 2000 people will be based at Westside.

Future plans

Changes are planned in working methods within BT and a number of experiments are under way. Some of these are being tried out within the Workstyle 2000 environment, for example:

- a 'wireless' environment (but with wires still needed for power and wide bandwidth for interactive video and other high traffic services)
- information compression – not yet available
- eye-to-eye video
- email to include video sequences
- disk storage of files and a completely paperless office
- automatic information decay

The overall objectives are to seek improvement by:

- reducing operating costs and increasing BT's competitive position
- providing appropriate space for people and equipment
- achieving greater flexibility
- creating space that enhances corporate image
- ensuring that real estate is not capital-intensive

It has been estimated that BT will gain savings of upwards of 150 000 m^2 of office space over the next 10 years because it will no longer be necessary for people to work from the same, or even any, workstation every day.

15.4   The real estate team

To achieve these changes BT's real estate team recognise that they have needed expertise spanning four key areas:

- effective linking of business and real estate strategy plans
- asset management: minimising cost and maximising value
- design and provision of world-class office environments and technology
- efficient management of the operational portfolio

It is noteworthy that the 'efficient management of the operational portfolio' is fourth on their list. In many corporations it is the main responsibility of the real estate or facilities management section – they do not offer the first three services.

BT has one of the first corporate real estate teams to achieve quality accreditation under BS EN ISO 9001, and the internal monitoring shows that it is continuing to improve the service it provides.

BT has begun to benchmark its buildings both internally and against other UK corporate real estate operators. They were one of the founder members of the IPD Operational Property Databank (see Chapter 11).

Despite its size the team is insufficient to cover all the surveying work. Consultants are therefore employed, but not to produce strategy. Strategic planning is in the hands of full-time staff who know the individual parts of the business and who understand corporate finance and strategy.

15.5   Marketing strategy

There has been considerable interest in the developments at Westside and many have asked to be shown the building. These visits have now become part of BT's marketing strategy, as, apart from the building, much of what makes Workstyle 2000 work are the products and services that BT sells!

15.6   Transferable experience

As BT Group Property turns round an under-managed real estate portfolio and executes a real estate downsizing exercise it has found that:

- a successful presentation to top management requires facts and figures, and follow-up reports are easier once a (computerised) property audit is in place
- top management support (main board level) is essential if real estate is to be included in corporate strategy
- successful incorporation of real estate issues into corporate strategy requires real estate professionals who understand corporate finance and strategy and for the remainder of the business to understand the role of real estate, which is easier when there are internal rents
- once real estate is part of corporate strategy, implementation will involve experts from all different parts of the operation, e.g. personnel and finance
- to make change happen requires resources, especially time, money and dedicated staff
- the real estate team can play a major role in changing corporate culture, especially when aims and objectives for real estate are well thought out and focused on the business's market needs
- learning from experience and future technical developments will make improvements possible, so taking change slowly is helpful – it is a continuous process
- siting top managers in new facilities helps to gain staff support

- much of the real estate work can be outsourced, but strategy matters are best retained in-house
- innovative approaches are needed to off-load real estate successfully, especially when it can affect local markets
- when new uses will be needed for redundant buildings the potential planning permission for new uses must be protected
- for a computer or communications business, making the best use of its products to run its business is also a good marketing strategy

16 Marks & Spencer plc

16.1 Introduction

The real estate management team at Marks & Spencer plc (M&S) cannot remember a time when real estate did not play a significant role in corporate strategy. Most retailers are very aware of the importance of location, but few are as committed to real estate as M&S, which has focused on retaining ownership of retail sites. This is a different strategy from that of other retailers, and shows that there is not just one 'best way' of using real estate within a business. This emphasises the importance of making decisions that best suit each business and therefore the importance of including real estate in the strategic decision-making process.

Real estate issues are fundamental to M&S's business philosophy, particularly:

- growth through expansion of retail sales areas
- control of its own destiny
- flexibility

Implementation of its strategies has meant that M&S has become the owner of a significant retail real estate portfolio, yet it outsources its warehouse/distribution centre needs.

16.2 Philosophy of the retail real estate strategy

M&S has had an almost continuous policy of only expanding through increasing floor space, either from opening new stores or by expanding existing sites. This policy has become even more entrenched after the difficulties experienced with Brooks Bros in the USA, which M&S acquired in 1988. There is a now a strong resistance to any expansion through acquisition.

M&S owns the freehold of 95% of all its UK retail stores. This is a key plank in its policy of controlling its own destiny. It does not want its business to be adversely affected by changes in the property market. It has seen too many of its competitors suffer. M&S's real estate team will talk of retail rents surging up during property and economic booms, but never falling in the subsequent recessions because of upward-only rent review clauses. They recall their competitors struggling to meet rent commitments from falling sales.

The 5% of retail stores that are leased account for a rent commitment of £100 million per annum, a sum which Chris Williams, the Estates Manager, was quick to point out comes straight off profits. M&S also actively manages all other costs which affect revenue, such as rates and service charges. It actively seeks to reduce rent and service charge commitment by buying out leases in all locations where retail sales and profitability are growing.

This is not always possible, as many of the leased stores are in shopping centres where freehold interests are not available. However, most of these stores are held on 125-year leases, usually with little or no rent, and even in some cases no service charges. The initial deal probably involved a premium – but not always paid by M&S: its strength as an anchor tenant is so high that developers and landlords will go to considerable lengths to attract it. M&S also seeks to control the part of any shopping centre in which it is located so that it has some control over its surroundings, including adjacent traders. Paradoxically, this strength when it is a tenant comes because it has demonstrated its preference and ability to be a freeholder.

In March 1995, the total value of the M&S group real estate was £2736 million. The freehold interests were worth £1672 million and the long leases £861 million, leaving £203 million (just 7%) as short leaseholds.

Satisfying demand for more space at the flagship Marble Arch store in London has been a constant problem over the years. Whenever adjacent space became available it was taken. The result has been a store that at times has seemed like a rabbit warren; it has also resulted in a very complex multitude of interlocking property interests. The real estate team constantly monitor all leases, reviews, notification dates and ownerships to attempt to draw the buildings into an M&S freehold.

The money invested in the freehold ownership of the retail stores does not bring as high a return as investing directly in trading. There are strong arguments in favour of renting, which frees investment in real estate fixed assets for other, more obviously profitable, purposes. These are counterbalanced by a number of considerations:

- the ability to predict over the long term most aspects of M&S's accommodation costs – only matters like rates and energy supply costs are likely to vary dramatically, and even these it seeks to limit
- the freedom to implement a life-cycle costing programme and invest in designs, materials and finishes which will bring low long-term maintenance costs
- the freedom to modify buildings to meet new trading needs
- consistent maintenance and occupancy costs assist consistent product pricing and consumer confidence

- it is a cash-rich company with funds (£735 million with their bankers at the end of 1995) to support a freehold ownership programme
- returns from prime retail real estate are predicted to grow faster than the returns from leaving excess cash on deposit with bankers

This last consideration is particularly pleasant for M&S. The predictions that M&S is receiving from the property world are for traditional retailing to consolidate and for key shopping areas to become more concentrated, with hot-spots around the M&S stores.

16.3   Implementation of the retail expansion programme

The importance of real estate for the retail operation is reflected by M&S's Footage Development Strategy Unit, which reports directly to the Capital Expenditure Committee. This is the most senior of the M&S committees, and is chaired by the Deputy Chairman and Joint Managing Director, Keith Oates, who is joined in the committee by the other joint managing directors and four directors, including Roger Aldridge, main board director responsible for Group Estates, Store Development and Equipment. It is the only committee to meet monthly.

The Footage Development Strategy Unit produces a three- to five-year footage expansion plan, which is the main platform for the capital plan. It is a fundamental cornerstone of the business. Unlike many businesses, top management at M&S through Keith Oates is actively concerned with real estate issues.

The Capital Expenditure Committee is involved with all issues affecting the location of M&S stores, both macro and micro. While M&S has moved into out-of-town shopping, the latest government policies have now focused its interest on edge-of-centre locations where adequate car parking can be created. Car parking has become essential, as the M&S product range has widened and customers want to carry home more than can be comfortably managed on public transport. M&S calculates that 75% of the UK population lives within a 45-minute drive of an edge-of-town store where large items can be bought. Each of these has good car-parking facilities.

Currently, 40% of stores are over 6000 m^2 in size, with 10 000 m^2 being considered large, but expansion plans include 'Marks & Spencer department stores' as large as 25 000 m^2. In 1990, M&S had 266 stores and 900 000 m^2 of space located in high streets and city centres. By 1995 it had 283 stores covering 1 100 000 m^2, with 17 large regional and edge-of-town stores. In 1995, £230 million was invested in the UK expansion programme, which increased sales floors by 40 000 m^2. This is expected to rise to 75 000 to 100 000 m^2 per annum towards the end of the century as some of the large schemes currently in planning come to fruition.

16.4   The role of real estate in physical distribution

Going back about 15 years, M&S, like other retailers, had more or less all its non-food stock in its high street stores either in stockrooms or under the counters. As the volume of sales increased, the in-store stockrooms could not cope and warehouses were leased to provide outside store capacity; almost a 'knee-jerk' reaction. Frequently, the pressure of sales resulted in the in-store stockroom being used to extend the sales floor. Ten years ago, M&S used 70 warehouses, known as 'outside stockrooms'. Some were large and served several stores.

At about this time point of sale computerisation gave the company accurate sales data which immediately highlighted the lack of accurate stock data. This coincided with the realisation that 70 small non-food warehouses were time-consuming to manage and not very economic. It was also clear that a computer-based stock control system would not work effectively with 70 sites.

A board-level policy decision was made to focus on large-scale regional distribution warehouses, with no stock in stores except that on display. At the same time, the then new Chairman, Lord Rayner, set in place a policy of increasing floor space by 50 000 m^2 per annum. It meant that the new warehouse policy had to be implemented fast. The new warehouses were needed immediately and the equivalent of four distribution centres were programmed for the following year. Within a year four were built, but only half opened, and short-term rental arrangements were made to fill the gap.

Overall, the changeover to regional distribution centres, once completed, reduced costs substantially – in absolute terms and as a percentage of ongoing operational costs. There were savings from the reduction in the amount of stock held as throughput increased, plus savings in real estate and physical distribution costs. Exact figures are not available, but overall, cutting costs has been important for M&S.

Figure 16.1 shows how, during the early 1990s, profitability (or operating margin, i.e. profit before tax ÷ turnover) increased from 10.5% to 13.2%. This has come by reducing costs so that more of the turnover is going straight to the bottom line. The difference may seem small, but the effect on profits growth is substantial – if costs had not fallen, profits growth would have been an unspectacular 18% over five years rather than the 52% which has kept investors very satisfied. The changes to distribution, including reducing real estate, helped to create this profit growth during an economic recession.

16.5   Implementation of the regional distribution programme

Between 1986 and 1991, 10 new purpose-built regional distribution centres have been constructed, and four of the largest original ones have been

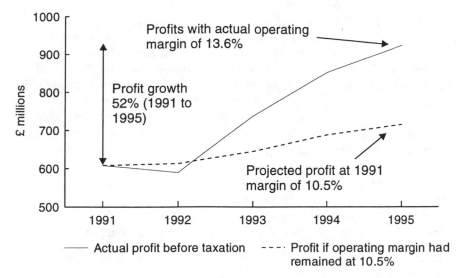

Figure 16.1 Marks & Spencer plc: the effect on profits of not increasing the operating margin. (Source: Marks & Spencer annual report 1995)

retained. In the UK, M&S now uses 14 regional non-food distribution warehouses, each up to 25 000 m² in size and all linked to a computerised stock control system. All of the remaining small warehouses were made available for disposal.

Disposing of nearly 70 small warehouses, many of them leased, has not been easy. The best were not a problem, but M&S is not the only company to have rationalised distribution, and there are many similar properties on the market. The physical distribution side of M&S ceases to bear responsibility for the warehouses once empty. They are now a problem for the real estate team. Those that have stuck on the market are generally away from the motorways, old, not high-bay and do not meet current specifications. Most are held on a lease, and M&S retains a rental liability. Where possible, M&S has sublet or assigned its leases. In a few cases it has bought the freehold interest because it found that it could sell the sites for development or to an occupier who did not want to rent. Like other empty warehouse owners, M&S claims rate rebates and spends heavily on security to stop vandalism and rave parties!

While the changes to the distribution organisation have helped to reduce costs, the accompanying real estate disposal programme has caused problems during the recession. The annual accounts have shown losses on the disposal of real estate and other fixed assets, for example losses of £17.3 million in 1994 and £5.4 million in 1995. These are very small sums when compared with the turnover, assets and profits of the company. Nevertheless, they show how real estate assets can and do, from time to time, fall in value.

M&S recognises that its skill is in retailing rather than distribution. Almost all the distribution is now outsourced. The 10 new warehouses were built by the outsourcing contractors to M&S's requirements, although the four original warehouses are still managed by M&S. The problems with the disposal of the leasehold interests in the redundant warehouses has confirmed to M&S the value of not having a real estate interest in a non-core business.

The outsourcing contracts cover the real estate, equipment, vehicle, management and staffing needs. The contracts are flexible and vary to suit the current needs of M&S, including those for real estate. Partnerships have been formed which focus on developmental and operational needs.

Nevertheless, M&S does review its warehouse real estate policies from time to time and includes all considerations in its appraisals, including the real estate market and current tax allowances. The balance is still in favour of not owning the warehouses but restricting its real estate investments to retail stores – the core business.

16.6   Management

The London-based in-house real estate team at M&S is responsible for overall implementation of policy, the provision of property market information to the Footage Development Strategy Unit and the effective management of the real estate services, both in the UK and overseas. The small team of seven surveyors and two assistants makes considerable use of outside consultants. There is also an in-house facilities management organisation that cares for the physical needs of all the property and occupants.

16.7   Future policies

Real estate is an important factor in M&S's European expansion programme, where the footage development philosophy is similar to the UK. However, implementation methods vary according to the real estate practices in each country. The real estate team mostly use the local offices of UK real estate consultants for advice and to undertake their real estate operations. Real estate issues are part of their strategies; for example, although M&S has been attracted by the valuable clothing market in Germany for many years, its decision in 1994 develop a store in Cologne was only finally taken when real estate prices fell.

Further afield, where expansion has been by franchising, real estate has not been a major concern. Again, local offices of UK-based consultants have been used. It is recognised that more extensive expansion in any of these markets would raise various real estate issues.

M&S has opened up a completely new field of business through its financial services operation, which began in 1985. Apart from small customer service facilities in its stores, this operation is not real estate-intensive. The M&S charge card is now the biggest in Europe, and many financial services are sold to these customers. Others are reached via radio advertising and telesales. They now have a highly profitable financial services business. The turnover for 1995 was £135 million (£170 million predicted for 1996) with operating profits of nearly £49 million, an increase of 18% on the previous year.

Given that M&S has made this formidable progress in a new sector, one cannot help but wonder how it will tackle the opportunities of online sales – at the moment it is not saying. What is clear is that, as in all of its other operations, the real estate aspects will be a consideration in its action plans.

16.8 Summary

Not only does M&S include real estate in its strategic planning, but within that strategy it makes individual decisions on real estate interests to suit different parts of the business. Table 16.1 shows how the key aspects of the retail operation and distribution generally meet the criteria given in Chapter 8 as to when to own and when to rent (which can include outsourcing, where the formula to fix the cost may mean that the rent most closely relates to the management fee or contractor's profit).

16.9 Transferable experiences

M&S is regularly held up as an example of the best of British business. Its strategies and tactical methods of implementation are frequently copied. The seriousness with which it considers the use of real estate within the business is another component of its success which other business managers would find beneficial to copy, although they may decide on different solutions.

There is nothing that is difficult, or particularly special, about the way in which M&S uses real estate – it is simply carefully organised to meet the business's needs. The following are the main points of interest:

- Marks & Spencer includes real estate in its corporate strategies
- real estate has been a central component of many of the successful strategies
- top management have been involved in real estate issues on a regular basis
- owning freehold shop premises guards against unpredictable rent increases and helps to stabilise costs
- freehold premises can be adapted more easily than leased premises

Table 16.1 Marks & Spencer plc: why shops are owned and warehouses rented (based on Table 8.1)

Retail stores	Own	Business factor	Rent	Distribution centres
	if		if	
Steady growth – strongest in market	Stable	OPERATION	Changing	IT and transportation changes and increasing sales volume
Strong individual internal finishes to high standards	Unique	ACCOMMODATION NEEDS	Ordinary	Latest industry norms
Wish to control own destiny	Control	MANAGEMENT	Flexibility	Many changes due to IT also outsourcing
Lack of downward rent reviews has harmed competitors	High	INFLATION	Low	Low inflation predicted
Cash-rich	Available	CAPITAL	Restricted	No interest in non-core operations

- a successful retailer can create real estate value just from its presence in a market-place
- holding real estate for non-core activities may be more risky than for core activities
- operational methods can change very fast within a business and across an industry, leaving a glut of obsolete real estate
- cost savings are possible from real estate measures and these can make a significant contribution to profitability
- real estate savings are often linked to changes in the use of IT and communications technology
- a small centrally based team can coordinate the work of consultants both in the UK and overseas
- new forms of trading can be very profitable without any major real estate input

17 J Sainsbury plc

17.1 Introduction

This chapter focuses on one event in the use of real estate by J Sainsbury plc – the way in which it developed an investment market for supermarket and superstore premises through the use of sale and leaseback. This happened at the end of the 1980s, so it is already historic, but this does not detract from the fact that it is a valuable example of the pivotal role of real estate in the finances of major corporate real estate users. It illustrates the importance of being able to conceptualise a different situation that will benefit a business and then taking the action to make it happen.

J Sainsbury plc, better known as Sainsbury's, the name the company uses for most of its business operations, also trades through the subsidiaries Homebase and Savacentre in the UK and Shaw's supermarkets in the USA.

Sainsbury's, like most of the major retailers, appreciates the importance of real estate and the value of the right location. The Director of Development, who heads the real estate team, is a main board appointment and has one of the five seats on the Chairman's Committee, the main strategic development and investment decision-making forum in the company. Ian Coull, the current incumbent, joined Sainsbury's in 1988 at a time when the company wished to broaden the financial support for its expansion programme, and immediately became involved in developing policy that would open up access to additional funds.

17.2 The established policy

The real estate policy of Sainsbury's is not written down and not rigid, but the company had become very comfortable with holding freehold, or virtual freehold interests (very long leases), on just 60% of their operational space, with the remaining 40% held on leases. This makes 60% of Sainsbury's real estate into fixed assets, while the remainder, while contributing to fixed assets, mostly affects the business through rent payments, which appear as a cost in the profit and loss account.

In Sainsbury's experience, this real estate policy gives it the best protection at both extremes of the property cycle. When the property cycle booms, only holding 40% of its property as leaseholds limits the adverse effect of high rent reviews (reduces 'the kick'). When the property cycle slumps, it suffers a loss in value of balance sheet assets for its freehold properties, but this will be less than from having an entirely freehold estate. Elsewhere in the accounts it gains, as the rent reviews will be lower in a slump, hence helping to hold back rising costs to the benefit of the profit and loss account.

17.3 Expansion without new equity and without high gearing

The expansion programme that Sainsbury's wished to fund from new sources of finance had been in progress throughout the 1980s and was able to continue uninterrupted once the sale and leaseback arrangements were in place. Figure 17.1 shows the mostly steady but rapid growth in the sales area during the 1980s and early 1990s. Over 10 years, the UK floor area increased by more than 2½ times. Additionally, many old stores were shut down and replaced with new properties. When Shaw's in the USA is included the floor space more than tripled in 10 years.

The easiest funding methods were not suitable. A share issue would have been attractive to many investors, but was rejected as the Sainsbury family did not want to dilute their interest in the business. This had remained substantially unchanged since 1973. Otherwise, growth until the late 1980s had been mostly funded by cash from the business and debt. Although this could have continued, the aim was to find a source of funding other than the reserves.

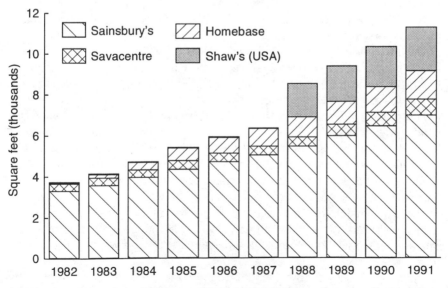

Figure 17.1 Growth in sales area. (Source: J Sainsbury plc annual reports)

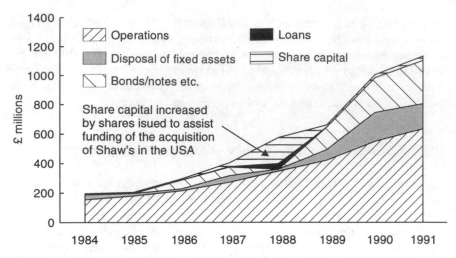

Figure 17.2 Sources of funds (deferred income and other sources of funds are too small to be shown at this scale). (Source: J Sainsbury plc annual reports)

One new component, the raising of debt through the issue of corporate bonds and loan notes, was implemented from the financial year 1988/9 onwards. These instruments opened up a new avenue of substantial funding, but they also pushed up gearing. There was concern that to meet Sainsbury's funding needs using long-term debt would result in the debt:equity ratio reaching 40%. While the debt:equity ratio had been increasing during the 1980s, 40% would be much higher than Sainsbury's had been used to, and the directors were not comfortable with this scenario.

The situation is well illustrated by Figure 17.2, which shows the sources of funds used by Sainsbury's to run the operation and support expansion. During the 1980s (until 1987) the vast majority of funding came from ploughing back profits from retail sales (operations).

The only significant use of share capital was in 1987, when a small share issue, totalling less than 5% of the company's issued capital, was used to support the acquisition of the final shareholding in Shaw's of the USA. The small amounts of share capital available in other years came from share option schemes and a profit-sharing trust. There were also small amounts issued as part of the earlier stages of the purchase of Shaw's.

The other major growth in funding comes from the disposal of fixed assets (which were mostly freehold and virtual freehold interests) through the major sale and leaseback arrangement that began in 1989 and which is the subject of this chapter.

Figure 17.3 shows how the debt:equity ratio rose steadily during the mid-1980s and then rose steeply in 1988/89. It rose to over 32% in 1988/89

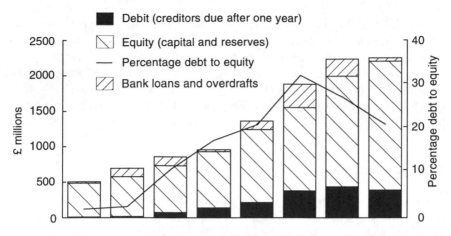

Figure 17.3 Percentage debt to equity. (Source: J Sainsbury plc annual reports)

and would probably have gone higher had Sainsbury's not been able to boost its profits from sale and leaseback, thereby increasing equity from retained profits and decreasing the need for debt finance.

Although not a consideration when calculating debt to equity ratios, it is interesting to look at the growing level of bank loans and overdrafts (a component of short-term debt), which is also shown in Figure 17.3. Bank lending was pulled back to its more traditional levels after the implementation of the sale and leaseback programmes.

The expansion that Sainsbury's planned included opening many completely new stores on edge-of-town and out-of-town greenfield sites. It had already begun a building programme and the new sites were proving successful with consumers, but developers and their funders were not attracted. Without the support of the property investment market Sainsbury's had had to retain control of the freehold interests for these new shops, which then featured in the business's fixed assets. It did not take long for freehold interests to build up to 70% of its real estate portfolio.

To the discomfort of a higher than desired debt was added the further discomfort of moving away from its 60:40 freehold:leasehold policy. The company's concern was further intensified when it viewed its store-opening programme for the next three to four years, which was entirely based on retaining freehold interests.

At that time the property market was strong and was going through an upswing in the property cycle. However, Sainsbury's management were aware of the cyclical nature of the property market and were concerned that during the inevitable slump the value of the real estate fixed assets would fall. The more the freehold interests grew as a percentage of the real estate holdings, the greater the potential for damage to the company's asset base.

The effect of these changes is not as clear in the annual reports, because the value of some real estate fixed assets has been included at historic cost. Although each year the directors give an actual figure or a percentage rate by which the total should be raised to give a realistic value, the division between the different property interests is blurred. Coull and his fellow directors were working with data based on the current valuations of each property.

17.4   Sale and leaseback

The directors, Coull recalls, wanted to find a strategy that would allow the expansion programme to continue without increasing either the debt:equity ratio or the amount of freehold property. They wanted more than just to end the growth in debt and the rising number of freehold interests. They wanted to reduce both and get back to the comfort of operating within their traditional financial boundaries.

They decided on sale and leaseback as a solution. This was not revolutionary, and was not unknown to Sainsbury's, which had enjoyed small profits from a surplus on sale and leasebacks of other types of real estate for many years. The difficulty was that the property investment market had already declined to become involved in the growing number of supermarkets and superstores.

17.5   Implementation

Lack of rental knowledge

Most of the new greenfield supermarkets and superstores were held freehold by one or other of the supermarket companies. They were trading from their premises and there was no need to sell the premises to other traders. In the early days of the move into greenfield sites property investors had not been interested, because there was no guarantee that the stores would be successful or that, if they failed, other retailers would want to buy or rent them. Consequently there was no market and little idea as to market value other than assessing an income derived from current trade, which might or might not be coming from the most profitable retailer and might or might not cover the cost of construction.

The only measurable market for real estate interests in supermarkets was for those in town centre locations, usually built as part of a shopping centre. In these cases the rent for the supermarket was part of a package of rents from all the tenants of a centre. If the head lease, or freehold interest, was sold, the interest in the supermarket would be just part of the total package.

Not only was there little or no market for investments in greenfield stores, there was little idea as to likely rent levels. Even for the town centre supermarket there was very little rental information. Normally, rental details get circulated in the market as property professionals contribute to rent review negotiations, but these were rare for supermarkets. Many of the major supermarket tenants had been welcomed into shopping centre developments as key occupiers who would attract other tenants. As a consequence, many had negotiated favourable terms with few rent reviews.

A product to suit the market

Sainsbury's decided to test the market. By the end of the 1980s it was clear that out-of-town and edge-of-town stores that relied on most customers using cars were successful. All the major supermarket companies were expanding in the sector. Yet at this point there was still no interest by property investors in funding a development programme.

The aim was to attract investors. Sainsbury's put together an investment opportunity containing a mixture of properties that were trading successfully. It was suggested that 10 to 12 of these would be a suitable investment package for one of the country's larger property investors.

The proposal included a guarantee that rents would increase at the first two rent reviews based upon rental growth. If rents failed to grow there was a fallback arrangement of a guaranteed increase based on a compound rate of interest which was fixed slightly below the predicted inflation rate.

Two real estate agency and property consultancy firms were commissioned to market the proposal. Coull was pleased by the result: the level of interest and the proposed yield was better than he had expected. The market did not see the proposal as being as risky as had been feared. No doubt the quality of the Sainsbury's covenant was a factor, and the risk, although related to the trading success of the various stores in one company, was with product ranges that included many staple items.

An additional factor which attracted investors was the way in which the proposal was marketed. In addition to the arrangements for upward rent reviews, the package included stores in various locations (which helped to spread the risk), and the number of stores was sufficient to create an opportunity attractive to serious investors. A further diversity came from some of the stores being leased to other retailers, such as The Boots Company.

The market is discovered

Most interest was shown by those property companies that were cash rich at the time. The insurance companies and other financial institutions were less interested, in part because the lack of rental evidence made it difficult to project rental growth. They needed rental growth to meet their projected

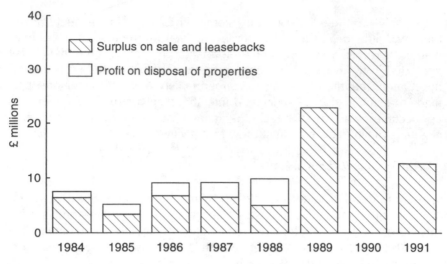

Figure 17.4 Operating income from property. (Source: J Sainsbury plc annual reports)

income flows, and were concerned that it could fall away; the guaranteed income was less than inflation and they feared the situation in future years.

Sainsbury's turned to the property companies and began negotiations with The British Land Company plc, which resulted in a deal being completed in March 1989. In the end the deal, which involved 20 stores and ancillary properties, was worth £90 million and covered 900 000 m^2 (1 million ft^2).

The detail of the terms of the arrangements between British Land and Sainsbury's are subject to a confidentiality agreement, so are not made public. Press reports suggest that Sainsbury's took 35-year leases with five-yearly rent reviews (*Shop Property*, 1989). The yields were reported to be between 8 and 9%, with individual properties yielding between 8 and 11.5% (*Estates Gazette*, 1989). Given the financial sophistication of both companies, it would seem reasonable to assume that the deals had been carefully worked out to bring the best taxation advantages to both parties (see Chapter 7).

The immediate effect for Sainsbury's was to increase operating income from sources other than retailing. Figure 17.4 shows just the profits from the disposal of properties and the surplus (profit) on sale and leaseback arrangements.

The small income from this source during the 1980s was boosted in 1989 by the surplus on the above deal. The £90 million deal contributed to a surplus of £22 million from sale and leasebacks in 1989. Figure 17.5 shows how the trading profits were boosted by the profits from property once the major sale and leaseback arrangements began.

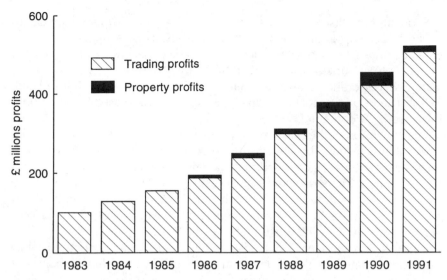

Figure 17.5 Trading and property profits. (Source: J Sainsbury plc annual reports)

At the same time, the real estate involved was removed from the balance sheet and the need for debt funding fell (see Figure 17.3). The only amount to remain on the balance sheet in the fixed assets would be any value from gaining a profit rent on the leases. As these were at rack-rents (current market rents) this would not arise immediately; it would happen only if they built up between the rent reviews because market rents were rising. The rent is a cost against the profit and loss account and does not affect the balance sheet. The released funding was available to drive the core retailing business.

17.6 Post-implementation

A developing relationship

The arrangement gave Sainsbury's greater financial freedom, and it enabled it to maintain the company structure within its preferred parameters. Building continued, with a programme that resulted in 38 new stores in a year – a new store every 10 days. The programme produced 116 000 m^2 (1.25 million ft^2) of selling space for supermarkets, DIY stores and garden centres.

Less than a year later, in January 1990, British Land purchased 11 more premises from Sainsbury's in another sale and leaseback deal, worth £88 million. Again the properties were from Sainsbury's and their subsidiaries in different parts of the country. The press again reported 35-year leases with rent reviews every five years (*Shop Property*, 1990).

Soon after the first Sainsbury's/British Land deal, other supermarket chains began to develop arrangements with various investors. A market had been created. British Land obviously liked the market, because it made further investments in supermarkets and in 1994 owned properties occupied by Gateway, Tesco and Safeway as well as 49 Sainsbury's stores (British Land, 1994). The result was that about 6–7% of the real estate used by Sainsbury's is owned by British Land.

The expansion of the sale and leaseback scheme from 20 to 49 properties came about, in part, because Sainsbury's was pleased with the service it received from its new landlord. British Land responded quickly to any requests by Sainsbury's for permission to make structural or other changes to the premises concerned. Otherwise, British Land is an almost silent landlord that has left Sainsbury's to devote its energies to making profits from its core business, which, after all, was the object of the deal.

It seems to have been a well-balanced 'win–win' arrangement, for while Sainsbury's gained its development funding, British Land has seen market rent exceed the guaranteed uplift for a number of the stores at the first review, five years after the original deal. The guaranteed uplift remains in place to be used at the 10 year review if market rents fail to continue to rise.

The wider perspective

Developing the sale and leaseback market has been very helpful in supporting Sainsbury's investment in new and improved stores. However, Coull points out some limitations, the foremost of which is that the financial rating companies, such as Standard & Poor's and Dun & Bradstreet tend not to be impressed by such arrangements and take little note of the decrease in debt that has been achieved. So Sainsbury's credit rating is unlikely to improve.

There is now a very healthy market in supermarket investment which has attracted developers and their institutional funders. Developers have been happy to spend time seeking out sites, investing in the time and cost of obtaining planning permission and putting together financed development packages to attract the major supermarket chains. The eventual occupiers have been involved at the planning permission stage, but have not needed to make a major financial commitment beyond agreeing to rent the finished building. They do not have to find long-term finance for the project.

The restrictions on out-of-town shopping development by the Government have reduced the development opportunities. However, as all retailers are now retrenching to some extent in response to the economic recession and concern over future shopping patterns, the restrictions overall have not been a major hindrance, particularly as many sites still have unimplemented planning permissions.

Sainsbury's continues to undertake developments and retain freehold interests. Its aim is to maintain the 60:40 freehold/leasehold split. In some locations its developments include accommodation for third parties, particularly where bringing other traders to a site will encourage more shoppers to visit. It is a landlord as well as a tenant.

17.7 Real estate management and corporate strategy

The development of the sale and leaseback market for Sainsbury's stores came about, at least in part, because Sainsbury's includes real estate in its corporate strategy. The Chairman's Committee of five main board directors, including Coull, is the main strategic and investment decision-making forum in the company, a group that meets fortnightly for most of the year.

The real estate team at Sainsbury's is centralised, and although consultants carry out much of the work, the team is sufficiently diverse and experienced to be able to undertake any real estate task in-house and, if necessary, maintain strict commercial confidentiality. Facilities management is undertaken in house, but estate management functions, such as rent and service charge collection, are outsourced. Nevertheless, Coull is able to draw on current experience from most aspects of the real estate and construction sectors through the experience of the real estate team and incorporate it into the corporate decision-making process.

17.8 Transferable experience

The successful introduction of sale and leaseback came as much from a good marketing exercise as anything else. This illustrates that, to be successful, corporate real estate teams need more than real estate skills. Points which may be useful to other corporate businesses include:

- provision of real estate is a core component of the financial provisions for many businesses
- there are gains from including real estate in corporate decision-making
- problems with the provision of real estate can hinder core business
- real estate decisions can affect the financial standing of a business
- a strong real estate team can influence the property market, but...
- ...it needs to match its product to the needs of the property investment market
- real estate managers need to have strategic vision and the skills to implement it
- good client relations are as important for landlords and tenants as in other service industries

18 The Boots Company plc

18.1 Introduction

The Boots Company plc incorporates various subsidiary companies, of which Boots The Chemists Ltd is by far the largest. The others include various healthcare companies, Halfords, Homestyle By Fads (A. G. Stanley Ltd) and a property company, Boots Properties Ltd.

This chapter discusses the corporate real estate strategies of the overall business with a specific focus on the contribution made by the Estates Department of Boots The Chemists, which is responsible for the management of that company's occupation of real estate.

Real estate at the heart of the business

The Boots Company has involved real estate closely in corporate strategy from the earliest days of the establishment of the company in 1877. By 1900, the company owned more than 250 shops nationwide, and in 1913 it had more than doubled in size, with 560 branches. Now there are over 1200 Boots The Chemists shops, serving 92% of the population from sites in the smallest local shopping parade to massive superstores. It has the highest footfall of any UK retailer and approximately 1.75% of all retail expenditure is in one of The Boots Company retail outlets. The group is still expanding, and in 1995 48 new Boots The Chemists shops opened as part of the plan to open 200 additional small shops over a three-year period.

18.2 Establishing a property company

During the later part of the 1980s The Boots Company became more aware of the financial implications of its real estate holdings. It decided to be more overt in the management of these assets and to clear confusion from the retail operation caused by the inclusion of real estate in the accounts of the retailing businesses.

240

'Modern' rents

The first move had been made in 1981, when the way in which the operational real estate was charged to the individual stores and businesses was changed. Until then, the different parts of the business had been charged a figure for using premises based on a return on the capital employed to acquire the premises – an historic, and usually not very realistic, cost.

An annual charge, which Boots called a 'modern rent', was introduced. It was effectively an internal rent. The principle was good, but the 'modern rent' levels were still somewhat unrealistic. The actual rent passing to the landlord was used where properties were held on short leases, but for other premises the rent was a notional figure, in part because the estate had not been fully revalued, and as a result some 'modern' rents were unrealistically low. Further, as market rent levels were rising even the actual rents paid for the shorter leasehold interests were soon below market levels.

Profit rents boosted trading profits

Although the modern rents were an improvement, the sum charged against sales for the cost of renting property was still below market rent levels. Part of what appeared to be profit from retail trading activities was actually a profit rent – the annual benefit of occupying property for less than current market rent. Property profits were boosting trading returns.

It was a distortion which clouded financial comparisons. For example, the profitability of a new store using premises rented at the current market rent would appear to be less than a store trading in premises for which the rent had been fixed several years previously. Extrapolated for the whole of The Boots Company, it meant that while current market rent levels were increasing, any increase in trade due to increased sales floor areas would increase profits at a declining rate, because the cost of all new stores or extensions would be higher than the 'rent' charged for existing stores.

Takeover risk

Furthermore, it was realised within the company that, despite top management's understanding of the potential of the sites, many of the company's real estate assets were underperforming. Working from day to day with a figure for rent below the market level tends to result in management being comfortable with trading returns which would not be profitable if market rents were being paid.

Also, without an emphasis on real estate the development potential was being overlooked by managers and resources were not directed at exploiting it. The senior management of the company felt increasingly vulnerable to a takeover by an investor who valued the real estate opportunities rather more than the core business of retailing.

Establishing Boots Properties plc

As a retailer, The Boots Company wanted to ensure that its profit from trading was transparent. It wanted to be able to distinguish clearly between successful trading growth and asset growth. This did not mean ignoring the real estate potential, but avoiding confusion of the two separate activities – retailing and property – to the detriment of both. There was also a growing realisation that about half of The Boots Company's assets were tied up in property, yet the group had no way of managing these assets to ensure that Boots was giving its shareholders the returns that they were entitled to expect – thus began the moves which established Boots Properties.

The first step, on 1 April 1989, was to set up Boots Properties plc, with the responsibility for improving the total return on property assets and for becoming progressively more involved in property development, and thereby providing an additional source of profit for the group. Boots Properties plc received the freehold and long leasehold properties of The Boots Company and the various subsidiaries. This included responsibility for rents paid to external landlords in respect of these premises.

The freehold and long leasehold real estate, excluding factories and specialised buildings, had been revalued as at 31 March 1989. The total amounted to £818.5 million, providing a surplus over book value of £568.9 million which was added to the balance sheet, boosting the assets of the company in the 1988/89 accounts. When the property transfers between the subsidiary companies took place on the first day of the new 1989/90 financial year (which was the day after the revaluation) the transactions were recorded at the revised values.

Boots Properties plc had been formed by renaming Timothy Whites plc, a company Boots had acquired some years previously. The new organisation started with the Timothy Whites property assets, which had amounted to almost £6 million in 1988 but with small changes and revaluation had become £75.8 million on 31 March 1989. The transfers of 1 April brought in properties worth £687.9 million (after revaluation) and by the end of the 1989/90 financial year the real estate assets of Boots Properties totalled £769 million.

The individual Boots companies were then charged a market rent for using the premises. This increased the rental charges for the companies. For example, Boots The Chemists' rent charge more than doubled, from £34 4 million in 1989 to £79.3 million in 1990, as shown in Figure 18.1. This affected its trading profit, which fell from £157 million in 1989 to £135 million in 1990, but the surplus arising from the transfer of the properties, £453 million, more than offset the difference for that year. Boots The Chemists managed to replace the lost profit rent by profit from sales during the following year and, by its close, in March 1991, trading profit had almost recovered, standing at £155 million.

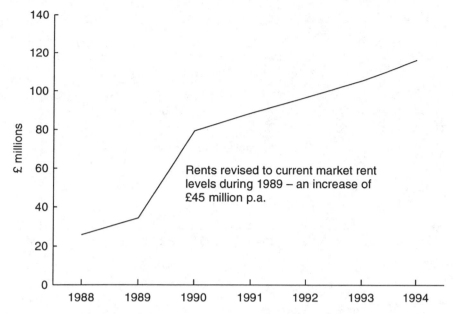

Figure 18.1 Boots The Chemists: rent payments. (Source: Boots the Chemists annual reports)

Although the effects of the change can be seen so clearly in the Boots The Chemists accounts, overall there was little difference, as Boots Properties Ltd is a subsidiary, wholly owned by The Boots Company. Apart from normal buying and selling of properties to meet trading needs, there was no sale of assets. The increased rent charges paid by the individual companies contributed to the profits of Boots Properties, all of which just moved money around in the parent company accounts while making it much easier in the future to see whether the real estate assets were being well-managed.

Nevertheless, changes which can be seen to involve a drop in trading profits can be unsettling for investors, so The Boots Company briefed its institutional investors about the changes to ensure that there was no alarm. It explained that a significant company asset would now be managed to produce the best return. Share prices undulated gently and then began to climb. It was successfully accepted, and the *Financial Times* called it 'a company that exudes confidence' (*Financial Times*, 1989).

The switch of assets

Figure 18.2 shows the revaluation and transfer of the real estate assets. In the financial year ending in 1988 most of the assets still belonged to Boots The Chemists and were shown to be worth £211 million. These were revalued

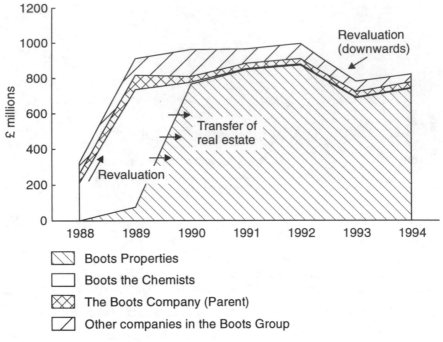

Figure 18.2 Property assets of the companies of The Boots Company plc. (Source: annual reports of Boots Group companies)

to £660 million by the end of the 1988/89 financial year, and then in 1989/90 most were transferred to Boots Properties.

This left just £9.6 million of real estate with Boots The Chemists at the end of the financial year 1989/90; this was mostly non-retail premises, such as the manufacturing plant and laboratories. Most of this has since been transferred out of the business. The value of the Boots The Chemists real estate holdings dropped to an amount so small that it fails to register on the graph in Figure 18.2 after 1991.

Boots Properties in action

Boots Properties has developed into a leading retail property investment and development company. It continues to hold most of the group's real estate, both freehold and leasehold, which is now valued at over £850 million and represents half of Boots' fixed assets.

The investment activity is important and is a major contributor to Boots Properties' profits. It is not a particularly high-profile activity, and is undertaken with the restriction that each investment purchased must have a Boots company as a tenant, but many of the investments are multi-tenanted.

The development activity is undertaken with the same restriction, so among the many tenants of each scheme are one or two Boots companies. The development activity started modestly and included a couple of joint ventures. Now the company is undertaking large projects which have included offices and leisure as well as retail as part of the overall scheme.

Two aspects of being part of a large corporate retail group have been very beneficial for Boots Properties. The first is access to retail trading data, which it can combine with econometric and demographic data to gain an enviable insight into its market (Boots The Chemists also uses similar methods to focus on its specific needs, and this is described in more detail later in this chapter). The second advantage is that projects are funded internally, making it possible to proceed without the involvement of external development finance.

Not only has the value of the portfolio increased, assisted by deals totalling £400 million over seven years, the quality of the portfolio has also improved. As part of the growth has come from both developing and purchasing investments in multi-tenanted properties, the percentage of third-party tenants has grown to 15%.

Boots Properties is maximising the revenue-generating and development potential of its retail estate, and there is no longer an unrecognised potential to cause a takeover bid related to under-exploitation of the real estate. The shareholders' value is realistically reflected by the share price, which means that the different business managers within the Boots group can focus on what they do best – the retailers managing shops and the property company managing real estate assets.

Hidden potential

Boots Properties operates as an almost independent property company. Most of its profits arise from the internal rent charges paid by the other Boots companies, especially Boots The Chemists – its main tenant. As the real estate is occupied by group businesses it must be valued as fixed assets used for operational purposes and not as investment properties. As discussed in Appendix A, valuations for operational buildings are undertaken on the Existing Use Value (EUV) basis according to the RICS *Appraisal and Valuation Manual* and Accounting Standards Board. This means that the valuation has to be on the basis that vacant possession is available.

The directors of both Boots Properties and the parent, The Boots Company, have commented in their annual reports (e.g. The Boots Company plc, 1993) that in their opinion the Existing Use Value is not a realistic indication of the value to the company of such properties. The EUV has to ignore the value of the covenant of the various Boots companies. If the real estate was owned by a non-group company, the fact that the rent was secured by a Boots company would increase the value of the investment. This would follow through to the owner's balance sheet, where fixed assets that are investment properties would be included at open market value (OMV), which reflects such matters as the covenant of the tenant.

When the economic recession and the property slump wrought their effects on Boots Properties' real estate holdings, a revaluation revealed a shortfall of £202 million. Whereas previously this would have affected the trading companies directly, in 1992/93 the revaluation shortfall was borne by the 'owner' of the real estate – Boots Properties. This can be seen in Figure 18.2.

The directors indicated in The Boots Company plc Annual Report of 1993 that, had the company been able to recognise the strength of the Boots covenant, the shortfall for the whole group of £223 million on the revaluation would have only been £175 million. This is an indication that the whole of the Boots Properties assets in 1995, which are recorded as being worth just over £800 million, would be worth on open market values well over £900 million. This 'hidden' potential is something that applies to many companies and relates to required accounting and valuation practices, which are constantly the subject of debate, so it is not as covert as profit rent masquerading as trading profit. The difference between EUV and OMV can only be released if properties are sold.

Investment properties

From 1993 Boots Properties began giving the value of the investment properties (i.e. occupied by non-Boots companies) on its balance sheet as fixed assets. Figure 18.3 shows how this has increased steadily in the following years.

Releasing development potential

Boots Properties has begun to release some of the development potential within the estate, and Figure 18.4 shows the ongoing profits arising from investment (i.e. rental income, mostly from other Boots companies) and the profits and losses from development. The profits from development are still a small part of the total, which is not surprising given the economic recession, but sufficient has happened for the potential to be demonstrated.

The contribution of real estate

When Boots Pharmaceuticals was sold in 1995, Boots Properties became the second largest company in the group – after Boots The Chemists. Figure 18.5 shows the operating profit of The Boots Company, with the contributions from Boots Properties and Boots The Chemists highlighted. This clearly shows the contribution of real estate to the group's success, but it is to be remembered that the rental income is mostly being transferred from other group companies. Boots The Chemists can be seen to have had substantial profits growth which,

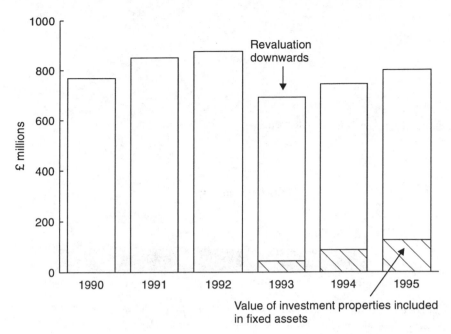

Figure 18.3 Boots Properties plc: growth in investment properties (occupied by non-Boots companies). (Source: Boots Properties plc annual reports 1990–1995)

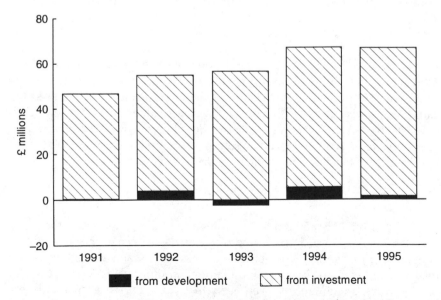

Figure 18.4 Boots Properties plc: source of profits. (Source: The Boots Company report and accounts 1995 (as restated))

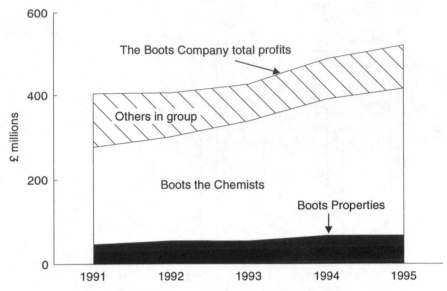

Figure 18.5 The Boots Company plc: operating profit before exceptional items. (Source: The Boots Company report and accounts 1995 (as restated))

as it no longer owns any substantial property interests, has come from its various trading activities. Boots The Chemists is the mainstay of the Boots Company – very clearly it is a retailer profiting from its core business activities.

Restated accounts

The figures used for Figure 18.5 were taken from The Boots Company's 1995 Annual Report, where a series of results are given on the same accounting basis. They do not align exactly with the other graphs in this chapter as the earlier years were restated to match current accountancy practice, which is not available for the accounts of the individual companies. The figures from the annual reports of the individual subsidiary companies are used elsewhere in this chapter because they contain more detailed information.

The occupancy handbook

The relationship between Boots Properties and other companies in the group is based on the internal arrangement that it has in place of leases. This is contained in a handbook which sets out the terms and conditions of the relationship, which is similar to a 'traditional' institutional lease (see Chapter 8). The rents, which are reviewed every five years, are set at market levels, with a system to use an external arbitrator in the case of disputes. There are two conditions that reflect the internal nature of the arrangement. The first is the provision for downward as well as upward rent reviews. Such a condition is not so rare today, but when included in the occupancy handbook in 1989 it was almost unknown in institutional leases.

The second is the proviso that the trading businesses only have to provide nine months' notice if they want to quit accommodation. The cost of owning unoccupied premises then falls to Boots Properties. This reflects the fact that only Boots Properties has the authority to relet or sell the premises, so the sooner the burden falls to it the sooner it has an incentive to take action. The short period of notice makes it easier for the Boots retailing businesses to react quickly to market changes. They can close down a shop in a weak shopping centre with very little cost burden to their individual accounts, while their competitors are bearing long-term costs against their trading accounts. Obviously there is a problem for the Boots Company, but it is shown to be a real estate and not a trading problem.

The Boots The Chemists Estates Department

Within the main retailing company, Boots The Chemists, is the Estate Department, headed by David Stathers, the Director of Estates. This is the operation that manages the occupation of the real estate and which contributes real estate expertise to the corporate strategy of the retailing businesses. While the retailing businesses normally take space owned or developed by Boots Properties, they are free to go to third parties for space if this is more suitable. If this happens, the freehold or lease is held and managed by Boots Properties.

Conflicting advice

After the establishment of Boots Properties as the group's separate property company, a link was established between it and the Estates Department of Boots The Chemists. This was achieved by Stathers being given the responsibility of advising both boards. It proved an impossible task. The objectives of the two organisations were too frequently in conflict. Landlord and tenant, even when within the same overall business, have different goals. In too many instances the advice that Stathers would have given to one board would not be in the best interests of the other company. The arrangement lasted less than 18 months, after which Stathers relinquished his role with Boots Properties and felt more comfortable.

Work of the Estates Department

It is the Estates Department that provides the real estate occupation component of the corporate strategy. Its role is to act as a support function for Boots The Chemists by providing value-adding estate and property services to maximise the potential of the Boots brand and give competitive advantage for the business. Its vision is to be the most successful and highest professionally regarded estate function operating in UK retailing. The objectives are set out as:

- satisfy the total strategic space requirement
- achieve the lowest affordable and sustainable cost of occupation
- resolve all issues to protect and enhance each property and its trading environment
- promote and influence beneficial change in the property market and professions

The real estate team provide the normal estate management services related to matters such as rent reviews, schedules of dilapidations, planning, and acquisition and disposal of properties. They also provide a service charge control and monitoring service. Finally, there is a very experienced in-house business rates team. The real estate team is not sufficient to provide for all the business's needs, and surveyors and lawyers are commissioned as necessary. Their aim is to have long-term relationships with consultants who perform to agreed briefs with quantifiable and benchmarked key quality criteria.

Forecasting

The real estate team takes their role as a contributor to corporate strategy very seriously. They are not hidebound by the valuation requirements of the RICS *Appraisal and Valuation Manual* (1995). Naturally, all formal valuations follow the manual's requirements, but when it comes to developing strategic policy they build their own forecasting models and use discounted cash flow (DCF) methods to bring more precision to their analysis.

When compiling the real estate contribution, they develop models incorporating everything which they believe will affect the business from a real estate context. The data they have on shopping centres is acknowledged to be among the best in the country. They have been collecting and updating it for 40 years. They have watched and recorded the growth of shopping centres, including the changing provision of retail services both in product ranges and accommodation.

The data from individual centres is analysed to produce regional and national trends. The real estate team will know where a centre is under- or over-represented in any particular product range, and will be able to predict the retailers most likely to succeed if they take any vacant space. They know which combinations of shops work well together. This may be used to relate to the plans of their own different retail specialists or to decide on the products to carry and the space to give them within existing Boots stores. An alternative use is to work out what other retailers would help to make a centre attractive if operating alongside The Boots Company stores.

The real estate team can view development opportun[ities in]
a shopping centre and make a good guess as to which m[?]
their competitors. They will attempt to ascertain the effect[?]
will have directly on the Boots group's operations in a ce[?]
assess the knock-on effect, whether good or bad, on other traders, both
competitors and non-competitors. They will be able to make calculated
predictions as to the future of the Boots businesses in the centre and make
any recommendations for pertinent changes in their own real estate before
the predicted financial effects, whether positive or adverse, are felt by other
traders in a shopping centre.

Many of these decisions are based on the team's understanding of the real
estate implications, which they then quantify by using DCF forecasting techniques. They also make use of a program that is producing 10-year forecasts
of rental levels in 600 key town centres.

These methods are used when a centre is subject to change, but they are
also used to produce five-yearly position assessments to evaluate their position
in the retailing and property markets. Stathers has found that the real estate
research data has been the basis for competitive gains over the years.

Rent reviews

A problem facing many retailers is producing evidence to support their
evaluation of rental levels for rent reviews. In recent years, the recession, the
property slump and the growth of out-of-town shopping centres have caused
many town centre shopping centres to experience a fall-off in trading. Profitability, indeed the very existence of a retail business, can be threatened if
rents are too high. Notwithstanding this, it is often possible for a landlord to
get a new tenant to pay a high rent, which is then used as justification to
push up existing rent levels. The failure of the new tenant's business, as
predicted by the existing tenants, will not occur until after the other rents
have been raised. Existing tenants may then also start to fail, or they may just
continue because even low profits, at least in the first instance, seem better
than the alternative of bearing the costs of closing down a shop.

Boots is able, from its databases, to predict where the rents that it is being
asked to pay are above what the locality can sustain and can make a strong
case to protect its interests. In centres where many tenants have the same
landlord, Boots has been instrumental in encouraging the retailers to commission consultants who, while providing confidentiality, can collect from the
individual businesses the vital information on trading and profitability to
illustrate whether a centre can or cannot support higher rents.

Boots is not acting in a philanthropic way. If a landlord sets any rents too
high in a centre where Boots trades, then Boots is affected, maybe directly,
but also indirectly. As the weakest and most vulnerable traders fail, the
ambience of a shopping centre changes and it becomes less attractive. This

begins to exacerbate the situation, because, as the centre becomes less attractive, fewer people shop there. Even though Boots may have had a fair rent for its operation, when trade declines it finds that its rent is too high for the reduced volume of trade.

Landlords are not oblivious to the risks of a shopping centre declining, and while they seek to maximise their resources, most are more interested in long-term sustainability and growth than high returns for the short term. It is an adversarial situation, but good real estate knowledge and acceptable forecasting techniques by a tenant will be taken seriously by most landlords. Stathers is very critical of any landlord who is still chasing rent increases when real estate values have declined.

The rental predictions are used to ascertain the overall profitable trading potential of Boots' individual stores. Where rent reviews were undertaken at the peak of the boom of the late 1980s the current rent levels can be well above market levels, and because of upward-only rent reviews they will remain excessive until market rent levels increase. Where properties are over-rented, this will be taken into account by the Estates Department when deciding on future policy in a shopping centre.

In many shopping centres changes in trading levels will arise because of changing layouts – a new competing development or a new car park may change passing trade. The effect may be marginal and not sufficient in normal circumstances to cause a retailer to move. Couple this with an over-rented location, however, and making a move may well be advantageous – the trading revenue will increase at the new location and the rent will be lower; additionally a profit rent may begin to develop – real estate growth is a possibility. There are still the commitments of the old accommodation, which may be a burden for a number of years because reletting may not produce an income to match outgoings. However, if the overall loss is less than that which was being experienced when the retailing business was tied to the over-rented building, the business has gained. These types of forecasting are important where the retailing business wants to expand its trading area or invest in new shop fittings in a property where rental growth is not expected (called ex-growth because it has already taken place). This level of real estate forecasting and appraisal is unusual. Most businesses do not have the research base.

Additionally, to understanding traditional markets Boots is taking on board consideration of substantial changes in the retail pattern. With many out-of-town stores, especially in its non-pharmacy businesses, it has interests spreading across the town centre vs. out-of-town shopping arguments. This wide base of information helps it to predict influences on retailing and how they will affect its business. One such development is the growth of home shopping and the development of teleshopping. All are carefully monitored and the company's own experience supplemented by specific research.

A general prediction is that prime property will succeed but that other shops, especially in areas where transport links and parking are poor, will fail to thrive. The Boots Company, with its diverse range of retailing outlets, can shift itself to reposition the types of stores that will succeed in the centres that will meet public requirements. Real estate decisions are a vital component of this survival process.

Stepping out of the straitjacket to add value

The real estate team work with strategists and economists from within Boots The Chemists to assist them in using these techniques to add value to the business. Much of what they do is well beyond the normal work of most property professionals. Stathers has to provide further education and training to develop the skills needed by members of his real estate team to produce the advice that will add the value demanded by corporate management.

Lord Blyth, the deputy chairman and chief executive of The Boots Company, has publicly expressed his view that the property industry is not serving the needs of corporate business (Blyth, 1994). Stathers has backed this with criticism of the restricted range of methods proposed in the Mallinson Report (1994) and later implemented by the new RICS *Appraisal and Valuation Manual* (1995) which is also the butt of his criticism (Stathers, 1996).

Together they have waged attacks on the property industry for being short-sighted, reactionary, arrogant and expensive. This, they say, is resulting in property professionals having little awareness of future real estate potential. They say that the property profession is ducking the need for modern financial appraisal to isolate and understand risk in decision-making that involves real estate. Given the wide-ranging use of a variety of valuation techniques by their staff to assist in the development of corporate strategy, they speak from a well-informed position. What they say is very relevant to the issues raised in this book.

Business rates

Another area in which the Estates Department of Boots The Chemists is driving through a new approach is in the valuation of the company's buildings for business rates. Traditionally, the Valuation Office provides a rating list giving valuations for all the business premises in an area. Any business that feels that its premises have been over-valued can appeal against the valuation. Since the publication of the 1990 Rating List, Boots The Chemists has received back £30 million after a large number of successful appeals. During the process there were severe peaks and troughs in the cash flow for a substantial overhead, which is not helpful to a business. Stathers felt that having to appeal was a time-wasting process which could be avoided to the advantage of all involved. The cause of Boots' success at appeal was that it could present very good evidence of values. It was information that had not been available to the Valuation Office when the list was prepared.

It would be better, Stathers reasoned, not to have incorrect valuations in the first place. This could be achieved in many instances by Boots presenting property value information to the Valuation Office ahead of the valuation exercise. Having found that consultants were unhappy about changing the traditional approach, an in-house rating team was established which is handling the 1995 Rating List/Valuation Roll. The aim is to provide a free flow of information for the mutual benefit of Boots The Chemists and the Valuation Office Agency and, in Scotland, the Assessors.

Boots' commitment to the exercise is highlighted by its published statement that they 'believe the withholding of information for short term gain damages our ability to both forecast future liabilities and manage cash flow' (Boots The Chemists, 1995).

The process, which has been welcomed by the Valuation Office, is not resulting in agreement on every entry on the Rating List. The Estates Department of Boots The Chemists is appealing against some valuations and is still using consultants for these representations. However, the number of appeals has fallen and the cash flow predictions for its business rate commitments are much easier to forecast than after previous valuations. This means that the businesses can invest funds in their operations rather than have them tied up and idle while appeals are in progress.

Having set up a specialist rating unit, the group makes full use of the resource, and even Boots Properties is a client.

18.3   Transferable experience

The Boots Company is particularly interesting because the changes in the arrangements for real estate were not brought about by some major event – they have been driven by ongoing and very ordinary corporate needs.

As a consequence, much of what was undertaken is of value to many businesses. While many will be too small or own too little real estate to set up a separate property company, the issues that drove The Boots Company to make this choice will be ones that others could need to address. A smaller company might address the issues by separating its real estate interests from the main business in other ways, such as by leasing rather than owning (clearly isolating the effect of profit rent) or setting about realising development potential.

The main points of interest are that:

- businesses needs to understand the role played by real estate in the success, or otherwise, of their operations
- real estate profits, if not isolated, can become confused with profits from other business activities
- accounting methods permit very inaccurate recording of the value of real estate assets

- some argue that current valuation and accountancy practice confuses the situation even when values are up to date
- when the full financial situation is not clear because of inaccurate real estate assumptions there is a risk of a takeover bid, even for a large company
- a company that understands the role of real estate can be influential in developing the future practices of the property industry and its professions
- internal rents only really work if they reflect market rents – otherwise they create a false impression
- internal arrangements for the occupation of real estate can encourage (or discourage!) rapid reaction to changing markets by the core business
- real estate teams are more effective if their own strategies and objectives are clear
- professional and industry practices and methodologies are not sacrosanct and should be reviewed and either improved or changed to meet changing circumstances
- research and information helps the decision-making process and information not available to others can give competitive advantage
- IT advances can handle information that was previously too difficult to evaluate
- making positive contributions to potentially adversarial situations can bring gains
- lateral thinking can result in new proposals and working methods – 'gains' previously held in high regard can be found to be lacking when wider issues are considered
- profitability can be improved by the real estate team working in ways that are not standard within the property world – it is essential to view real estate from the business perspective

19 Conrad Ritblat Group plc

19.1 Introduction

The Conrad Ritblat Group plc is a commercial property services consultancy offering professional and agency services to property owners, investors and users. It is a practice used by many corporate property owners and occupiers. Its core business comprises services related to real estate. It has been included in this book because it has actively used real estate-based strategies to gain competitive advantage in a difficult market-place.

19.2 A fundamental difficulty

Much of the income for a property services firm arises in various ways from property advice and deals. It comes either directly from agency fees or from providing professional services to assist owners and users to protect their interests in these deals. The firm also gains from fees earned by enhancing clients' property interests, either by physical improvements or by managing these interests to gain financially from a wide range of activities, such as obtaining planning permission, assembling development sites and managing tenants. The work can be very profitable in a property boom, but during an economic recession and a property slump the margins fall and professional firms find it hard to make financially adequate returns (London, 1995).

Professional service firms that can come through the difficult periods in sound financial shape are well placed to expand their activities as demand increases again. During the 1990s many of these firms have found it difficult to maintain their business during the dearth of work. Although many have left the market, there is still fierce fee competition. Barriers to entry are low, and when large practices stop trading, merge or retract by making staff redundant, the ex-directors, partners and employees frequently start new practices with lower overheads and lower fees, although often not offering the same level of service.

Conrad Ritblat has used a real estate strategy to enable itself not only to survive through this difficult period but also to strengthen its financial standing so that it can increase its share of this very fragmented market.

While the original partnership of Conrad Ritblat began life in the 1960s, the current group was only formed in 1993, with the reverse takeover of Sinclair Goldsmith plc by the then incorporated Conrad Ritblat & Co. The new business was called Conrad Ritblat Sinclair Goldsmith plc until the name was changed to Conrad Ritblat Group plc in 1995.

19.3   Acquiring fixed operational assets

During 1993 and 1994 the company acquired the freeholds of four office buildings which it was already occupying or moved into after acquisition. As they were all partially operational buildings, they were, at least in part, operational fixed assets rather than investments. These purchases meant that Conrad Ritblat had succeeded in avoiding the handicap of high accommodation rental costs that were being borne by many of its competitors. Some of the purchases were financed by debt and others through the issue of new share capital. Conrad Ritblat switched from paying rent to receiving rent from tenants in its buildings.

19.4   Real estate investments

In August 1995 Conrad Ritblat moved very clearly into real estate investments with the purchase of 109 public houses let to a public company brewery for the next 22 years. The deal, financed by debt, provided the practice with a net cash flow after debt charges of £400 000 per annum, which went straight to the bottom line. Synergy came from using the company's core surveying skills to manage the estate, including rent reviews, and to implement redevelopment proposals. The marginal cost of managing these investments is negligible. Conrad Ritblat paid £10.6 million for the portfolio and it pushed its total gross assets to over £40 million.

The public house investment was an interesting choice. A Monopolies and Mergers Commission report and the subsequent Beer Orders of 1989 ended the dominance of brewers in the ownership of pubs. Investors and analysts who have monitored the subsequent performance of this sector found that, unlike most property, public houses had performed well during the recession and the income from these properties is from traditional full repairing and insuring leases at market rents. So although Conrad Ritblat has invested in a core skill – the management of property – it is one that has performed differently from most of their property industry-related income. There was also an understanding that the vendor, Allied Domecq, which was already a client, would place more professional property work with Conrad Ritblat, hence creating an additional potential gain.

A few months later, in December 1995, the company purchased another real estate investment portfolio. This portfolio had been acquired by the Royal Bank of Scotland when it foreclosed on clients who went into receivership. The mixed portfolio included industrial and office premises and a London theatre currently used as a music venue and night club. Although diverse in character, the income from the estate is more closely aligned to core surveying income than in the case of the public house investment.

The purchase increased the gross fixed assets of the company by 24% to over £53 million. The purchase price of £9.9 million was paid by £5.5 million in cash and a further £4.4 million was satisfied by the issue of shares to the Royal Bank of Scotland. This increased share capital by 13% and resulted in the Royal Bank of Scotland holding 12% of the equity. There was again the expectation that the deal would result in more consultancy work, this time from Royal Bank of Scotland, which has the incentive of being a shareholder. In return, Conrad Ritblat intends to utilise the bank's services where appropriate.

19.5   Gaining core business market share

The second real estate investment acquisition with the Royal Bank of Scotland coincided with the acquisition of Colliers Erdman Lewis, a major surveying practice which had gone into administrative receivership. The cost of acquisition from the receiver was calculated as the redundancy payments plus cash to a total of £400 000. A further £1.8 million has been written off against the reserves to cover trading losses during an initial management contract and for other exceptional expenses. It was not a problem for Conrad Ritblat, with its strong balance sheet.

Immediate rationalisation of Colliers Erdman Lewis just prior to acquisition reduced its turnover by 50%. The remaining 50% was sufficient to double the turnover of Conrad Ritblat. A doubling of turnover would have been hard to achieve by organic growth. At the same time, the acquisition broadened the range of professional services that the group could offer.

As the focus of this book is real estate strategies, the details of this transaction are unimportant except for the fact that the real estate strategies of Conrad Ritblat had placed it in a position where it could make this strategically important gain of market share.

19.6   Structured for a profitable future

The three acquisitions which occurred between August 1995 and January 1996 have resulted in a substantially different company structure – the income source has diversified but remained within core competencies, gearing has substantially increased and turnover from professional property services is set to double. Shareholders have traded a dilution of their holdings by 13% for the prospect of higher profits and asset growth.

Operating margins (based on profit on ordinary activities before taxation) since the merger in 1993 until the last reported figures in November 1995 have remained above 10%. This is significantly higher than some of Conrad Ritblat's major competitors, many of whom have to bear high rental charges in their cost structure. A 10% margin on the increased turnover would produce a profit increase well above the levels experienced by property consultants since the onslaught of the economic recession and property slump.

In the short term the effect could be dulled because the business might take time to absorb all the changes. However, this is unlikely to be a problem with the property acquisitions, where the profit rents should go straight to the profit and loss account. With £1.8 million in the reserves to cover the short-term costs and losses during the acquisition of Colliers Erdman Lewis, profitable trading will be immediately reflected in the profit and loss account.

Conrad Ritblat's real estate-based strategies are bringing them significant competitive advantage – diversity of income streams and increased turnover – in very difficult market conditions. It will be well placed to reap the benefits of an expanding economy.

19.7 Transferable experience

A significant feature of this chapter was Conrad Ritblat's use of an existing core competence in real estate to gain competitive advantage. It is a possibility for any business that employs real estate managers. The experiences that could be transferable are that:

- real estate competencies can be strategically leveraged
- real estate assets can bring financial flexibility to a business
- the real estate on the balance sheet can be of strategic importance in supporting strategies for growth
- more generally, devising ways to overcome the major problems facing participants in a market opens up opportunities for gaining competitive advantage

20 Z/Yen Ltd

20.1 Introduction

This study is of a much smaller company. This is not one of the major UK corporate businesses. Z/Yen is of interest as a practical example of the development of a company that shows how the future is forming. Its virtual company arrangements are a step on the path to Mitchell's *City of Bits* (1995; see Chapter 5).

Z/Yen offers services that match those of many traditional companies, yet it has a core office of only 46 m². Its operation shows how new organisations, without the sunk costs of an existing operation, have the freedom to run with new ideas and use new practices that others only dream about.

20.2 A traditional service

Z/Yen is a management consultancy. It has a diverse and substantial client list comprising some of the UK's largest companies and government departments, leading international and European companies, and a number of charities. Z/Yen and its client list have shown healthy growth since the company was founded in 1994.

The consultancy's successful growth is clearly due to a number of factors. Most of them are completely unrelated to its futuristic *modi operandi* and include:

- services which focus on the key strategic need for risk/reward management
- a practical methodology consisting of a strategic framework, supporting software, procedures, case studies and report formats
- key issues are identified before expensive in-depth research and analysis are undertaken
- experienced well-qualified consultants with wide-ranging skills
- an initial core group of excellent clients

These factors would not be changed by Z/Yen having a large city centre office. Z/Yen's success is due to many traditional features. It earns its living by providing consultancy services which are, in practical terms, much like many other consultants. While the Z/Yen directors will say that their success is due to the unique and client-focused range of services, this is no different from the claims of directors or partners of other successful consultancies.

The key point is that Z/Yen has been successful in a traditional market providing traditional services. Clients do not feel that they are being especially adventurous when they engage Z/Yen's services. No doubt many client companies have added confidence that, as Z/Yen consultants have sorted out their own organisation so effectively, they will be equally able to develop effective, workable but innovative ideas to assist their clients' businesses.

20.3   Founding Z/Yen

The foundation of Z/Yen was also not particularly unusual – the initial directors came together because most of them worked for accountancy and management consultancy firms that amalgamated, and they decided to sidestep the new operation and start up their own. Several clients followed. This initial group of directors had been working in different cities – Leeds, London, Manchester and Milton Keynes. Had they all lived around one city they would not have been faced with the prospect of major upheaval to replicate their previous working patterns. Like others before them, the business plan could so easily have included capital to solve their accommodation problem.

20.4   Seeking flexibility – a good life

This group wanted to work together, but none wanted to be burdened with unnecessary travel. They wanted flexibility, yet they also wanted their clients to have at least the same level of service as that provided by a traditional large, international consultancy – ideally it would be better.

All the consultants now work from studies in their homes, but at any time they can be at clients' premises, in hotels or travelling anywhere in the world and accessible only via client or hotel switchboards or by mobile phone. Anyone telephoning Z/Yen in normal UK office hours will receive a personal reply and will be connected to their consultant – anywhere in the world, without any indication of where the call is being routed. Consultants can speak to each other with ease, yet enjoy the peace of their own quiet study to think and write. The answer has come by investing in IT and connectivity rather than bricks and mortar.

The core of the business is the telephone system supported by ordinary PCs. Each consultant has a PC. This is nothing unusual – it is now the norm for management consultancy. In addition, each has two home telephone lines to support telephone, fax machine and modem. Each consultant also has a mobile phone. They use email.

Despite email, the telephone system is very important to the practice. Voice mail is used not only as a telephone answering system but also as a way of linking the consultants. The system allows individuals to dictate one message which will be left on the voice mail of all or some of the other consultants.

Another major use of the telephone is conference calls. These are easy to set up with BT, and allow all the consultants to use their home telephones to join a conversation in which they can all be heard. 'Meetings' held in this way have saved them a considerable amount of travelling time and expense.

Z/Yen's operational core is just one small office staffed initially by one, but now two, organisers. This is where the company phone lines are answered and calls routed to consultants at home or to most places around the world. This office is served by four ISDN lines, which are needed to match the connectivity standards of clients and to assist global networking.

Alongside the telephone system is the network, with its file server. Consultants can work on this system if they are in the London office, but mostly they link up to it using their modem and ordinary telephone connections from wherever they happen to be working. The organisers receive reports and letters prepared by the consultants as files sent via their modems. They then finish off the work in the company format and send it out. Most consultants can print from home, if they wish. Files can also be sent by modem direct to the company's printers, an outsourced service for printing and binding reports. A simplified model of the system is shown in Figure 20.1. The boxes with thick borders represent the core office in London and locations where the consultants can be working at any particular time.

Figure 20.2 shows a stylised cross-section of an office block that could be the alternative accommodation for the company without a virtual framework. In this the shaded areas show where the consultant's have permanent space to work – even if they are travelling, at a client's office or at home. Each will probably have a support office, and there will be other provision such as the board- or meeting room(s), reception, car parking and the telephonist. Other space could be required for a library, canteen, smoking room etc. The space for the telephonist has been shared, as this is similar to the core office of the virtual company. All the non-shaded space is the stylised representation of the additional accommodation needed to run a traditional office. Even with all this space, unless similar IT to the virtual office is installed the accessibility of consultants away from the office will be weak.

20.5   No wizardry

The systems used to create the Z/Yen virtual company are not at the vanguard of IT development. There is nothing in place that is amazingly expensive or

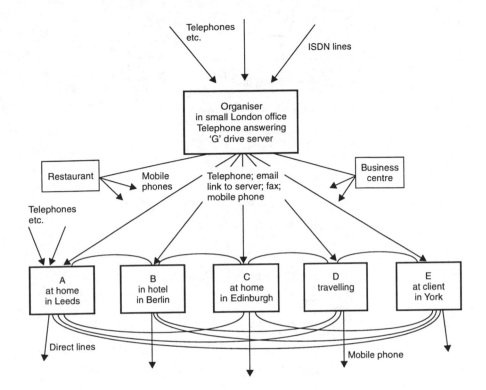

Figure 20.1 The virtual company.

complex. The cost of the initial IT equipment would not have bought a modest starter home – and certainly not office accommodation in London for all the consultants. Indeed, most of the IT would have been needed for report writing and communications when travelling, even if the consultants had an office block. The additional IT costs to set up the virtual company were small.

Z/Yen has formed a virtual company without using mind-blowing technology. This very ordinariness is important. It shows what is possible. The flexibility gives it dynamic possibilities. When the group decided to expand and offer a post to another consultant they were still able to go ahead when the would-be new member said 'I would love to join you, but I am moving to Edinburgh'. Now Z/Yen has a presence in Scotland and its network has been able to absorb the new consultant's work even though he is an Apple Macintosh user!

Z/Yen expect to upgrade the IT capacity of its network. Taking on a second organiser has given it the capacity to build a graphics library. The next step will probably be the introduction of more a sophisticated groupware system by installing Lotus Notes. It will make the interchange of ideas easier and will

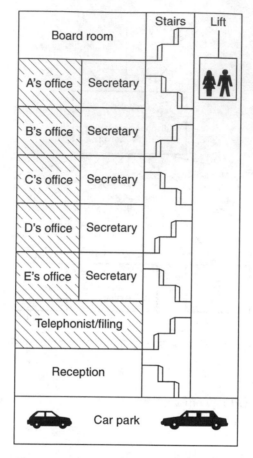

Figure 20.2 Offices for the traditional non-virtual company (stylised cross-section.

form a structured system for the network, including greater replication of databases. This development is probably essential if it is to continue to expand without pushing this simple system to breaking point.

20.6   Working with the information revolution

IT is turning the world upside down. In the past the library of any consultancy practice was a resource that others could not easily replicate. It was an entry barrier for individual consultants to offering services which needed the backup of research facilities. An individual cannot afford the wide range of books and journals shared by those working from a large practice. Now, with easy access to numerous online databases, the library is, for the most part, redundant. Indeed, the online services are probably more up to date. Interestingly, the allure of books has not faded, and Z/Yen consultants still maintain a small London office library and have personal libraries in their studies at home.

There are charges for using online databases. These are not excessive, but for an organisation that maintains a full library they are an expensive duplication, which has caused some established practices to reject or only partially use online services. This is yet another illustration of how sunk costs can be a millstone to fast reaction in an ever-changing world.

20.7   Cost-effective and enjoyable alternatives to offices

Without large real estate commitments, Z/Yen's operating costs are different from those of many other businesses. After salaries, IT is the largest outgoing. The company does need places to meet together and with clients. An arrangement with a firm with whom their business has a synergy gives them access to meeting rooms adjacent to Z/Yen's core office, but these rooms are rarely used.

Z/Yen consultants meet in restaurants, hotels, business centres and when travelling to appointments. Health clubs and yachts make attractive venues for their monthly management meetings (see Figure 20.1). These venues are a little grander than the motorway service stations predicted by Hillman in *Flexicities* (1993; see Chapter 5). The costs seem high for businesses also paying for office accommodation, but for Z/Yen, which does not have other real estate costs, it is more than manageable, as are the travelling costs of running a small business with near-nationwide coverage. Furthermore, they are not leaving expensive office space empty when they meet or travel to client's premises.

20.8   Hot-desking

Z/Yen is still working out its need for touchdown or hotelling space for consultants who would like to spend a day in London. Demand is not high, and it has been using a desk in its small core office. The company thinks that it will soon expand, but it is clearly not a major issue. Like most management consultants they also spend a lot of time working at their clients' premises. If the virtual consultant has to meet a virtual client, then the short-term hiring of space in a business centre will surely be the way forward!

20.9   Sharing the benefits

The success of the business is based on the initial list of factors. It is also clear that the virtual company arrangement is not causing clients any problem. There is not really any reason why it should. Z/Yen offers high-value services and receives commensurate fees. Cutting out many of the real estate costs increases operating profits, but without wholesale cutting of fees Z/Yen is able to offer its clients the opportunity to share in the benefits of their lower costs – an attractive proposition.

20.10 Services to suit corporate clients

The Z/Yen consultants have realised the dream of working from home without becoming sole practitioners. Large corporations fear the unreliability of the sole practitioner with no backup in case of illness. For many projects the single consultant just does not have the resources to tackle several issues at once. Z/Yen consultants, while working from home, are part of a company with resources that equal, or even surpass, those of many of the larger practices.

20.11 An indication of the future

This study has been included because it illustrates that personal computers, their software and connectivity can, and are, changing working methods without resorting to the use of complex and expensive technology. It shows that it is possible for businesses that are not large, do not have a technology base and have only small resources to use changing IT-based working practices. These methods are not just the preserve of companies such as IBM and BT.

20.12 Summary

This chapter shows how Z/Yen Ltd is operating in a mostly virtual format, using very little office space, yet providing clients with high-value consultancy services. The key points of interest are:

- the service to clients is as good, if not better than, traditional consultancy
- well-known, tried and tested IT supports the practice
- IT costs are higher than the real estate costs
- the IT costs incurred to create the virtual company are less than a similar size business would spend on real estate
- the Z/Yen consultants are enjoying their working arrangements
- meetings in expensive restaurants, hotels or leisure locations are affordable
- the company is profitable and expanding

- expansion can usually be undertaken without acquiring additional offices (these are only needed if the number of organisers becomes too high for the existing core office)
- new consultants can join the business without moving home
- a geographically widespread presence does not add to costs
- most support services are available either online or by outsourcing.

Part 6:
Conclusion

21 The Steps Ahead

UK corporate business has begun to appreciate that real estate decisions can be of strategic importance. Some leading companies involve real estate experts in their strategic planning teams and on their main boards so that their corporate strategy incorporates real estate considerations and vice versa. However, many companies have yet to take this step.

Seeking to be competitive while ignoring the deployment of 30–40% of the company's assets and the source of 16–17% of costs is hard work – like tying one's hands together and trying to write. It is possible, but the results are less than ideal and twice the necessary resource has been engaged in the process.

For many businesses real estate is a significant resource. This is the tradition, but in recent years many choices have arisen about how and where (or even if) it will be used. The choices are arising as technological developments are freeing operations from both geography and time.

For many services, especially in the financial field, it is of no consequence to the client where the decisions are made. The service by telephone is the same whether the client is a mile or 1000 miles away from the provider.

Even products that are transported from manufacturer to customer can pass rapidly through the process, individually and electronically monitored from production to consumer, without spending any time in storage. These operational developments often require less real estate: Marks & Spencer found it much easier, and also cheaper, to have fewer warehouses when it installed electronic stock control methods. Potential cost savings in other areas, such as real estate, can have a significant impact on the decision to spend on IT equipment. More important for business success is that investment in IT operational systems frequently gives managers a wider choice when considering real estate needs. No longer are there obvious answers to questions of location, type and quality.

Many decisions involving real estate have the capacity to make a significant difference to profitability. A 5% cut in real estate costs may increase profits by 10%, as the saving directly cuts costs, frequently fixed costs.

Each real estate decision has the capacity to bring competitive advantage or, conversely, the risk of falling asset value and high unexpected costs. The real estate implications of decisions will not be highlighted by businesses that do not involve real estate experts in their strategic decision-making processes.

Many business managers allow their lack of interest to extend to the point of complete ignorance of what they spend on real estate. Many more have no idea of the indirect costs linked to real estate decisions. The situation is improving, but very slowly. All the time they prevaricate, they are spending potential profits.

Change must come, and will probably come much too rapidly for the survival of some businesses. Once competitors address the changing opportunities and make competitive gains, the visionless can only be followers. These followers will be left only to hope that the first movers make a mistake. If the first movers succeed, the followers will see the value of their businesses fade and even disappear.

It is not only the visionless non-property businesses that can suffer. Those in the property world, developers, landlords and professional advisers, need to educate themselves to understand the changes. If they do not change their own business operations to serve their markets, they will be facing a similarly difficult future. Property people must know their clients' needs, whether as tenants or purchasers of professional advice. Services offered must focus on the future and not remain as just those that have worked in the past. They must address the smallest nuances in their clients' needs or face losing their corporate clients. This approach is attracting and keeping tenants for BAA.

It is not always easy to move in the way that is best for the business. Strategic vision and intent have to be carried out. Looking back, Sainsbury's programme of sales and leaseback of trading buildings looks mundane. Yet at the time, the financial environment and the nervousness of traditionally minded investors made their requirements very ambitious. Sainsbury's had to market its idea by producing an investment product to overcome the concerns of prospective partners. Eventually, the money tied up by holding real estate assets was released to help fund its development plans.

The overall role of real estate in a business will be very particular to each operation. So while Sainsbury's sold real assets to expand the business, the Conrad Ritblat Group did the opposite. To support its expansion, Conrad Ritblat acquired real estate both as operational assets and investments. In its market of professional services many competitors are tied to paying high rents and to occupying particular buildings because of lease commitments. Owning its operational buildings gives Conrad Ritblat greater freedom – and less risk. Additionally, its well-chosen real estate investments have diversified its income flow and provided an asset base to support debt finance and the expansion programme.

For many businesses, using less real estate is bringing advantages. However, even those that make little use of real estate, such as the consultancy Z/Yen Ltd, with its virtual office, have to make decisions that involve real estate. The Z/Yen consultants must each have a place at home to work. Teleworking shifts the burden of providing working space – an issue that looks set to become more important for many in the future. Teleconferencing is very useful to Z/Yen, but the consultants still meet and use restaurants, hotels and health clubs for accommodation. The substitution of the virtual office and varied meeting places for fixed accommodation works well for Z/Yen. As others follow, the advantages will be experienced by many and the value of the virtual office may be of no strategic importance.

The case studies have shown that much is gained when real estate considerations are incorporated into the business's strategy. However, as IBM has found, the consideration of real estate issues needs to spread throughout the business. It affects the work of everyone, and their day-to-day decisions have a direct bearing on real estate occupation. It is not easy, and IBM is still working towards finding solutions. Strategy, and especially strategy involving real estate, is an iterative process. It changes in response to factors from within and external to the business. Being sufficiently unconventional to step out of the reactive framework and boldly into the future is frightening, and always seems very risky.

It is risky. Strategists aim to be well informed when they plan future action. The same applies when considering real estate, except that few have the research base and analytical skills to make these judgements. Boots The Chemists has a competitive advantage just from being well informed by holding records of town and shopping centres going back 40 years and linking this with current research and statistics to produce econometric models to assist forecasting. It is a factor supporting its profitability.

It can be daunting to change the way in which a business uses real estate but, as BT has shown, even the largest businesses can draw real estate into corporate strategy and make significant gains, not only from reducing requirements but by contributing to the environment of cultural change.

This book has not only shown that real estate is of strategic importance; it has paved the way towards helping corporate real estate managers and business managers to understand the role of real estate in their businesses and then develop their own real estate strategies and move on to the point where their corporate strategies incorporate real estate.

Management strategy itself is still developing, having been an academic discipline for only 25 years. Over the coming years our understanding of the strategic role of real estate should expand. But it will not happen unless its importance is appreciated and efforts are made to realise the potential.

As the book has shown, corporate real estate managers must understand traditional business skills in addition to understanding property, and business managers need to be able to appreciate the role of real estate.

However, this is not enough: in today's climate of rapid change all managers need to understand the latest developments in information technology and connectivity. This is not a one-off issue but an ongoing need – there is always something new. All of the time managers need to focus on the opportunities that the new developments will bring to their industry, some of which may also present massive threats to the profitability of their current operations. As real estate is one of the most cumbersome of fixed assets, the effective real estate manager needs to be among the first involved with changes within the company if the real estate requirements are to be effectively met. Economically activating real estate to serve the precise needs of a business takes time.

As businesses appreciate the importance of their real estate and the role that it plays in achieving profitability, opportunities are opening at the highest levels for those who can combine excellent property and business skills and have the capacity to visualise the future. There is every reason for the ambitious to equip themselves to take the lead – they are needed on the main boards of UK companies. As many shareholders, chairmen and chief executive offices still do not appreciate the significance of real estate decisions, it will not be an easy ladder to climb. Those who gain main board appointments will have had to prove their worth to their colleagues. As the case studies show, some UK top businesses have already demonstrated the wide range of areas where real estate is of strategic importance.

It is always to be remembered that real estate for non-property companies is mostly an operational asset. However well real estate serves the business financially, its main role is to support production. IBM UK's innovative real estate management programme was successful because its main aim was, despite saving costs, to support staff in gaining profitable business.

This book has dwelt on the neglected interface between business and real estate, and is a bid to widen understanding of the role of real estate within UK business. There is no thesis within the book that suggests that current practices can be forgotten – they should just be enhanced and brought much closer to central decision-making. Consequently, nothing is removed from the wide range of issues already of concern to corporate real estate managers – businesses need buildings that work: lifts that are efficient, roofs that do not leak, a comfortable environment for staff and space efficiency – but these should be provided in the way most suited to the business and its profitability.

Businesses should seek to profit from the contribution of real estate in their operations. Managers should be gaining the competitive edge from corporate strategy that includes the role of a major resource – real estate.

Appendices

Appendix A: Real Estate in Annual Reports

A.1 Introduction

This appendix reviews aspects of the company accounts, the annual report, to provided supplementary information on matters of strategic interest for those who have not previously considered company accounts with regard to real estate issues. Those who have no experience of reading company accounts would find a basic reference book, such as *The Meaning of Accounts* by Reid and Myddelton (1992) and copies of some annual reports useful.

As explained in Chapter 7, the accountancy profession is debating accountancy practice. This appendix is based on current practice, which for many companies is 'modified historical cost accounting' with the revaluation of some assets – usually real estate.

A.2 Parts of the annual report

The following numerical and written statements in the annual report provide valuable information, including real estate items:

- Profit and loss account
- Consolidated statement of total recognised gains and losses
- Balance sheet
- Cash flow statement
- Note of historical cost profits and losses
- Directors' report
- Notes to the accounts
- Report of the auditors

A.3 The four main numerical statements

The profit and loss account

Under the Companies Acts companies have to show certain figures in the annual accounts, but there is no requirement to show the amount spent on real estate-related costs. The main profit and loss account gives turnover and operating costs (cost of sales and other expenses), and by taking one from the other provides the operating profit (or net profit).

The supporting notes normally provide details on the make-up of the operating costs. Staff costs and depreciation allowances are shown, together with any major amounts, especially those that occur irregularly, such as large-scale redundancy payments. The remaining items are usually grouped together as other operating costs. Most companies give more information than this; some provide details of the amounts spent on rents or rent and rates, some provide a breakdown for maintenance and others include an item called 'other property costs'. All also have to provide details on interest payments, audit fees and directors' pay.

It is not usually possible to get a precise idea of actual real estate costs. For example, the staff costs of an in-house real estate team would come under the staff costs heading, while consultants' fees would be listed as a real estate cost or included in 'other operating costs'. The figures can be further confused by the inclusion of rents received and other operating income.

Nevertheless, the figures could be sufficient to get an understanding of the way in which a business is using real estate. It could be helpful when undertaking competitor analysis as part of a strategic analysis, but there is always a risk that the breakdown is inadequate and that the result confuses rather than enlightens!

Consolidated statement of total recognised gains and losses

The consolidated statement of total recognised gains and losses, a new component in the annual report, is where individual components of gains and losses are listed. This is an important addition to the annual report, as individual components are often more significant than the total (which may be negligible if the gains and losses balance). The information shown here makes it easier for shareholders and others to judge the health of the company. All will contain either a profit or loss figure. Companies trading international usually have a gain or loss on currency transactions to report.

Gains or losses included are ones that have been recognised during the accountancy period, normally a year. So, if balance sheet assets are revalued it is probable that the change in value has been building up (or declining) over a number of years, but the result is shown as a lump sum in the year of the revaluation. The gain or loss only has to be recognised. It does not have to be realised through the sale of the asset.

The balance sheet: operational and investment property fixed assets

Real estate which is owned by a business appears in the balance sheet as a fixed asset. If the real estate is used for operational purposes then it is valued in much the same way as other fixed operational assets, although special methods apply for real estate. When the real estate is not used for the business's operations it is normally treated as being held for investment purposes and dealt with on this basis.

Many of the proposals for changes to accountancy practice focus on the balance sheet – especially as to whether fixed assets should only be shown in the accounts at their historic cost, which is what the company invested in them, or at their current value. There are no strict rules about what can or cannot be done, so comparing company results is not easy, because the value at which assets are held in the accounts will be reflected by the profit and loss account whenever their value is realised.

The note of historical cost profits and losses in the annual report has been designed as a way to overcome this. When a company has revalued assets it must provide information in each following annual report on what the profit would have been if no revaluations had taken place.

Cash flow statement

The cash flow statement (or source and application of funds) shows the expenditure on fixed assets and the funds raised from their sale. Some companies break this down to show the real estate items separately. It will show when a company is funding its operation from the sale of real estate. Whether it is selling real estate to prop up a weak trading position, or whether it is using it to fund expansion, will be found from the reports on the company's activities (for an example, see Figure 17.2).

A.4 Other information

The directors' report, together with other general information in the report, may help to explain why various accounting practices have been undertaken. It will also include comment on the valuation of real estate interests if the figure in the main account differs substantially from market value. The notes to the accounts are where the detailed figures to support the main accounts are given. They are a vital source of information when attempting to understand the financial position of a company. The note of historical cost profits and losses has been mentioned above in the section on balance sheets.

Although it is rare for the accounts of major companies to be qualified by the auditors, anyone investigating a company should read the report of the auditors.

A.5 Group and subsidiary accounts

Most major corporations are organised as a group of companies with lots of wholly and partially owned subsidiaries. The published annual report will contain the results of the holding company plus those for the overall group, including the subsidiary companies, in the consolidated group accounts. Brief financial details about the subsidiary companies may be included. Where, as is often the case, these subsidiary companies are wholly owned there are no individual shareholders who need to receive copies of their accounts and therefore these documents are not produced for distribution. They are available from Companies House, where copies of all company accounts must be deposited.

The accounts of subsidiary companies can be consulted for an in-depth company search. Some subsidiary company accounts contain more information on the financial aspects of a company's real estate. The differences in the detail given in the group accounts and those of the subsidiaries can be large, but for many major companies the difference is not great because they take pride in producing comprehensive group accounts.

A corporate real estate manager who wants to compare one company's performance with another may only be successful if the accounts of subsidiary companies are consulted. This will reveal which of the subsidiaries have real estate holdings – this may not be as expected. When the different subsidiaries and the main company agree transfer payments for occupation of each other's real estate the situation can be become very confused. Such a search can be time-consuming, as the subsidiaries in turn may have their own subsidiaries.

There may be differences between the documents, as the parent company may break information down into divisions which do not exactly match the main subsidiaries. The different companies in a group may have different accounting periods. When accounting methods are changed the previous year's account will be restated. Comparisons between details in the subsidiaries and those in the group accounts can be done on a year-by-year basis, but if there has been a restatement it is hard to make historic comparisons. The real estate manager can rapidly reach the point when the information gained is not worth the work involved!

In general, the major companies are very open and helpful in the way that they present information, but there are always exceptions. Apart from moving assets off the balance sheet, companies determined to confuse can also constantly adopt different accounting practices, change their accounting periods and provide no restated figures beyond the statutory minimum.

A.6   Sources of information

For information on acquiring copies of annual reports see Section 7.16.

Appendix B: Aspects of the Valuation of Real Estate Fixed Assets

Guidance and mandatory requirements on the valuation of corporate real estate is included in the Royal Institution of Chartered Surveyors (RICS) *Appraisal and Valuation Manual* (1995), known as the RICS Manual or 'Red Book', which includes the requirements of the Accounting Standards Board (ASB).

When providing valuations for company accounts and financial statements, valuers of real estate have to produce figures that meet the ASB requirements. The RICS Manual enables valuers to achieve this by matching and adapting the RICS standard approaches to real estate valuation to the ASB's wording.

A company that is to continue in its existing business at the same or a growing volume will be required to value properties occupied for the purpose of the business at Existing Use Value (EUV). This is a methodology developed solely for business accounts purposes. The requirements may be different if a decision has been taken to reduce the operations of the business.

For those buildings occupied for the purpose of the business for which there is no market for sale, the value is normally agreed with the directors and auditors to be the Depreciated Replacement Cost (DRC). Such buildings are known as specialised properties and include, for example, chemical plants. Depreciated Replacement Cost can also be used in conjunction with Existing Use Value for any works of special adaptation to make a building fit for occupation for a particular purpose.

Depreciated Replacement Cost is the aggregate amount of the value of the land for the existing use or a notional replacement site in the same locality, and the gross replacement cost of the buildings and other siteworks, less allowances for depreciation normally for economic and functional obsolescence or environmental factors. It may well result in the existing property being worth less to the business than a new replacement.

The Depreciated Replacement Cost value assumes adequate potential profitability from the business. If the business is not sufficiently profitable to warrant carrying the facility in the balance sheet at the Depreciated Replacement Cost, the directors can adopt a lower figure. The RICS Manual contains many comments on the different circumstances that can arise with Depreciated Replacement Cost valuations. Clearly, the circumstances that have resulted in the figure finally included in the accounts could reveal information about the profitability of the company, both as it currently operates and, if it had to bear the full cost of its operational assets, about (for example) an expansion programme.

The Existing Use Value is similar to Open Market Value (OMV), but with the additional assumptions of vacant possession of those parts occupied by the business and that the building will be used for the foreseeable future only for the existing use.

The RICS Manual's assumption that, where a property is fully developed for its most beneficial use, the Existing Use Value will equate to Open Market Value is contested by major businesses. They feel that the EUV undervalues their real estate assets, as the assumption of vacant possession removes much of the value that comes just because they are the occupiers. They contest requirements that the covenant of the particular owning company and any value attributable to goodwill are generally excluded. The valuation cannot include any increase in value that could come from special investment or financial transactions, such as sale and leaseback.

There are strong arguments for and against the different methods. As the differences between the resulting valuations are high, it seems likely that the pressures for change will continue. However, if a change were to be introduced, once the initial financial adjustment had been made the year-on-year differences would not be so different from now.

Similar Existing Use Value methods apply for properties, such as hotels and pubs, that are valued fully equipped and trading as an operational entity. In these cases the valuation will include the effect of any management contracts, and there will not be an assumption of vacant possession. Real estate that is fully equipped as an operational entity and is valued having regard to trading potential involves a variety of extra requirements, related to the trading accounts etc., that are beyond the scope of this book. Special considerations also arise for valuing turnover rents and inducements agreed as part of leasing arrangements.

Existing Use Value is intended to replicate the cost of purchasing the remaining service potential of the asset in use by the business. It does not include any hope value of alternative uses for the operational buildings that require planning permission. It can include hope value for extensions, refurbishment etc. for the existing use if the work can be carried out without disturbing the business. Likewise, hope value can be included for parts of the business's assets, such as a sports field, which are not used for operational purposes and where development (for existing planning use) could be undertaken without any major interruption to the operation of the business.

Unused parts of the building which physically could not be sold off separately are valued at Existing Use Value. If surplus property could, in the opinion of the valuer and the directors, be sold off separately, it is valued at Open Market Value.

Existing Use Value can be higher than Open Market Value. This can occur, for example, when the business holds a valuable personal planning permission that would lapse if it vacated, if covenants restrict the right to sell or if a new owner would be obliged to decontaminate land whereas the existing business is exempt.

The more common situation is where development potential means that Open Market Value is higher than Existing Use Value. Open market value will include the value that would be obtained from the highest achievable alternative use, assuming that the business stopped trading. All the assumptions about planning consent, landlord's consent etc. must be realistic.

When there is a significant difference between Existing Use Value and Open Market Value the valuer has to report it to the directors. The directors must include the information in any published reference, but only if the effect on the aggregate valuation figure reported is material. The development potential of a single building on a large estate, while of considerable size, could be immaterial overall and would not be highlighted publicly.

B.1   Sources of Information

The Royal Institution of Chartered Surveyors *Appraisal and Valuation Manual* (1995) is available from the RICS bookshop (Tel: 0171 222 7000).

Appendix C: Fiscal Allowances

C.1   Capital allowances

When property prices were rising fast and inflation was high, capital allowances were less interesting. The most common allowance, which is for plant and machinery, is calculated on the declining balance method. Consequently, this allowance is higher in the early years after purchase (or refurbishment or development) than in following years. So for every £100 of allowable plant and machinery expenditure, the allowance would be £25 in the first year, but by the fifth year the allowance would be worth just £7.91. This is an allowance against taxable profits, which are normally taxed at 33% – so an allowance of £25 will mean saving tax of £8.25. When inflation is high, the real value of the allowances is falling year by year, so that after a couple of years or so they lose much of their attraction.

In these circumstances it is far more productive to concentrate time and energy on gaining a real estate interest that has potential for capital growth faster than the rate of inflation – due, say, to good location, facilities or development potential – rather than focus on the capital allowances, if this is the choice. Obviously, whatever the economic situation, a building that has both capital growth potential and capital allowances will be the best deal, if it meets a business's needs.

With low inflation, the potential cash savings from capital allowances are an incentive to be given serious consideration when assessing the viability of a building purchase or a development for owner occupation or investment. Some corporate finance directors are considering the capitalised value of these types of allowance when choosing between various investment options, including whether to own or rent (see Chapter 8).

Understanding and claiming capital allowances related to buildings has become a very specialised skill. The need to understand construction and construction contracts makes it difficult for accountants without building experience to appreciate the issues. Most surveyors have little knowledge of the specific requirements of the Inland Revenue. It is a dynamic subject, with details regularly changing; as a result, there are a number of specialists, usually with a surveying background, who focus their consultancy work on giving this advice.

Property companies are usually well versed in the gains to be had and the required procedures, and know when to seek expert advice. Those whose interest in real estate is limited to acquiring just what is needed to run their businesses often have little or no understanding of the requirements and do not come into contact with those who do – or not until it is too late to make the best arrangements.

As with many specialised tax matters, pre-planning often brings the best results. It is also the case with capital allowances that a purchaser can often be financially substantially better off if the vendor is ignorant of the taxation possibilities and remains so until after the deal is done. It is a case of *caveat emptor* – let the buyer beware – but the vendor must also beware, as either of the parties can lose out if they do not understand the importance and potential value of the tax opportunities.

There are five categories of capital allowances covering specific situations, and some are more generous than others. Circumstances change from case to case, but if allowances have not already been claimed the most valuable, if it applies, is the Enterprise Zone Allowance, which is up to 100%. Another 100% allowance is the Scientific Research Allowance, but few qualify. The remaining allowances, in descending order of value, are the Plant and Machinery Allowances, followed by the Industrial Building Allowances and finally Hotel Allowances.

Many parts of a building may be considered, for tax purposes, as plant and machinery. It varies building by building and owner by owner, depending on the trading operations undertaken in the property.

Table C.1 gives an estimate of the percentage of the purchase price that may be considered to be plant and machinery and eligible for plant and machinery capital allowances. It can be seen that, for a prestige owner-occupied headquarters building, the plant and machinery can be as much as 50% of the value. For a £10 million building the capitalised value at the time of purchase/development of the allowances over the following 10 years could exceed £1 million, effectively reducing the cost of the building by 10% or more. If these have already been claimed by a previous owner the available allowances may be less.

To achieve allowances with a capital value of 10% of the building value needs pre-planning and good records of the information that the Inland Revenue requires. The taxpayer also has to demonstrate that the items are plant within the terms of various statute and case laws.

In the case of purchased property, the allowances are based on the value of the plant and machinery as indicated by the sale price. This means that the sale price has to be divided between land, building and plant and machinery to assess the 'just apportionment'. The sale price may be more or less than the cost of providing the plant and machinery. The value is likely to be higher than cost in a property boom and could be lower than cost in a recession or property slump.

The Inland Revenue was not comfortable with the potential increase in capital allowances available with purchased property on a sale-by-sale basis.

Table C.1 Guide to capital allowances on purchased property. (Source: Property taxation Index, Datacard, by Crosher & James, September 1994)

Offices	Range (%)
Low-rise basic	12–18
Medium/high-rise basic	15–25
Air-conditioned	20–30
Prestige air-conditioned	25–40
HQ owner-occupied	30–50
Retail	
Shopping centres – open	5–10
Shopping centres – covered	10–20
Retail warehouses	5–10
Industrial	
Industrial/warehouse units	1–5*
B1 industrial/office units	10–20*
Hotels	
City centre luxury	40–60*
Provincial	25–45*
Specialist buildings	
Leisure centres	15–20
Computer centres	40–60
Private hospitals	25–35

*Plus Industrial Building Allowance or Hotel Allowance where applicable

Recent statute law has attempted to restrict the amount of plant and machinery allowances available to the vendor's claim for capital allowances, and is dependent upon the purchase date. This is complex and also depends on whether the vendor has made a claim for a plant and machinery allowance.

If, instead of purchase, a new building is constructed, the allowances are similar, but records required by the Inland Revenue include contract documents and final account breakdowns. The most effective claims will come if capital allowances are considered from the inception of the project.

It is not unusual for the Inland Revenue to consider claims very carefully, and while it can dismiss a claim, the most usual arrangement is for an agreement to be reached. Claims have to be made within two years (extending to three years in some cases) of the event, such as purchase, that made the claim possible. If the claim is late the allowance is not deleted but it may delay payment, and a claim for those years which have been ignored may well fail.

C.2   Revenue expenditure

While capital allowances are important, with two exceptions which give 100% allowances (Enterprise Zones and Scientific Research), they only succeed in reducing the amount of tax over a drawn-out time-scale during which the largest claim will relate to 25% of expenditure. Claims for revenue expenditure are much more attractive. A revenue item is a cost against profits, and therefore, in effect, a 100% tax allowance. Not surprisingly, the Inland Revenue prefers capital allowances to revenue expenditure.

A straightforward repair or replacement should be revenue expenditure, but if any part is an improvement this will constitute capital expenditure, which may or may not be subject to the benefit of capital allowances.

So, for refurbishment works it is clearly more beneficial, i.e. tax efficient, to have the highest claim for revenue expenditure and then aim to claim as much of the remainder as possible against capital allowances. The ways in which revenue expenditure and capital allowances are claimed are different, and much will depend on the details of the construction work. It is therefore important to plan the tax claims as part of the design and construction process under the guidance of a property tax planning expert. Leaving it to the accountant to sort out after the event is unlikely to be as successful and it will be very demanding on the accountant and therefore probably much more time-consuming and costly in professional fees.

C.3   Development finance and finance lease of plant and machinery

Potential capital allowances have a value if they can be offset against taxable profits. When development is planned, the potential capital allowances can be used to secure a loan from a dedicated financial institution which may give preferential rates.

The finance lease possibilities are most attractive to those businesses that cannot use the allowances, either because they are exempt from tax or have made no profits, say in the early years of an operation. It is an arrangement designed to meet a need and will be easier to organise for those businesses with a good covenant.

C.4   Landlord/tenant relationships

There is considerable scope for arbitraging the tax system by parties to a leasing deal seeking the most favourable deal both financially and for tax efficiency. The tax status of possible landlords and tenants can make them more attractive to each other. Fiscal requirements can affect the arrangements made by different parts of the same business or arrangements in a sale and leaseback (see Chapters 16 and 19).

The tenant, a profitable tax-paying business, pays rent, which is a cost against the tenant's income before taxable profits are calculated. A non-tax-paying landlord, for example a pension fund, pays no tax on the rent it receives. Such a non-tax-paying landlord loses nothing by passing the ownership of the plant and equipment to the tenant, who makes the claim for the capital allowances attaching to these items. This reduces the tenant's tax liabilities, which can be seen, in simple terms, as a contribution to the rent. The principles will remain the same while the tax systems remains unchanged, but the details of deals will vary according to the state of the property market – each party will be seeking the best arrangements.

C.5   VAT

VAT requirements are subject to change, and in recently months have contained different liabilities for the seller and buyer which could be influenced by decisions about when notification is given to Customs and Excise. The best way forward is to obtain expert advice before being party to a sale involving VAT.

C.6   Capital gains tax

Like VAT, this tax has its own set of rules and these vary according to the type of interest in real estate that is being sold. These provisions are unlikely to be of strategic importance, but could influence the implementation details when specific options are under consideration. Yet again expert advice is needed.

C.7   Other opportunities

The main taxation and fiscal matters have been raised in this brief guide – there are many other possibilities (for example, lease premiums and landlord's inducements) which have tax implications. As tax liability often depends on how the deal is structured, taking professional advice before a property deal is made can be advantageous.

C.8   Sources of information

The *Property Taxation Index* (Crosher & James, 1996) gives up-to-date general guidance on capital allowances. It is available from Crosher & James, 1–5 Exchange Court, London WC2R 0PQ (Tel: 0171 836 1221; Fax: 0171 831 1233).

Bibliography

References

3i (1994) *plc UK: A Focus on Corporate Trends: Outsourcing*, Survey No. 12, 3i Group plc, January.

Accounting Standards Board (ASB) (1994) *Reporting the Substance of Transactions, Financial Reporting Standard 5 (FRS5)*, Accounting Standards Board, April.

Accounting Standards Committee (1981) *Accounting for Investment Properties: Statement of Standard Accounting Practice 19 (SSAP 19)*, Accounting Standards Board, November.

Accounting Standards Committee (1987) *Accounting for Depreciation: Statement of Standard Accounting Practice 12 (SSAP 12)*, Paragraph 10, Accounting Standards Board, January.

Alder, J. (1995) Rough ride ahead for property managers as industry shake out continues, *National Real Estate Investor*, USA, March.

Alsop, P. (1991) Document store offers fast payback, *Industrial Handling and Storage* **13**(5), November.

Ambrose, W. B. (1990) Corporate real estate's impact on the takeover market, *Journal of Real Estate Finance and Economics*, **3**(4).

Arthur Andersen and Co. (1991) *Managing the Future: Real Estate in the 1990s*, Institute of Real Estate Management Foundation, USA.

Arthur Andersen and Co. (1994) *Real Estate in the Corporation: The Bottom Line from Senior Management*, Arthur Andersen, San Francisco.

Andrews, K. (1971) *The Concept of Corporate Strategy*, Dow Jones-Irwin, New York.

Apgar IV, M. (1995) Managing real estate to build value, *Harvard Business Review*, Nov–Dec.

Asset Information (1996) *A Market Audit of the Facilities Management Market 1996*, Asset Information Ltd, Cambridge.

Avis, M. and Gibson, V. (1995) *Real Estate Resource Management*, GTI, Reading.

Avis, M., Gibson, V. and Watts, J. (1989) *Managing Operational Property Assets*, GTI, Wallingford, Oxfordshire.

BAA plc (1995) *Annual Report and Accounts*.

Baker, S. and Baker, K. (1993) *Market Mapping*, McGraw-Hill, London.

Bannock, G. and Partners (1994) *Property in the Boardroom: A New Perspective*, Hillier Parker and Graham Bannock and Partners.

Baum, A. (1991) *Property Investment, Depreciation and Obsolescence*, Routledge, London.

Bauman, Z. (1992) *Intimations of Postmodernity*, Routledge, London.

Bayliss, J. (1996) *Service, Quality and Ethics: Question Surveyors*, Inaugural Address, RICS, 9 July.

Becker, F. and Steele, F. (1995) *Workplace by Design: Mapping the High Performance Workscape*, Jossey-Bass Publishers, San Francisco.

Bernard Williams Associates (1994) *Facilities Economics Incorporating Premises Audits*, Building Economics Bureau, Bromley, Kent.

Blackley, N., Lamming, G. and Parekh, M. (1995) *The Electronic Retailing Marketplace*, Global Research, Goldman Sachs, 16 February.

Blyth, J. (1994) Keynote Address, *Third Commercial Property Conference*, Cardiff, 23 May.

Boots The Chemist Ltd (1995) *Introducing the Rating Team*, Boots The Chemist Ltd, Nottingham.

The Boots Company (1993) *Annual Report and Accounts*, The Boots Company plc, Nottingham.

The Boots Company (1995) *Annual Report and Accounts*, The Boots Company plc, Nottingham.

British Bankers Association (1996) *Annual Abstract of Statistics*, Vol. 13, British Bankers Association.

British Council for Offices (1994) *Specification for Urban Offices*, British Council for Offices/College of Estate Management, July.

British Institute of Facilities Management (1995) *Measurement Protocol*, British Institute of Facilities Management, Saffron Walden.

British Land Company (1994) *Annual Report and Accounts*, The British Land Company plc.

Brown, E. (1995) Clear views from a troubleshooter, *Estates Times*, 17 November.

Brown, G. (1991) *Property Investment and the Capital Market*, E. & F. N. Spon, London.

Brown, R. K. (1987) Competitiveness, the CEO and the Real Estate Decisions, *National Real Estate Investor*, USA, October.

Brown, R. K. (1993) *Managing Corporate Real Estate*, John Wiley & Sons, New York.

BT (undated) *Future Business: Engaging Customers Across the Information Superhighway*, BT plc.

Buchanan, J. (1995) The wonders of wireless, *Property Week*, 6 July.

Buckley, N. (1995a) Check out the television, *Financial Times*, 8 August.

Buckley, N. (1995b) Technology: check it out, *Financial Times*, 8 August.

Building Research Establishment (BRE) (1990) *Building Research Establishment Environmental Assessment Method (BREEAM) Offices*, Building Research Establishment, CRC Ltd.

Building Research Establishment (BRE) (1991) *Building Research Establishment Environmental Assessment Method (BREEAM) Superstores and Supermarkets*, Building Research Establishment, CRC Ltd.

Building Research Establishment (BRE) (1993a) *Building Research Establishment Environmental Assessment Method (BREEAM) Existing Offices*, Building Research Establishment, CRC Ltd.

Building Research Establishment (BRE) (1993b) *Building Research Establishment Environmental Assessment Method (BREEAM) Industrial Buildings*, Building Research Establishment, CRC Ltd.

Building Research Establishment (BRE) (1995a) *Energy Efficiency in Offices – Small Power Loads*, Energy Consumption: Guide 35, Building Research Establishment, Watford.

Building Research Establishment (BRE) (1995b) *Office Toolkit*, Building Research Establishment, CRC Ltd.

Business Publishing (1996) *The City in 2020: The Official Report of the Symposium held at Disneyland, Paris in 1995*, Business Publishing.

Carpenter, A. (1996) Worth the argument, *Property Week*, 11 January.

Cash, H. and Taylor, G. (compilers) (1995) *PCS Property Software Directory*, Property Computer Show Ltd.

Catalano, A. (1996) BL in £200m Tesco Store JV, *Estates Gazette*, 1 June.

Central Statistical Office (1991) *Retail Prices 1914–1990*, HMSO, London.

Central Statistical Office (1995) *Annual Abstract of Statistics 1995*, HMSO, London.

Chalk, M. B. (1994) Last word: measuring the quality in corporate real estate, *National Real Estate Investor*, USA, February.

Clift, M. R. and Butler, A. (1995) *The Performance and Costs-in-Use of Buildings: A New Approach*, Building Research Establishment Report, CRC Ltd.

Cochrane, P. (1995) The information way, *First Institute of Direct Marketing Symposium*, Institute of Direct Marketing, Teddington.

Collis, D. J. and Montgomery, C. A. (1995) Competing on Resources: strategy in the 1990s, *Harvard Business Review*, Jul–Aug.

Cookson, C. (1995) Technology: ultra-miniaturisation: the benefits of thinking small, *Financial Times*, 28 December.

Coopers & Lybrand (1996) *The Future of the Food Store: Challenges and Alternatives*, The Coca-Cola Retailing Research Group – Europe.

Crosher & James (1996) *Property Taxation Index*, Crosher & James.

Currie, D. and Scott, A. (1991) *The Place of Commercial Property in the UK Economy*, Centre for Economic Forecasting, London Business School, January.

Davies, M., Paterson, R. and Wilson, A. (1994) *Generally Accepted Accounting Practice in the United Kingdom (UK GAAP)*, 4th edn, Macmillan, Basingstoke.

DEGW and Tecnibank (1992) *The Intelligent Building: Executive Summary*, Occasional Paper, British Council for Offices, Reading, September.

Doidge, R. (1995) How to improve financial returns, *Shopping Centre Progress 1995–96*, British Council of Shopping Centre and Estates Gazette, bound into *Estates Gazette*, 11 November.

Drivers Jonas and Investment Property Databank (1995) *Commercial Leases: The Structural Revolution*, Drivers Jonas.

Debenham Tewson & Chinnock (1992) *The Role of Property: Managing Cost and Releasing Value*, Debenham Tewson & Chinnock, June.

DTZ Debenham Thorpe (1993) *Distribution 2000*, DTZ, January.

Duckworth, S. L. (1993) Realising the strategic dimension of corporate real property through improved planning and control systems, *The Journal of Real Estate Research*, USA, Fall.

Estates Gazette (1989) Sainsbury's have agreed a sale and leaseback deal with British Land, *Estates Gazette*, 25 March.

Ferguson, J. (1995) The state of GPS in 1995, *Professional Surveyor*, BPA International, Professional Surveyors Publishing Company, Arlington VA, July/August.

Financial Times (1989) Boots treatment working, *Financial Times*, 22 June.

Frampton, K. (1980) *Modern Architecture: A Critical History*, Thames & Hudson, London.

Frost & Sullivan (1994) *European Data Communications Services Markets*, Frost & Sullivan, 24 June.

Gates, W. (1995) *The Road Ahead*, Viking, London.

Gillespie, A., Richardson, R. and Cornford, J. (1995) *Review of Teleworking in Britain: Implications for Public Policy Prepared for the Parliamentary Office of Science and Technology*, Centre for Urban and Regional Development Studies, University of Newcastle upon Tyne, February.

Grimley (1996) *Survey of Property Confidence and Future Requirements*, CBI/Grimley, Summer.

Goold, M. and Campbell, A. (1987) *Strategies and Styles: The Role of the Centre in Managing Diversified Corporations*, Blackwell Business, Oxford.

Gourlay, R. (1995) Management: the growing business: working like clockwork, *Financial Times*, 8 August.

Grant, R. M. (1995) *Contemporary Strategy Analysis: Concepts, Techniques, Applications*, 2nd edn, Blackwell Business, Oxford.

Gray, M., Hodson, N. and Gordon, G. (1993) *Teleworking Explained*, John Wiley & Sons, Chichester.

Griffiths, J. M. (1990) *ISDN Explained*, John Wiley & Sons, Chichester.

Griffith, V. (1995) Club class on the Internet, *Financial Times*, 30 October.

Hall, A. (1996) Cable's blurred picture, *Sunday Telegraph*, 4 February.

Hamel, G. and Prahalad, P. K. (1994) *Competing for the Future: Breakthrough Strategies for Seizing Control of Your Industry and Creating Markets of Tomorrow*, Harvard Business School Press, Massachusetts.

Harding, J. (1995) Oliver Group seeks funds for growth via sale of head office, *Financial Times*, 19 December.

Hendley, T. (1995) *An Introduction to Document Management*, Document Management Suppliers Group, Worcester.

Hill, P. R. (1995) The impact of small power loads on offices, paper to *Blue Print to the Green Office*, Museum of Science and Industry, Manchester, Building Research Establishment, 18 January.

Hill, T. (1991) *Production/Operations Management: Text and Cases*, 2nd edn, Prentice-Hall, Englewood Cliffs NJ.

Hillman, J. (1993) *Telelifestyles and the Flexibity: A European Study: The Impact of the Electronic Home*, European Foundation for the Improvement of Living and Working Conditions/Publications Office of the European Communities, Dublin and Luxembourg.

HMSO (1984) *Data Protection Act 1984*, HMSO, London.

HMSO (1989) *Companies Act 1989* HMSO, London.

HMSO (1995) *Landlord and Tenants (Covenants) Act 1995*, HMSO, London.

Hollington, J. (1986) Obsolescence – turning white elephants into lucrative assets, *The Workplace Revolution*, Healey and Baker, London.

Hollis, J. (1995) Smart store for a changing world/breakaway strategies, *Retail Technology: Smart Store Europe*, Anderson Consulting, Windsor, Autumn.

Holdsworth, P. (1995) Benchmarking: taken to the cleaners?, *Property Week*, 26 January.

Huws, U. (undated) *A Manager's Guide to Teleworking*, Department of Employment/Cambertown Ltd, Rotherham.

Investment Property Forum (1995) *Property Securitisation*, RICS, London, November.

Investment Property Databank (IPD) *et al.* (1994) *Understanding the Property Cycle: Main Report: Economic Cycles and the Property Cycle*, RICS, London.

Investment Property Databank (IPD) *et al.* (1995) *Understanding the Property Cycle: 1995 Update*, RICS, London.

Isakson, H. R. and Sircar, S. (1990) The critical success factors approach to corporate real asset management, *Real Estate Issues*, Spring/Summer, USA.

Isaac, D. and Steley, T. (1991) *Property Valuation Techniques*, Macmillan, Basingstoke.

Johnson, S. (1993) *Greener Buildings: Environmental Impact of Property*, Macmillan, Basingstoke.

Joroff, M. *et al.* (1993) *Strategic Management of the Fifth Resource: Corporate Real Estate*, Industrial Development Research Foundation, USA.

Jones Lang Wootton (1987) *Obsolescence: The Financial Impact on Property Performance*, Jones Lang Wootton, London.

Kehoe, L. (1994) Internet purchase to put home shopping on-line, *Financial Times*, 8 September.

King Sturge and Co. (1995) *Office Occupier Trends*, King Sturge and Co., London.

Lambert, S., Poteete, J. and Waltch, A. (1995) *Generating High-Performance Corporate Real Estate Service*, International Development Research Council, Norcross GA, USA.

Lawson, D. (1994) Arctic weather on the job, *Financial Times*, 20 April.

Lay, R. (1988) Real estate portfolio valuation, *Journal of Valuation* **6**(3).

Lex Column (1994) Electronic shopping, *Financial Times*, 8 September.

Liow, K. H. (1995) Acquisition and disposal of corporate real estate: some UK evidence, *Journal of Property Finance*, **6**(4).

London, S. (1991) Loosening the debts that bind: how small companies may limit bank dependence, *Financial Times*, 31 July.

London, S. (1995) Profits after the pain, *Financial Times*, 13 January.

London, S. (1996) Windfall from property not guaranteed, *Financial Times*, 18 April.

London Stock Exchange (1996) *Consultation Document*, 24 May.

Lowe, K. (1995) Reckoning it'll help, *Property Week*, 9 November.

Mackenzie, J. A. and Phillips, M. (1994) *A Practical Approach to Land Law*, 5th edn, Blackstone, London.

McLocklin, N. (1993) *Flexible Working Practices*, unpublished MBA dissertation.

McWilliams, D. (1992) *Commercial Property and Company Borrowing*, RICS Research Paper No. 22, RICS, London, 5 November.

Mallinson (1994) *Mallinson Report*, RICS, London, April.

Mills, L. (1994) State of chaos in *Estates Gazette*, 1 October.

Mitchell, B. R. and Dean, P, (1962) *Abstract of British Historical Statistics*, Cambridge University Press, Cambridge.

Mitchell, W. J. (1995) *City of Bits: Space, Time and their Infobahn*, The MIT Press, Cambridge MA.

Monopolies and Mergers Commission (1989) *Report on the Supply of Beer for Retail Sale in the UK*, Cm 651, HMSO, London.

Morgan, D. (1996) Mend your ways, *Property Week*, 23 May.

Murray-Brown, J. (1994) Fibre optic bridge in *Financial Times*, 28 December.

Nass, M. D. (1995) Excelling at the top – what it will take in the twenty-first century, *The Real Estate Finance Journal*, USA, Summer.

Neate, S. (1995) The threat from new technology, *British Council of Shopping Centres Conference*, Harrogate, GMA Planning, Twickenham, 9–11 November.

Nourse, H. O. (1990) Corporate real estate ownership as a form of vertical integration, *Real Estate Review*, USA, **20**(3).

Nourse, H. O. and Roulac, S. E. (1993) Linking real estate decisions to corporate strategy, *The Journal of Real Estate Research*, USA, Fall.

The Oliver Group plc (1995a) *Report and Accounts 1994*, The Oliver Group plc, Leicester.

The Oliver Group plc (1995b) *Interim Results 1995*, The Oliver Group plc, Leicester.

The Oliver Group plc (1995c) *Trading Statement*, The Oliver Group plc, Leicester, 9 August.

The Oliver Group plc (1995d) *Company Announcements Office: The Oliver Group plc – Castle Acres*, The Oliver Group plc, Leicester, 8 December.

The Oliver Group plc (1996) *Report and Accounts 1995*, The Oliver Group plc, Leicester.

Oxford Brookes University and University of Reading (1993) *Property Management Performance Monitoring*, GTI, Reading.

Panel on Takeovers and Mergers (1993) *City Code on Takeovers and Mergers and Rules Governing Substantial Acquisitions of Shares*, Panel on Takeovers and Mergers, November.

Park, A. (1994) *Facilities Management: An Explanation*, Macmillan, Basingstoke.

Paterson, R. (1996) We regret nothing – it had to be done, *Accountancy Age*, 7 March.

Pollock, A. (1995) The impact of information technology on destination marketing, *EIU Travel and Tourism Analyst*, No. 3, Economist Intelligence Unit, London.

Porter, M. (1980) *Competitive Strategy: Techniques for Analyzing Industries and Competitors*, Free Press, New York.

Porter, M. (1985) *Competitive Advantage: Creating and Sustaining Superior Perform-ance*, Free Press, New York.

Reading, C. (1993) *Strategic Business Planning*, Kogan Page, London.

Reid, W. and Myddelton, D. R. (1992) *The Meaning of Company Accounts*, 5th edn, Gower, Aldershot.

Richard Ellis/Harris Research Centre (1995a) *Volume I: Occupiers' Preferences*, Richard Ellis, London.

Richard Ellis/Harris Research Centre (1995b) *Volume II: Tomorrow's Workplace*, Richard Ellis, London.

Rodriguez, M. and Sirmans, C. F. (1996) Managing Corporate Real Estate: Evidence from the Capital Markets, *Journal of Real Estate Literature*, **4**.

Rondeau, E. P. (1988) Corporate manager's success built on service, *National Real Estate Investor*, USA, December.

Royal Institution of Chartered Surveyors (1995) *Appraisal and Valuation Manual*, RICS, London.

Salway, F. (1986) *Depreciation of Commercial Property*, College of Estate Management.

Seeley, I. H. (1996) *Building Economics*, 4th edn, Macmillan, Basingstoke.

Shop Property (1989) Sainsbury's in £90m sale and leaseback deal with British Land, *Shop Property*, 24 April.

Shop Property (1990) J. Sainsbury confirms a sale and leaseback deal with British Land involving 11 stores, *Shop Property*, 14 January.

Sinderman, M. (1995) Outsourcing gains speed in corporate world, *National Real Estate Investor*, **37**(8), USA, August.

SJT Associates/Centre for Facilities Management, University of Strathclyde (1994) *Facilities Costs and Trends Survey '94 (FACTS '94)*, SJT Associates.

Spring, M. (1995) Plus points, *Property Week*, 31 August.

Stathers, D. (1996) How do valuers add value? at *ISVA Conference*, Bristol, ISVA, 10–11 May.

Sullivan, K. (1995) Backroom to backwoods? International relocation, *The Cutting Edge 1995*, RICS, London.

Sullivan, L. (1956) *The Autobiography of an Idea*, Dover Publications, New York.

Taylor, P. (1995) Technology: the information superhighway: like a double decker bus in a country lane, *Financial Times*, 27 December.

Thame, D. (1995a) Boxing clever, *Property Week*, 3/10 August.

Thame, D. (1995b) Speed limits, *Property Week*, 20 July.

Tighe, C. (1995) Sunderland stadium scheme backed, *Financial Times*, 26 July.

Veale, P. R. (1988) *Managing Corporate Real Estate Assets: A Survey of US Real Estate Executives*, MIT, Cambridge MA.

Waters, J. (1996) Property valuation: time to call ASB efficiency proposals to account, *Property Week*, 30 May.

White, A. and Taylor, N. (1995) Development plans: BT's response to the Planning and Compensation Act 1991, *Chartered Surveyor Monthly*, March.

Whitmore, J. (1996) Attacking formation, *Property Week*, 11 January.

Periodical publications

Academic journals

Business Strategy Review (quarterly): Oxford University Press, Oxford.

The Economic Outlook (quarterly): Blackwell Publishers, Oxford.

Harvard Business Review (bi-monthly): Harvard Business School Press, Masschusetts, USA.
Journal of Property Finance (quarterly): MCB University Press, Bradford.

Professional journals and newspapers

Estates Gazette (weekly): The Estates Gazette Ltd, London.
Facilities Management (bi-monthly): and Facilities Management: Management Guides (quarterly), The Eclipse Group, London.
Financial Times (daily Mon–Sat): The Financial Times Ltd, London.
Property Week (weekly): The Builder Group plc, London.

Commercial publications

Cimtech (annually): Document Management Yearbook, St Albans.
DTZ Debenham Thorpe/Property Managers Association (annually): Index of Retail Trading Locations, DTZ Debenham Thorpe, London.
Grimley (bi-annually): Survey of Property Confidence and Future Requirements, CBI/Grimley, London.
Hillier Parker (quarterly): Property Market Values Index, Hillier Parker, London.
Hillier Parker (quarterly): Rent Index, Hillier Parker, London.
Investment Property Databank (annually): Annual Review, Investment Property Databank, London.
Jones Lang Wootton (quarterly): Jones Lang Wootton UK Property Index, Jones Lang Wootton Fund Management, London.
Jones Lang Wootton (annually): OSCAR: Office Service Charge Analysis, Jones Lang Wootton, London.
Richard Ellis (half-yearly): Corporate Real Estate Bulletin, Richard Ellis, London.
Richard Ellis (monthly): Richard Ellis Monthly Index, Richard Ellis, London.
Royal Institution of Chartered Surveyors (weekly): RICS Weekly Briefing, RICS, London.

Annual reports and accounts

A number of annual reports and accounts, company announcements, internal documents etc. were consulted. Where specific textual information from such a document has been referred to in the main text of the book, the document has been included in the References section of the bibliography. Most company publications were used to gain numerical information that has been incorporated into the illustrations. The full list of official company documents consulted is as follows:

- BAA plc, London
  - Annual Report and Accounts, 1995

- The Boots Company plc, Nottingham
  - Annual Report and Accounts, 1987, 1988, 1989, 1990, 1991, 1992, 1993, 1994, 1995

● Boots The Chemists Ltd, Nottingham
  – *Annual Report and Accounts*, 1988, 1989, 1990, 1991, 1992, 1993, 1994
  – Boots Properties plc, Nottingham
  – *Annual Report and Accounts*, 1989, 1990, 1991, 1992, 1993, 1994, 1995
  – The British Land Company plc, London
  – *Annual Report and Accounts*, 1994

● BT plc, London
  – *Annual Report and Accounts*, 1994
  – *Managing Corporate Real Estate*, BT Group Property
  – *Workstyle 2000: Westside Story*, BT Group Property, 1994
  – *Imagine the Future: Stockley Park*, BT Group Property, 1995

● Conrad Ritblat Sinclair Goldsmith plc, London
  – *Annual Report and Accounts*, 1995

● Conrad Ritblat Group plc, London
  – *Interim Results*, 1995
  – *Press Release*, Conrad Ritblat Group, 15 December 1995
  – *Conrad Ritblat Group: Corporate Review*, Panmure Gordon & Company Ltd, March 1996.

● IBM United Kingdom Holdings Ltd, Southampton
  – *Annual Report and Accounts*, 1988, 1994

● IBM United Kingdom Ltd, Southampton
  – *Annual Report and Accounts*, 1987, 1988, 1989, 1990, 1991, 1992, 1993, 1994

● International Business Machines Corporation, Armonk NY, USA
  – *Annual Reports*, 1990, 1991, 1992, 1993, 1994

● Marks & Spencer plc, London
  – *Annual Report and Accounts*, 1995
  – *Interim Results*, 1995

● The Oliver Group plc, Leicester
  – *Annual Report and Accounts*, 1994, 1995
  – *Interim Results*, 1995
  – *The Oliver Group plc – Castle Acres*, Company Announcements Office, 8 August 1995
  – *Trading Statement*, Leicester, 9 August 1995

● J Sainsbury plc, London
  – *Annual Report and Accounts*, 1985, 1986, 1987, 1988, 1989, 1990, 1991, 1992, 1993, 1994
  – *Interim Results*, 1994

Index